6-4-69

Guido Gregorietti

JEWELRY
THROUGH
THE AGES

Foreword by Erich Steingräber
Translated from the Italian by Helen Lawrence

American Heritage
New York

Contents

1511502

Foreword
by Erich Steingräber

Since time began man has felt an instinctive need to adorn himself. Superstition and prejudice, awareness of social position and the desire for secure investment were, and still remain today, the fundamental urges behind man's desire to emphasise the solemnity and prestige of his person with ornamental symbols.

Leaving aside the primitive custom of painting the body, today when we talk of personal ornaments we refer in a strict sense to objects of apparel made by the goldsmith and the jeweler either for clothes or for the body. While ornaments for clothes such as buckles or brooches often combine practical and decorative uses, those for the body have a purely decorative purpose. We must, however, guard against judging ancient ornaments exclusively as art: their numerous decorative aspects are also indissolubly linked with man's history and often clearly reflect his joy and sorrow, love, sadness, pride, fear and humility.

Until the time of the French Revolution there was no 'pure' jewelry as such; pieces were significant according to their purpose as momentoes, amulets, talismans or as signs of social distinction. The numerous sumptuary laws and statutes passed in ancient times to regulate the rights of the various social classes show that until the end of the 18th century the wearing of jewelry was, and indeed in most non-Western civilisations still is today, a matter of social privilege. Jewelry which was not in any way linked with social functions or had any other particular significance was introduced for the first time in the 19th century.

Another interesting aspect of the application of jewelry is that up to and including the 18th century the wearing of jewels was by no means the sole preserve of the gentler sex. It became a feminine privilege only after the French Revolution when European fashions for men, following the sober English example, saw the establishment of the type of masculine attire still worn today in most advanced societies.

Guido Gregorietti, director of the Museo Poldo-Pezzoli for over twenty years and professor at the Accademia di Brera in Milan, has made a deep study of the minor arts and has given of his vast knowledge with generous enthusiasm in this work, to which we wish every success.

Woman with a necklace and diadem, from a bronze mirror, Etruscan, 6th century BC. Museo Nazionale di Villa Giulia, Rome.

Introduction

The story of jewelry is as old as human vanity. Even in the earliest times, though scarcely yet in a position to organise his society, man found a pretext for satisfying his narcissism by creating hierarchies which required signs of rank. These badges were usually precious objects or, if of low intrinsic value, objects enriched by the craftsmanship of particularly talented individuals. The value of the materials is relative to the era in which they were used: a necklace made of seashells some twenty thousand years ago from a particular area is comparable to a necklace of large pearls belonging to an aristocrat of Louis XIV's time. The earliest evidence of personal ornaments has been found in excavations of the paleolithic era and in some rock paintings of later epochs. Archaeologists call prehistoric ornaments 'personal works of art'; of these, the ones which are relevant to our subject are those which were considered precious in their time: works of ivory (from mammoth tusks), reindeer antlers and more rarely amber or lignite. They are mostly small objects (2-2½ inches), roundish or square in shape and sometimes, according to the region and period, engraved with zoomorphic or anthropomorphic figures or geometric designs.

Prehistoric finds made to date vary in time from approximately 40,000 to 10,000 years and extend geographically in an arc from the Algerian Sahara, through Spain, France, across Germany, with two long arms finishing in the north in Sweden (north of Göteborg) and in the south in Sicily and from there stretching towards eastern Europe finishing east of Kiev in Russia.

A curved band of carved ivory was found at Mézine north of Kiev; it has three holes at each end, through which thongs would have been drawn to fasten it to the wrist as a bracelet. Other objects from various places with similar perforations were probably used as pendants. In some the quality of the engravings or the relief is so refined that it suggests a highly developed aesthetic sense as well as a surprisingly sophisticated technical ability. Presumably the most important uses of these objects were magical but, nevertheless, many apparently also had a decorative purpose.

Wooden ritual mask with geometric designs, Africa. Private collection, Paris.

13

During the prehistoric period the earth's surface was still undergoing great changes. It is thought that the great thaw of the last ice age raised the sea level by about 250 feet, and many areas perhaps rich in interesting evidence are today submerged. Hunting and fishing were for many of these peoples the only way of life, and coloured feathers from rare birds, horns and skins of animals which were difficult to catch, the bones and teeth of certain fish and seashells were the materials first chosen to embellish valued items of adornment, often strangely shaped and gaudily coloured. These might be worn at magic, civil or religious rites or as marks of social rank. In more recent times the craftsmanship of the Pre-Colombian epoch, which represented an ancient and continuing tradition, gives us a good idea of how feathers were chosen and prepared in earlier times. Brilliantly coloured plumes were used in making clothes,

14

Female figures in a ritual dance. Prehistoric rock paintings from J. D. Lajoux, *Les merveilles du Tassili N'Ajjer*. By kind permission of Editions Larousse.

cloaks, headdresses and symbolic ornaments, executed with the most refined taste and painstaking skill. Horns and antlers of deer, reindeer and other animals and seashells were skilfully cut, shaped, engraved, pierced or carved to make necklaces, bracelets, pendants, rings for nose, mouth and ear and elaborate headdresses, with colour, composition, material and style varying distinctly according to the different regions of origin.

The next phase of man's development was his discovery of mineral materials. He was attracted by the colour, shape and the reflection of certain glassy pebbles. He found out how to pierce them so as to make them into gay ornamental objects, first in their natural state and later rounding and polishing them. He learned

below Mask decorated with ostrich feathers and coloured pearls, Tanganyika. Linden Museum, Stuttgart.

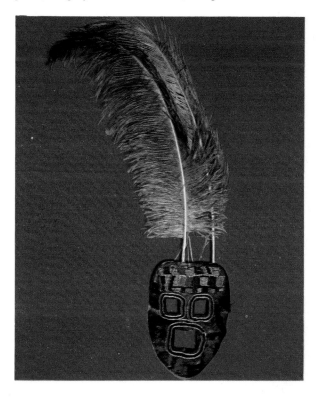

below and below centre Shell bracelet and necklace, New Guinea. British Museum, London.

above Shell necklace, New Guinea. British Museum, London.

above Mask decorated with shells and pearls, Bakuba. Von der Heydt collection, Rietberg Museum, Zurich.

15

to distinguish the regions where his search would be most fruitful and, without knowing the reason why, he looked in alluvial deposits, that is, in dried-up river beds and streams where water carried and deposited all kinds of minerals which had formed during the period of upheaval and disintegration. Experience taught him to remove the topsoil and examine the underlying stratum covered with loam. There he found pebbles of various shapes and sizes which, with slight cleaning or polishing by rubbing them against other stones, reflected the sun. They were of solid substance, and even the most violent blows did not shatter them, but instead would flatten them out.

How, when and where gold came to be discovered is not known, but it seems certain that it was one of the first metals discovered by man.

16

Bronze sculptured figure in ceremonial costume, Ife, Nigeria, 11th-15th century.

Gold pendant with human mask, Africa. Centre of Human Sciences, Abidjan, Ivory Coast.

I

Gold

Its physical properties and methods of working

In contrast to silver, which traditionally symbolises the gleam of the moon, gold is the symbol of the sun's splendour. It is a metal which in its natural state offers an unequalled stability and beauty. Moreover its malleability permits the manufacture of almost transparently thin leaves, while from one ounce of gold it is possible to draw a fine wire fifty miles long. This gives some idea of how inviting its early discoverers found it to work with. The ductility of gold diminishes in relation to the amount of other metals alloyed with it. Its melting point is between 1000° and 1060°C, and it is not subject to normal oxidisation; it is insoluble in common acids, but dissolves in acqua regia, a mixture of hydrochloric and nitric acids, (*cf* Basilio Valentino, 1624) and in a mixture of telluric acid and strong sulphuric acid, with a little nitric acid, heated above 230°C; it will corrode with various degrees of speed in solutions of chlorine, bromine and iodine.

Ore Deposits Gold in its natural state exists to a greater or lesser degree in almost all rocks, in the sea as well as in rivers and streams, in sand and even in plants. However, the areas where it can be extracted in large enough quantities to be of economic importance to the community are few and situated in regions scattered throughout the world.

The geological origins of gold are not fully understood, but it is believed to come, as other metals do, from the deepest recesses of the earth. The mineral most commonly associated with gold, apart from silver, is quartz, while iron pyrites is often mistaken for gold because of its apparent similarity to it.

Gold is almost never found pure, but generally alloyed with silver in varying degrees from at least 10% to about 50%. When the natural alloy exceeds 20% the yellow metal tends to be very pale and greenish in colour, and was thought in antiquity to be a different metal known as white gold or electrum. Apart from silver, gold in its natural state can contain small quantities of copper and traces of other metals. Gold distributed in rocks is usually invisible to the naked eye, although sometimes it can be seen quite clearly in grains and crystals or in veins of various lengths and thicknesses, gener-

top Auriferous quartz.

centre Rare octahedron-shaped gold nugget (actual size 2mm).

far left Auriferous quartz.

left Gold nugget from a Californian mine.

below Gold washing from a 16th-century engraving.

below centre Gold beating from an engraving of about 1640.

ally in quartz reefs. It is also found in sulphite veins of other metals particularly pyrites.

Auriferous deposits can be divided into primary and secondary types. The primary ones are veins of metal found in volcanic rock and the secondary ones are the alluvial deposits formed by the disintegration of these rocks by the continuous action of running water. The secondary deposits were the first to be discovered and tapped by man, because the grains and chips are easily seen shining on the sand of dried-up river beds and even through shallow water. The density of gold is about 19·3 times the weight of an equal volume of water and about seven times that of a flint pebble of the same size. This explains how the flow of hot spring waters, carrying the mineral debris of shattered or eroded rocks, created rich deposits of auriferous mineral. Around the middle of the last century a nugget found at the Ballarat gold mines of Victoria in Australia weighed nearly 160 pounds. It was named Welcome Stranger.

The opinion of the scholar Humboldt that the history of man's exploitation of gold deposits follows the development of civilisation is largely correct. In fact the earliest proof of the discovery of gold comes from western Asia and Egypt, then from Macedonia, Italy, France, and Spain. Gold was next discovered in America, then Africa again and finally distant Australia.

Extraction Even though the people of antiquity who discovered gold did not possess the means of weighing it as we do today, they realised that its weight in relation to its volume was significant and using this information were able to devise ways of separating the gold from particles of mineral dispersed in sand or in

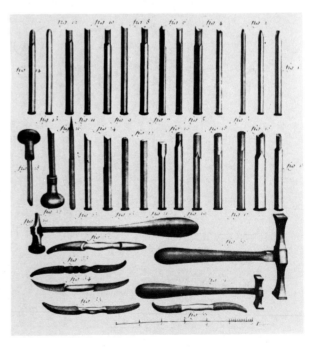

above and left Engravers and goldsmiths and their tools from *Recueil de planches sur les sciences et les arts*, Diderot, 1772.

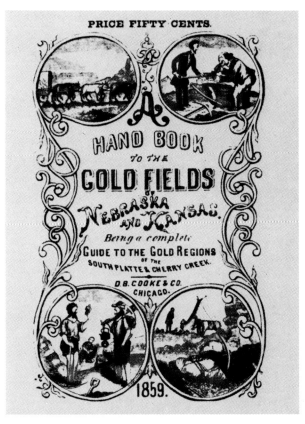

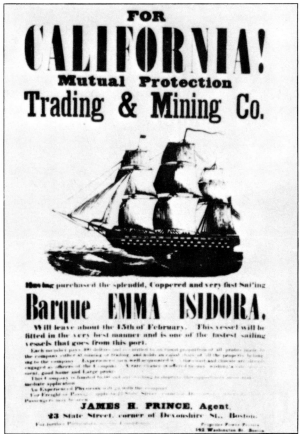

above Poster advertising a departure for the Californian gold mines, 1849.

auriferous rocks. They hammered and ground the minerals to powder which they then washed with a current of water over fleece. The heavy particles of gold sank to the bottom and were held by the grease in the wool, while the other mineral debris, being lighter, was carried away by the water. When it was dry the gold was shaken out of the fleece into a receptacle, ready to be melted into ingots. The legend of the Golden Fleece may owe its origin to this process.

Egyptian paintings of the 18th dynasty illustrate a process of washing the pulverised auriferous mineral by means of a sluice made of sloping wooden channels, with obstacles to trap the precious metal. Gold panning is another very ancient method used until the last century; the auriferous material was placed in a wooden bowl with some water; this was gently gyrated so that the water dislodged the lighter materials which floated to the top and were then carefully strained off. The process was repeated and fresh water occasionally added, until only the heavier material, which was, of course, gold, remained at the bottom. A very old system consisted in crushing a small quantity of auriferous material in a stone, iron or bronze mortar together with double the quantity of mercury, which amalgamates only with the gold particles. The excess mercury was filtered through a chamois skin, and the amalgamated mercury was liberated from the gold by distillation. Mercury was also used in the channels of the wooden-sluice method described above.

More efficient modern methods using machinery and chemicals have made it possible to extract still more gold from the old debris from mines and to take a larger percentage of the precious metal from auriferous minerals. The

above Gold washing machine used in California around the middle of the last century, from a contemporary engraving.

21

best system was invented by J. S. MacArthur and R. W. and W. Forrest in 1886. It is based on a cyanide process. Very finely ground gold-containing powder is put in a watery solution of cyanide and sodium which transforms it into potassium aurocyanide. Then by a complicated process, during which zinc and oxygen are used, the gold is precipitated and dried and treated with dilute sulphuric acid to dissolve out the zinc. The gold is then fused into ingots which are sent to a refinery to be finally purified of other metals.

According to the writings of Herodotus, gold would appear to have been quite easy to find. He recounts how in India ants the size of foxes would pile up heaps of nuggets extracted during the course of making their underground passages; the Indians would come in the heat of the day, while the ants were asleep, and take away armfuls of the precious metal. To a certain extent this story is corroborated by fact, as it is true that deposits of gold have been discovered in the materials thrown out by animals in the course of digging their lairs.

Ancient Deposits The most ancient extractions of mineral gold came, to the best of our knowledge, from Asia Minor. Herodotus, in writing about India, was probably thinking of a region whose limits at that time were vague and indefinite; he was quite possibly referring to the area of southern Mesopotamia where in the 4th millennium BC the Sumerian civilisation developed. Other deposits were mined in Nubia and Arabia by the Egyptians. The most ancient documentary evidence of these is a papyrus map of some gold mines dating from the 14th century BC, which is preserved in the Museo Egizio in Turin.

The Greeks found gold on some of the islands of Cyclades and in Macedonia and Thrace, and during the Hellenistic period Alexander the Great's conquests probably resulted in great quantities of gold flowing into Greece from Iran, Asia Minor and Egypt. During the period of the Roman empire, Italy, the Iberian province and Gaul assumed some importance as sources of gold. In his *Natural History* Pliny recounts that in the Vercellae region the employment of more than five thousand miners in the excavation of gold was prohibited.

Modern Deposits With the discovery and Spanish colonisation of America in the 16th and

22

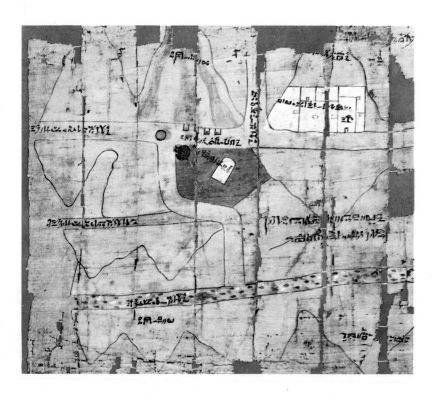

Egyptian gold-mining map on papyrus. Museo Egizio, Turin.

Goldsmiths at work, from a Theban fresco, Egypt, 18th dynasty.

17th centuries large quantities of gold and silver reached Europe, partly through plunder of the Indians and partly from the products of the Mexican and Colombian mines, which became substitutes for the exhausted mines of the old world.

In 1848 in North America gold nuggets were found by a sawmill builder in the American river near Colonna, California. The news of this discovery attracted crowds of prospectors and adventurers to the area, and in a few months the population of California had increased tenfold. At the end of the century new deposits, still productive today, were found in the region of the Yukon river on the Alaskan frontier with Canada.

In 1851 a miner, returned from California, found gold in the state of Victoria, Australia, in an area which he was certain manifested the same geological features. Important gold deposits were discovered in 1884 in the Transvaal in South Africa, and from that time South African mines have produced more gold than any other country. In modern times gold has been found in Europe, Transylvania and Siberia.

It has been calculated that in the twenty-five years from 1850 Australia and California together produced more gold than the total world production in the previous 385 years.

Gold Alloys Ancient craftsmen nearly always used gold in its natural form for the manufacture of jewelry even when they knew how to alloy it with other metals, because the purer it was, the more malleable it was. When alloyed with silver, the point of fusion diminishes in proportion to the amount of silver used. Silver and copper can be mixed with gold, in both liquid or solid form, in all proportions, but if the amount of copper exceeds 18% the gold becomes fragile and difficult to work. The larger the percentage of copper used in the alloy the redder the colour of the gold. The most common alloys used in modern jewelry are: 25% silver (green gold), 30% silver (gold leaf), palladium, nickel and not more than 75% gold (white gold), 15-20% iron (grey gold), 25% iron (blue gold).

24 The standard of a gold alloy is the percentage of pure gold it contains. The standard alloys most used in modern jewelry are: 916/000 = 22 carats, 833/000 = 20 carats, 750/000 = 18 carats, 625/000 = 15 carats, 500/000 = 12 carats, 375/000 = 9 carats. In the United States the most usual alloys are 10 and 14 carats. All alloys diminish the malleability of gold and increase its resistance. Thus something made of gold gains in permanency as it looses in delicacy of workmanship. While working on a piece of gold it is necessary to re-soften it constantly by heating, so that it does not become hard and therefore brittle.

Working No gold of any type is susceptible to compression or condensation while it is being worked; the molecules move and alter position according to the pressure they receive in such a way that, for example, when beaten gold increases in surface area while losing thickness.

In ancient times gold was at first worked with tools of wood, flint, copper and bronze and later of iron and steel. After being fused into lumps it would be beaten into sheets of the required width and then cut to dimensions approximating to the size of the desired object. The technique for reducing gold to thin leaves has been known since the earliest civilisations. Some Egyptian sarcophagi have been found covered with gold foil of a fineness which almost compares with what we can produce today. Gold beating is a lengthy process requiring great skill. In the past the sheets of gold, refined in advance, were placed between layers of carefully selected and prepared skins or parchments and then beaten; gradually the leaves of gold would become thinner and broader. The process of beating would continue until the required fineness was obtained; sometimes the gold leaf was almost transparent. An infinitesimally thin gold leaf was used for gilding metal or other objects and was applied by beating while it was hot or by means of special glues or other fixatives.

The making of gold leaf is not strictly within the bounds of our subject, but it does exploit the malleable properties of gold to an even greater extent than any other method of working.

Evidence shows that the first gold ornaments were sheets of various forms decorated in relief,

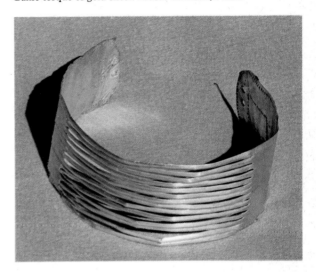

beaten or stamped onto stone, wood or bronze. Skill in doing relief decoration on gold developed very early. An important work dating from the 3rd century BC is a beautiful helmet in the form of a wig found in one of the Royal Tombs at Ur in Mesopotamia. This masterpiece shows that the technique of relief work was already highly developed. It is apparent that a sheet of gold of consistent thickness was beaten on a wooden or stone mould to make the rough shape and then hammered in *repoussé*; finally the detail was finished off on the right side with engraving tools.

There are various methods of making relief designs on sheet metal. The *repoussé* technique, particularly suitable for delicate work, consists

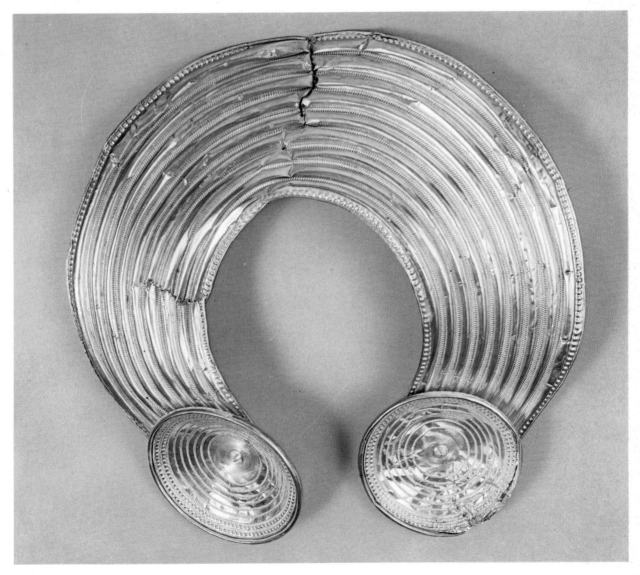

25

Gold collar with *repoussé* work, Ireland, 7th century BC. Victoria and Albert Museum, London.

Gold helmet with *repoussé* work and engraving, Ur, *c.* 2700 BC. Bagdad Museum.

of beating the sheet from behind as it rests against a yielding material such as lead or a pitch mixture, controlling the work constantly on the reverse side. The relief is then finished off on the right side with hammers and engraving tools. With this technique it is possible to obtain highly complex designs in high relief. Relief obtained with a cameo or intaglio stamp tended to be less prominent and was particularly useful for making jewelry with a repeated pattern as, for example, on the pieces of sheet

gold which, since the earliest civilisations, have enriched the robes of princes and dignitaries. A pointed tool made of agate was sharp enough to trace the outline of a pattern lightly on a sheet of gold resting on a background of wax.

To obtain completely round objects such as human or animal heads or amphoras a piece of metal was hammered into a hemispherical mould and then soldered to another similar hemisphere.

Engraving and Casting Another ancient

below Statue of king wearing a gold pectoral worked in
repoussé, Assyria, 883-759 BC. Museum of Fine Arts, Boston.

below Pendant made of gold sheet with *repoussé* work and
stamping, Noicattaro, 6th century BC. Museo Archeologico,
Bari.

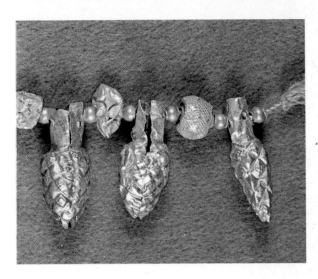

technique, used on ring bezels or pendants, was
to carve figures, scenes or designs in relief by
cutting the metal from the front with an engraving
tool of flint or bronze.

For reasons of cost it was rarely considered
worthwhile to cast from precious metals even
in the most advanced cultures. If the desired
relief from the cast was only to be visible from
one side, it was sufficient to fill the cast obtained
from a mould with melted metal and then to
finish it off with a chisel. If, however, the object
in question was to be fully modelled, the *cire* 27

above Gold necklace made of stamped pieces, Etruscan, 5th
century BC. Museo Nazionale di Villa Giulia, Rome.

below Gold ring with *repoussé* mask on the bezel, 3rd century BC. Victoria and Albert Museum, London.

below centre Gold ring bezel engraved with writing, 6th century. Victoria and Albert Museum, London.

perdue (lost wax) process was used. This consists of making a wax model, with a funnel at the base through which the melted wax escapes when heated. The model is then encased in a thick layer of clay; when it has dried it is put into a kiln with the dual purpose of baking the clay and melting the wax which then runs out. The gold is then poured in before the mould cools, through the same funnel. When the clay is finally removed the gold object is finished off with an engraving tool.

Filigree In addition to the various methods of relief work described above, the technique of making and using gold wire was also known from earliest times. It was used for framing, subdividing, decorating or supporting the elements of a jewel and in the making of rings, brooches, earrings, bracelets or buckles. From the beginning filigree, in a profusion of various shapes and sizes, played a very important role in the decoration of all kinds of goldwork. Before the invention of wire drawing the preparation of these threads was obtained by twisting a thin strip of metal into a spiral or by rolling fine strips of sheet metal between two very hard surfaces (possibly stone) until they were cylindrical.

While it is easy to see how plain wire was twisted in ancient times, there are many opinions about how threads were made into the shape of beads, bobbins, spheres and various other more complex forms which today would be made on a lathe. In ancient jewelry these pieces are minute, and their shape is so regular that it is difficult to imagine how they were made without any mechanical aid, however rudimentary. A beading tool actually described by Theophilus consisted of two small rectangular grooved blocks of bronze or some other substance harder than gold. When the indented faces of the blocks were placed together the semicircular grooves corresponded with each other and with marks on each side indicating the necessary position. Gold wire was then placed between the blocks, which were bound and hammered together forcing the wire to take the imprint of the patterned grooves. By using differently cut blocks various patterns and sizes of beads could be simply, quickly and accurately

above Gold ring bezel with *repoussé* work, Greece, 4th century BC. Victoria and Albert Museum, London.

Gold earrings in the form of Eros, Hellenistic, 4th-3rd century BC. Museo Nazionale, Taranto.

Spiralled gold wire from a necklace, Etruscan, 6th century BC. Museo Nazionale di Villa Giulia, Rome.

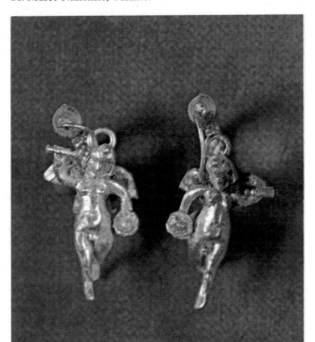

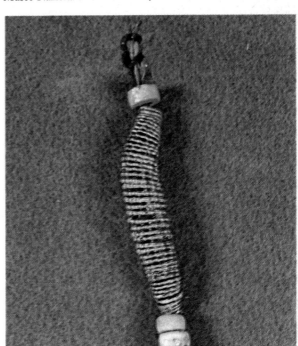

Gold earring with filigree work, chains and gold sheet, Hellenistic, 4th century BC. Museo Nazionale, Taranto.

obtained. This probably accounts for the wide application of this type of decoration in ancient jewelry in every area.

The fine gold wire could be used singly or any number of strands could be twisted together; in the hands of a highly skilled craftsman it looked like a plait, which was relatively flexible and often used in important pieces of jewelry.

The decorative use of simple or rounded wires is called filigree. The wire, bent by various methods into the desired design, is soldered onto a backing of sheet gold. Often the design can be made from two or three threads arranged parallel to each other. Filigree can also be used in openwork patterns without a background, which, of course, adds to the technical difficulties.

Chains Finally, gold wires in various lengths can be used for making the chains which have played an important part in jewelry throughout its history. The simple chain has been used at all times and does not require description. One of the most ancient type of chain used in decorative work is called loop-in-loop and can be made in various degrees of complexity. Whereas in the simple chain each link is made separately as the work progresses, the loop-in-loop variety is made from previously prepared links, which are pressed into an elliptical shape and folded in half. The single chain is obtained by slipping the looped ends of one link through another which is bent ready to receive the next link and so on, the last ring of the chain being closed by soldering. The double loop-in-loop, more solid than the single one, is made by passing each successive link through the looped ends of the two preceding ones, thus producing a more compact chain. This sort of chain can also be cross-linked to make a broader chain, perhaps four, six or eight links across. Highly flexible belts, necklaces, diadems and bracelets were made in this way.

Granulation One of the ancient goldsmith's techniques is granulation, and evidence of its use dates from about the 3rd millennium BC. It was in use in western Asia, Egypt, Greece, the Aegean islands and was intensely developed by the Etruscans between the 7th and 6th centuries BC. Then the use of the technique began to decline until it disappeared completely, apart from some rare example in north-west Europe in about AD 1000. Granulation is a form of decoration obtained by soldering tiny spheres of gold onto a background. The granules were probably made by placing pieces of gold (usually cut from a wire or sheet) between layers of powdered charcoal in a crucible. When heated the pieces of gold melted into minute spheres separated from each other by the charcoal. The charcoal was then washed away, and the granules graded for size by passing them over a punched sheet till each slotted into a hole of its own diameter. In some of the oldest examples the granules measured as little as 1/60 inch (0·4 millimetre), while in the finest Etruscan work granules measuring about 1/100 inch (0·25 millimetre) and even smaller were used.

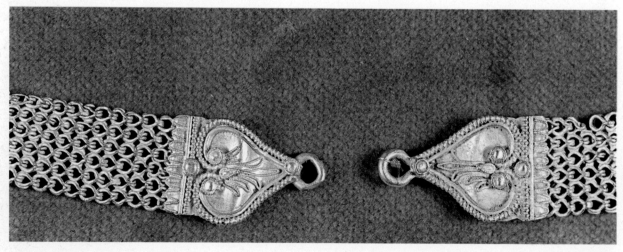

30

above Gold sheet fastening of a chain necklace, Greece, 4th century BC. Museo Nazionale, Taranto.

opposite Chain necklace with small pendants, from a tomb at Canosa, Hellenistic, 3rd century BC. Museo Nazionale, Taranto.

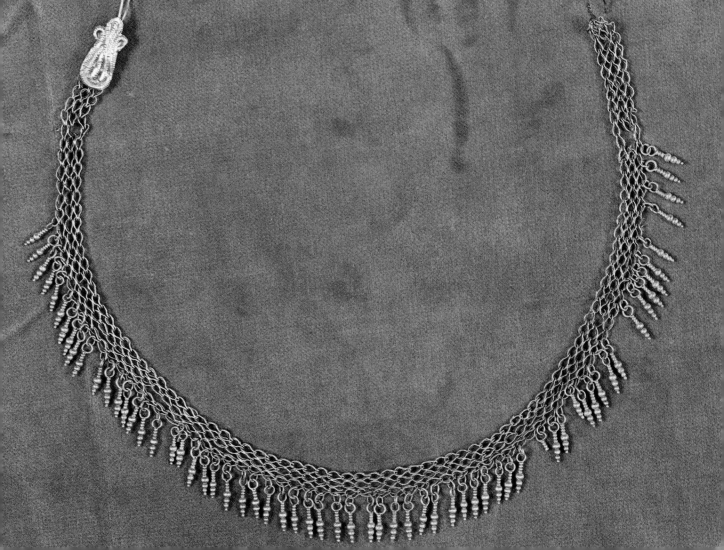

Filigree gold earrings, early Christian. Benaki Museum, Athens.

The granules could be arranged in simple linear or geometric patterns or massed to cover parts or all of the ornament. Occasionally they were used as a reversed silhouette: the background was filled in with grains, while the main embossed features were left plain.

After centuries of disuse the Roman goldsmith, Augusto Castellani (1829-1914), made various unsuccessful attempts to rediscover the art of granulation. The main difficulty was in soldering the granules both to each other and to their gold base so that the soldering was not visible. Then in 1933 an Englishman, H. P. Littledale, patented a process that he called colloid hard soldering which was undoubtedly very similar to, if not the same as, the method used by the ancient goldsmiths. The process is based on the fact that when copper is heated in contact with gold the melting point of the two metals together is noticeably lower than when they are separated. Littledale, therefore, used a copper-salt mixture to weld the granules to each other and to the base. The melting point could be achieved at 890°C, leaving a large safety margin for a piece of jewelry entirely in gold of which the melting point is 1060°C.

In Rome F. Magi and the chemist V. Federici have experimented with another process. They were convinced that the Etruscans made granules and powdered gold by pouring melted gold from a height of about $1\frac{1}{2}$ feet onto a slab of marble or some other polished stone. With this method they obtained granules of varying diameters and dust. To weld the granules into the desired pattern on the sheet which they were to decorate the two men experimented with a resin which they brought to red heat by means of a rudimentary blowpipe. Welding occurred as a result of certain residual tars in the resin which when heated acquire adhesive properties.

German experts have also studied the problems, coming to various technical solutions, all of them based on precise modern physio-chemical theories which in the past would have had to be found by trial and error.

It remains a mystery whether the men of antiquity were able to measure the melting point of gold and of other metals. Diodorus describes how the Egyptians ground and washed

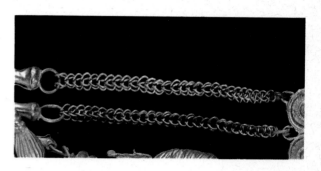

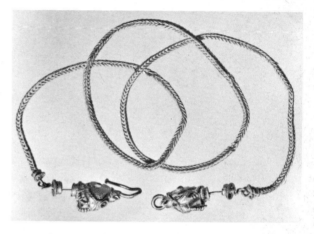

above Gold necklace of 'loop in loop' chains. Private collection, Switzerland.

gold-bearing minerals and then put them with equal proportions of lead, salt, tin and barley into earthenware pots which were sealed and baked in kilns for five days and five nights. This process apparently served to obtain pure gold. In other words a massive purification took place. The time mentioned by Diodorus must relate to the time it took to bring the metal to the correct temperature. Evidently, therefore, the ancients must have had some sort of system unknown to us of measuring temperatures.

It is apparent from the fineness of the gold leaf used in ancient jewelry and the application and soldering of various decorations often of minute proportions that a high degree of visual control was required. The theory of Magi and Federici of the use of the blowpipe is, therefore, convincing. The method used by the Greeks and the Etruscans to fix granules of gold would appear to be the same as that used to fix filigree and to weld together moulded hemispheres. The most amazing thing about the jewelry of this period is the microscopic proportions of

33

its components. Some of the tools used by the ancient goldsmiths for their work must have had needlefine points.

Soldering The various parts which go to make up a piece of jewelry are worked separately and then finally put together. They can be joined by such methods as hinges, by two pieces folded together and burnished and with pieces of binding wire. Soldering, which belongs to the most highly developed phase of the goldsmith's art of ancient times, was used in Mesopotamia from the 3rd millennium BC and in the Minoan civilisation of the 2nd millennium. Two pieces of gold are joined by a binding material with a lower melting point, so that the binding can melt without damaging the gold ornament. As all base metals oxidise when they are heated, the surfaces are coated with a substance known as a flux (in antiquity probably burnt sediment of wine or natron) which stops the metal oxidising when red hot, and chips of solder are placed between them. The two parts are then secured with strips of binding wire to ensure and maintain the correct position during the heating.

Stamped figures on a granulated background, from a sword belt from the Aliseda treasure, Phoenician-Punic, 6th century BC. Museo Arqueológico Nacional, Madrid.

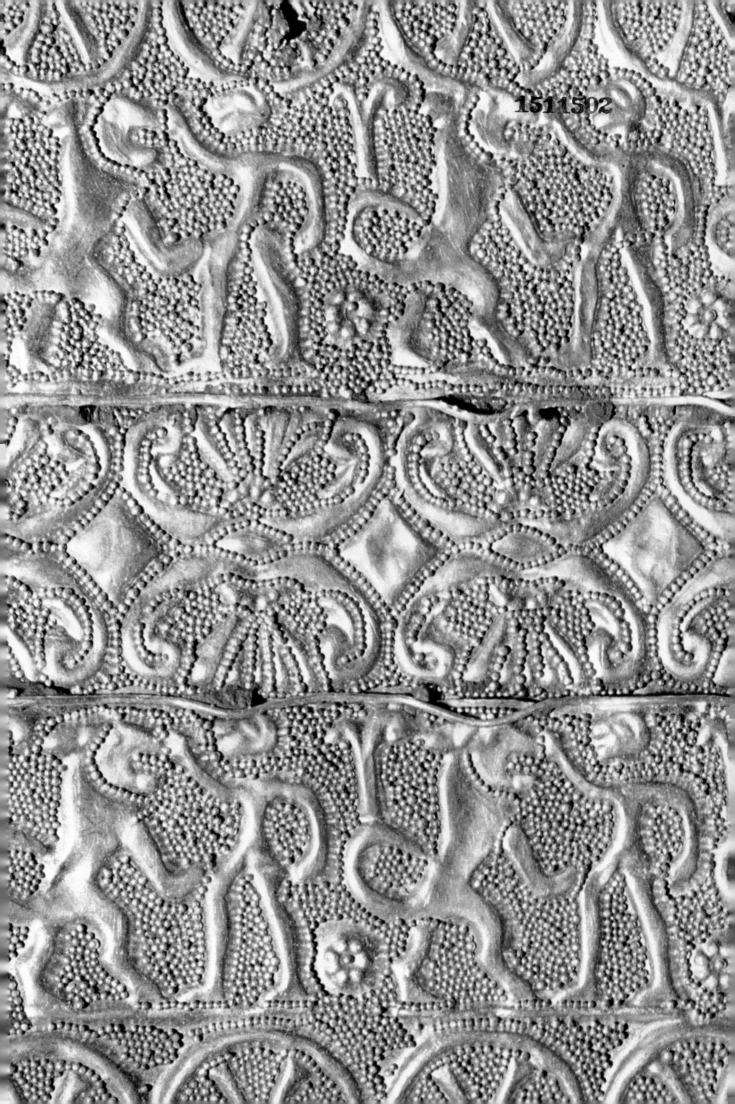

Gold

The use of gold in the ancient world

The history of the development of jewelry is linked with the most advanced civilisations of the past. Today, thanks to archaeological finds, we can trace the development of the styles and forms characteristic of the jewelry from the various areas or regions of the earliest cultures known to us. Relics of the distant past are scarce for obvious reasons: jewelry is relatively small, easily transportable and liable to be damaged or melted down and remade; in addition gold has always been the chief object of booty in sackings and robberies. Fortunately many tombs containing funeral treasures have been found intact. These have been, and continue to be, sources of interesting precious objects, which, in accordance with religious beliefs, were buried with or on the body of the person to whom they had belonged.

It would appear that by the 4th millennium BC various tribal groups of the ancient world were beginning to reject their nomadic life for a more settled existence, and by the beginning of the 3rd millennium important social groups were rapidly developing. The largest organised societies, or at least those whose expansion is registered in history, appear to have chosen fertile river valleys for their settlements. These areas were also untapped sources of precious minerals, which were the primary materials in the manufacture of jewelry.

Thus the movement of peoples when the civilisations of the world were just evolving was bound to that of the rivers. The Sumerian civilisation of Mesopotamia began in the regions of the Tigris and the Euphrates, the Egyptian civilisation developed around the Nile, Troy was situated on the Scamander, the Indian civilisation arose on the banks of the Indus and the Chinese one along the course of the Hwang, the great Yellow River.

In attempting to trace the broad outlines of the history of jewelry and in order to gain some idea of the vast panorama which precedes the Christian era we must be guided by the evidence of the most significant archaeological finds. From these it seems logical to start with Mesopotamia where, by the 3rd millennium BC, we find indications that the Sumerian civilisation was already well developed. Turning our atten-

Cult object in the shape of a woman's arms, made of cast bronze decorated with gold serpentine bracelets, Hellenistic, 3rd-2nd century BC. The hands are fixed on a pivot hinge so that they are mobile. Museo Nazionale, Taranto.

37

tion to jewelry we can establish that most of it was made entirely of gold. Primitive ornaments of feathers, seashells, animal bones and coloured stones had already been superceded. In fact if any material other than gold was used, even precious or semiprecious stones, the object was considered less valuable. Apart from the ancient civilisations of the Indus and the Nile, which showed from the beginning a predilection for coloured jewelry, until the Alexandrian period jewelry was made entirely of gold.

Before examining the important Mesopotamian developments in jewelry, it is interesting to point out that at about the same period in Troy, which was relatively far away, Priam's treasure was also being made entirely of gold. Unfortunately this, though important, is an isolated piece of evidence and many centuries away from the first Mediterranean civilisations, while the Mesopotamian region affords us richer and more continuous evidence of jewelry styles. In particular, the most often recurring motifs of the 3rd and 2nd millennia served as points of departure for the evolution of this art which was inherited by the Assyrians and Babylonians, handed down to the Iranians and interacted with the Scythians to the north and the Hittites to the west. Through the Scythians the goldwork of Mesopotamia was to influence lands as far off as China. Meanwhile, in the Mediterranean region the Phoenicians enlarged their sphere of activity and spread their art; and the Iranian culture thrived and was enriched, transmitting and receiving influences as far as Greece.

The Sumerians The ruins of the city of Ur, situated in the south of the Mesopotamian region about twelve miles from the Euphrates, were visited for the first time in 1625 by Pietro della Valle. However, the region was identified as the Ur of the Chaldees of the Bible only in 1854 by J. E. Taylor, the English consul in Basra, through a cylinder seal which he found at the site. From 1922 widespread systematic excavations were carried out by an archaeological expedition sponsored by the British Museum, London, and the university of Pennsylvania and led by the English archaeologist Sir Leonard Woolley. During these excavations

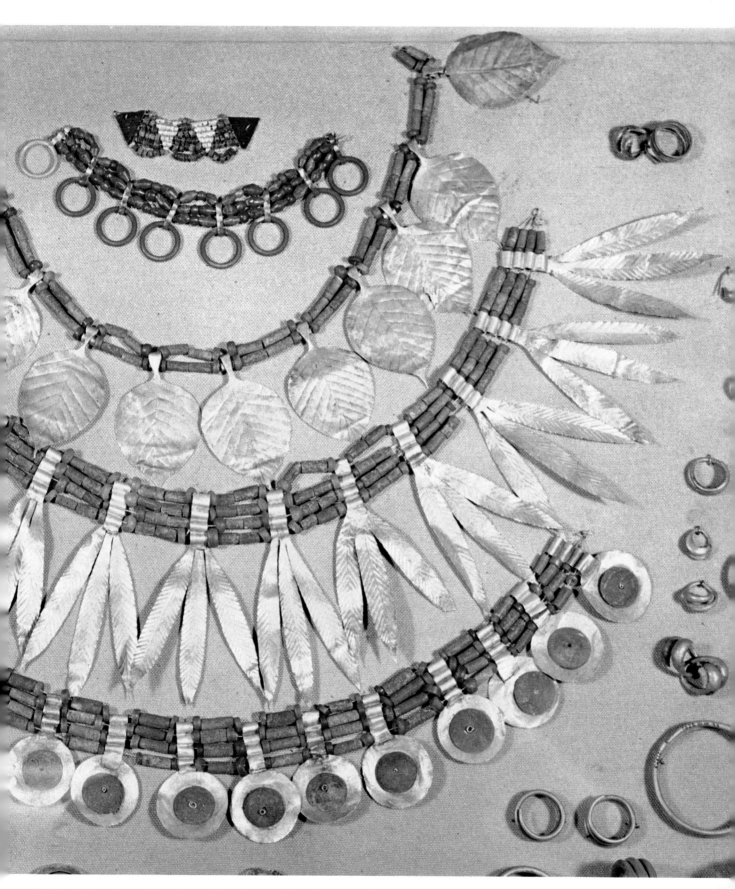

Gold and faience jewelry from Queen Shubad's tomb, Ur, 2685-54 BC. British Museum, London.

Man with a necklace and earrings, from a relief fresco. The Apadana Palace, Persepolis.

the discovery of the so-called Royal Tombs constituted the greatest and richest archaeological discovery since Tutankhamen's tomb.

It was Queen Shubad's tomb which aroused the most excitement. In the spacious burial chamber lay the body covered with a sort of robe made of beads of gold, silver, lapis lazuli, cornelian, agate and chalcedony, bordered by a fringe of small tubes of gold with lapis lazuli and cornelians. The relative abundance of stones is accounted for by the fact that this was a richly embellished costume rather than a piece of jewelry. Lying beside her right arm were three long gold hairpins with lapis lazuli heads, three amulets in the shape of fish, of which two were gold and one lapis lazuli, and a fourth amulet in gold bearing the figures of two seated gazelles. A headdress, which must have been worn over a very wide thickly padded ceremonial wig, consisted of a wide gold band surmounted by three delicate golden diadems of decreasing diameter one on top of the other. The first, worn low over the forehead, was made of large interlocking pendant discs, the second was made out of long gold willow leaves in groups of three, and the third was a wreath of thin gold beech leaves, so naturalistic that even the veins are visible. In addition there was a comb with five teeth decorated with upright golden flowers to fix into the back of the wig. Enormous gold earrings in the form of two linked, tapered semitubular hoops completed the dazzling headdress. Round the neck hung a necklace of three rows of semiprecious beads, supporting a gold central ornament consisting of a ring attached to a flower.

The high degree of refinement of these pieces is found also in the goblets, plates and bowls, the decoration on the chariots, the symbolic animals and musical instruments all of gold or silver which were also found in the tomb. They are the culmination of a mature and long tradition of goldwork.

The Royal Tombs of Ur also contained the bodies of servants and ladies-in-waiting, the animals which pulled the funeral carts, and the guards and dignitaries of both sexes who had formed the funeral processions of their sovereigns and who died and were buried with them

below Alabaster statue with amber and gold jewelry, Persia, 6th century BC. Louvre, Paris.

below centre Gold pendant, Ur, 2500 BC. British Museum, London.

so that they could render their service in the afterworld. Ceremonial costumes interwoven with gold and valuable headdresses were made for their burial.

Sumerian jewelry fulfilled practically all the ornamental functions which were to occur during the course of history; in fact there were more different types of jewelry than there are today. Men wore bracelets round their wrists and on the upper part of their arms, earrings, gold pectoral ornaments, rings and necklaces. Women of high social rank frequently wore great padded wigs surmounted by diadems, and even women of lower rank would wear a gold headdress or some fabric interwoven with gold. Five linked bracelets were frequent; tubular shapes were widely used whether in necklaces, bracelets or earrings; circular and disc shapes were popular, as were small joined hoops. Later the stylised flower motif with up to thirteen petals occurs and was for many centuries the distinctive motif of Mesopotamia, with the same significance as the lotus flower in Egypt and the palmette in Greece. Objects from the Royal Tombs show that in the first half of the 3rd millennium BC forms of expression were orientated towards a highly developed naturalism. Besides the plant motifs, many figures of animals have been found which must have constituted some sort of cult symbols or had some magico-religious significance. Uniform geometrical designs executed with fine precision, such as those which decorate Queen Shubad's rings, were also used during this first period.

There then followed an era of development which lasted, with various stylistic modifications, up to and including the whole of the 1st millennium BC. The changes were expressed particularly in the representation of animals. Their form is often adapted to the limits of a particular object; and they are characterised by a strict likeness and a powerful suppleness obviously derived from a thorough knowledge of anatomy, achieving a free, harmonious and rhythmic effect.

The Scythians This style of Mesopotamia spread towards northern Persia and was later assimilated by the Scythians, seminomadic or nomadic tribes of the Eurasian steppes, who

41

above Man with a diadem and earrings, from a relief fresco. The Apadana Palace, Persepolis.

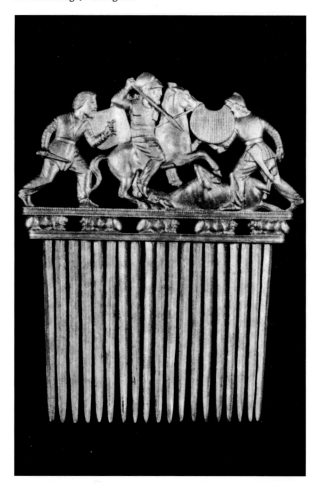

Gold comb with openwork figures of a battle scene between infantry and cavalry from Solokha, Scythian, 5th-4th century BC. Hermitage, Leningrad.

inhabited the regions between the Danube and the Don dispersing in the east towards north China and in the west towards the Balkans. The animals, which so frequently occur in Scythian works, have a characteristic bold expressive force and a high degree of stylisation on the most sophisticated artistic level. The representations of deer, wild beasts or bulls suggest magical rather than ornamental functions. The oldest Scythian gold ornaments are very basic in form. A great quantity of plaques and gold sheets of various shapes and sizes worked in relief have been found; they are often pierced with holes which suggests that they may have been used on clothing. A small gold comb from a king's tomb near the city of Nicopoli (Hermitage, Leningrad) depicts a battle between infantry and cavalry. This is not the sort of theme one would expect to find on a woman's ornament, and, despite its appearance, it may not have been used as a comb at all. Women's jewelry is rare in Scythian art; far more frequent, however, are harnesses and gold ornaments for horses. These horse trappings have been found on animals which were buried with their masters.

When some of the Scythians came into contact with the Trans-Caucasian civilisations and absorbed their way of life and social organisation the skilled Scythian metalworkers swiftly adapted the new influences. The Ziwiye treasure shows the stylistic modifications which occurred. After a landslide between Kurdistan and Azerbaijan an Assyrian bronze sarcophagus containing treasure was found. Its contents were immediately pillaged by the local inhabitants, but recovered by A. Goddard in 1949 for the Teheran Museum and can now also be found dispersed among various American museums and in the Louvre, Paris.

The exquisite items of the treasure were probably made in the royal workshops by the best available workmen of many different origins. A large quantity of women's jewelry is included: necklaces, earrings, rings, bracelets, brooches and buckles. There is also a very unusual ornament, now in the Archaeological Museum, Teheran, which consists of a gold glove made of diamond-shaped net, with a fine

double chain covering the palm and the back of the hand held at the wrist by a chain circlet and clasped over the fingers by five rings, one for every finger (three are missing).

Another object of great artistic significance also in Teheran is a gold half-moon-shaped breastplate. The front is decorated with parallel ornamental bands and bordered with a fringe of cones supported by small arches. Between the two bands is a carved scene depicting a procession of fantastic hybrid beings, mostly animals of obscure symbolism, converging on a sacred tree. A gold belt, formed of equal divisions, every alternate one containing carved figures of deer and goats, is notable for the combination of decorative balance and perfection of taste which place these ornaments among the most beautiful in the world and indicate how much this strong centre of Scythian origin imbibed from south Caucasian culture.

Towards the end of the 6th century BC the

below Gold bracelet from the Ziwiye treasure, Persia, Achemenean period. Archaeological Museum, Teheran.

Front view of the bracelet illustrated above.

Gold griffins from the Ziwiye treasure. Archaeological Museum, Teheran.

position of the Scythians in Central Asia altered. Pushed back across the Caucasus they extended their hegemony to southern Russia.

While the Ziwiye treasure probably belonged to a Scythian sovereign, the Oxus treasure, discovered in 1877 on a tributary of the river Oxus or Amu Darya which marks the frontier between Afghanistan and the USSR, would appear from its mixed contents of precious objects of various origins to have been a trophy of war. Most of its rings, necklaces, bracelets, chains and pendants bear the influence of Iranian style.

To conclude this survey of the production of jewelry in Central Asia and Eurasia, it can be said that the Sumerian civilisation initiated a period in which the highest standards were attained, both in technical perfection and artistic expression, and that the various civilisations which later followed in this vast area consolidated this tradition without equalling it, perpetuating its stylistic and thematic characteristics which were Iranian in inspiration and which for a long time remained unaltered by outside influences. Moreover, the Trans-Caucasian nomads of the Steppes, some of whom returned as conquerors and absorbed a higher level of civilisation, attached particular significance to the little gold objects used as personal ornaments apparently with ancestral significance.

Crete and Mycenae In the course of history contact was established with the Mediterranean civilisations of Egypt, the Aegean, Greece and Rome, and the ornamental styles of Central Asian gold jewelry passed into the western tradition. While the eastern civilisations were slowly declining, the Aegean civilisation was asserting itself in the Mediterranean. The jewelry in Priam's treasure is almost contemporary with those of the Royal Tombs of Ur, but has completely different stylistic characteristics; it is related rather to the Mycenean products of several centuries later. However, there is no lack of examples of jewelry in a naturalistic style from the Aegean area, as, for instance, the floral patterned jewelry discovered on the little island of Mochlos near Crete.

Excavation has revealed the great developments which took place in goldwork in general and jewelry in particular between 1800 and 1400 BC in Crete, Mycenae and other island and mainland centres. The most important finds were those at Knossos and Mycenae. The styles and subjects found in Minoan-Mycenean metalwork are wide ranging, dominated by an intense interest in nature, which is often represented with a high level of realism. The rich

Gold bracelet from the Oxus treasure, Persia, Achemenean period, 5th century BC. British Museum, London.

Gold bracelet with winged animals from the Oxus treasure, 5th century BC. British Museum, London.

variety of decorative subjects ranges from sea creatures to flowers, from wild beasts to timid deer, from fierce hunting scenes to the dynamic rhythms of popular dances. All are characterised by great expressive vitality, even when the complicated linear patterns, which so richly embellish the designs, are contained within a basically symmetrical framework. Technical advances were made, and filigree and granulation were introduced. Another new process was the technique of stamping for mass production.

One of the earliest things to be found was a pendant of the middle Minoan period (17th century BC) now in the Heraklion Museum. It is in the shape of two hornets, their curved bodies seen in profile, forming an irregular circle in the centre of which they hold with their legs a honeycomb of granulated gold; their tapered wings, which are spread out on each side, have indented edges; three discs with granulated edges hang one from each wing and one from the bottom of the joined bodies.

Many earrings have been found, particularly in the shape of bulls' heads, with curved horns forming the ring by which the ornament was attached to the earlobe. This motif occurs frequently, depicted either highly naturalistically or in a stylised way in the form of a disc with spirals at each side of the top. Massive rings, with gold bezels carved with figurative scenes, recording costumes, legends, ceremonies, men and beasts fighting, symbolic animals and dances, offer a vivid and animated picture

Gold plaques decorated with stamped figures of a winged Artemis, from a necklace, Rhodes, 7th century BC. British Museum, London.

above centre Gold ring bezel depicting a scene of offering, Tirinto, 15th-14th century BC. National Museum, Athens.

above Gold ring, Mycenae, 15th-14th century BC. Victoria and Albert Museum, London.

45

Gold pendant of hornets, from the necropolis at Chrysolakkos, Mycenae, 17th century BC. Heraklion Museum, Crete.

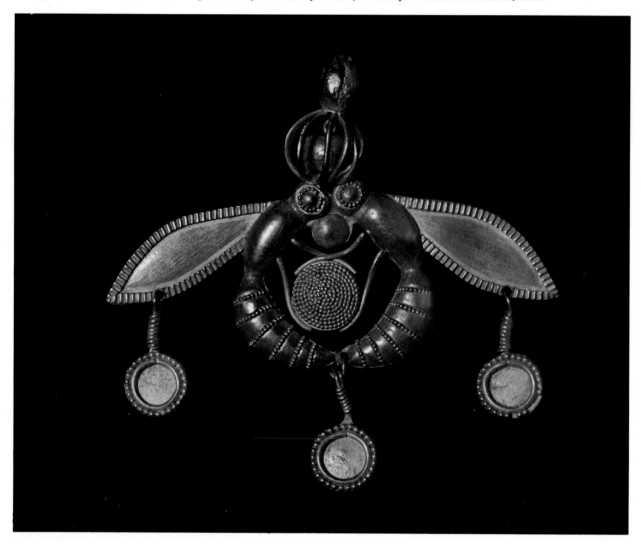

of a world of dynamic activity portrayed with spontaneous freshness and unprecedented effectiveness, in a style which, although sometimes summary, is always full of expression.

Very often several metals would be used together on one object: gold, silver, bronze, iron, lead and copper. An unusual bracelet from Mycenae consists of bands of gold and silver and gold foil; it has a central ornament in the form of a flower with sixteen fluted petals and a bronze and gold centre.

There are also many pins decorated with stamped heads of reliefs of animals and sea creatures. Beads, stamped from sheets of gold, are particularly numerous; they are decorated with a variety of designs: geometrical scrolls, intertwined ribbons, rosettes of various shapes and stylised shells.

With the expansion of the Creto-Mycenean culture towards the 6th century BC the mass production of the jewelry was increased still further by the use of stamps. At Mycenae Schliemann found 701 stamped discs in one tomb alone. Cyprus, Rhodes, Troy and Syria were part of the Creto-Mycenean culture, which spread through the intense commercial trading which was carried on throughout the Mediterranean area.

The Phoenicians Among the most important and skilful traders and colonisers at the beginning of the 8th century BC were the Phoenicians, who through their trading activities helped to spread eastern art forms. Other influences came from Phrygia and Lydia, while Egyptian contacts came indirectly through Syrian art. Finally ancient Minoan-Mycenean motifs reappeared,

46

Gold and silver bracelet decorated with a gold rosette, from shaft grave IV, Mycenae, 1550-1500 BC. National Museum, Athens.

probably through some ancient art which had preserved them.

In the earliest times the Phoenicians inhabited the area of Syria and Israel, but by the 8th century BC they had been expelled and had moved to the African coast east of the Syrtis and had colonised Utica near Carthaginia, Marsala in Sicily and Cadiz in Spain. Their trade centres became centres of culture. It is impossible to assess with any accuracy just how great was the role played by these seafaring profiteers in the circulation of artistic ideas in various regions, but gold objects excavated in places where the Phoenicians exercised dominion provide evidence of an eclectic art which often expressed itself in the spirit and character indigenous to the various places.

Among the Aliseda treasure in the Museo

above centre Circular gold clothing ornaments stamped with stylised butterfly and octopus, from shaft grave III, Mycenae. National Museum, Athens.

above Earrings made of double gold sheet from grave III, Mycenae, 16th century BC. National Museum, Athens.

47

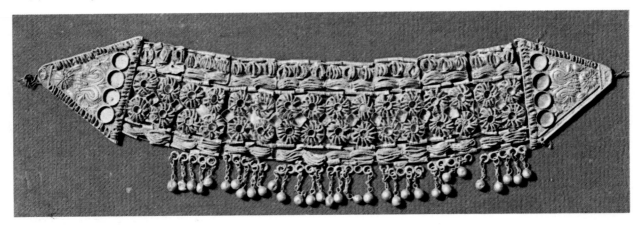

Arquelógico Nacional, Madrid, is a sword belt made of squared pieces of plate gold which is decorated with the repeated theme of a fight between a man and a lion, clumsily copied from a plaque found among the Ziwiye treasure. The granulated background of the repeated scenes and the unusual character of the relief in the Aliseda objects indicate Arabian influence. In a pair of earrings from the same hoard the tasteful richness and grace of the designs based on palms, bells, tendrils and birds are reminiscent of the richness of Spanish Baroque. Another interesting object is the famous sculptured bust of a goddess known as the Lady of Elche in the Prado, Madrid. She wears a headdress consisting of two wheel shapes hanging one over each ear, her forehead is adorned with several gold bands and a sumptuous necklace hangs around her neck.

A different spirit pervades the jewelry from Tharros, Sardinia. A five-part bracelet, with a winged scarab as its central subject and patterns arranged symmetrically around it, suggests an Egyptian origin with Greco-Cypriot influences. The same elements and the same taste are present in a drop earring, consisting of a succession of pieces suspended from each other, which show Egyptian, oriental and Greek derivation. The fact that granulation is widely found in these pieces gave rise to the erroneous supposition that the process inherited by the Etruscans was found in jewelry of much greater antiquity,

above Gold pierced bracelet with palmette-shaped finials, from the Aliseda treasure, Phoenician-Punic, 6th century BC. Museo Arqueológico Nacional, Madrid.

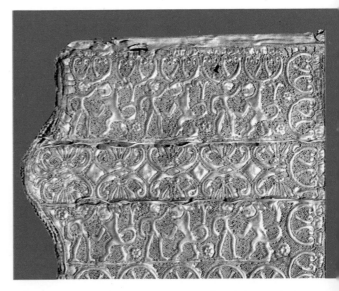

above Fragment of a sword belt of a sheet of gold decorated with granulation, from the Aliseda treasure, 6th century BC. Museo Arqueológico Nacional, Madrid.

The Lady of Elche, Phoenician-Punic, 6th century BC. Prado, Madrid.

although it is highly probable that the Etruscans did learn it from the Phoenicians who used it extensively.

During this period, when the Phoenicians were expanding and the Mycenean culture was declining, various Greek mainland and island centres displayed stylistic manifestations using geometric designs still showing oriental influences. These characteristics are clearly in evidence in the jewelry from Aegina acquired by the British Museum in 1892. Greek dependance on oriental styles during the 7th century is apparent in these pendants and necklaces, which have a composite style primarily dominated by oriental decorative and symbolic elements. The products of the Greek islands, especially Rhodes, are richer and more interesting than those of the mainland. On Rhodes have been found necklaces made of gold plates stamped with repeated designs, earrings also of great originality, pins, bracelets and decorated gold plaques, which form a collection of undoubted decorative interest, although somewhat lacking in creative originality.

The Etruscans The Etruscan work of the same period is very different. Many influences were at work shaping the early styles of Etruscan art, in particular that of the Phoenicians, who through their vast trading activities were in contact with all the Mediterranean centres and brought with them traces of oriental culture. At Caere, Tarquinia, Vulci, Praeneste, Vetulonia and elsewhere all these influences became assimilated and formed an original style and technique which was entirely Etruscan in character.

Granulation was the most important decorative technique; it was used on animal and human figures or in ornamental motifs either outlining the pattern or silhouetting it. Fibulae, breastplates, necklaces and sword belts are decorated with minute and elaborate tracery of various different kinds of granulation, resulting in a new and arresting richness and effect. The excellent and frequent use of granulation by Etruscan goldsmiths indicates that the process was rapid and sure.

Particularly original were the complex and varied designs of Etruscan earrings and fibulae. Characteristic earring designs were *baule* (named after their resemblance to a bag) in the form of a cylinder, tubular hoops, metal bands

below Gold pendant with decorative elements of Egyptian influence, from the Aegina treasure, Creto-Mycenean, 18th-17th century BC. British Museum, London.

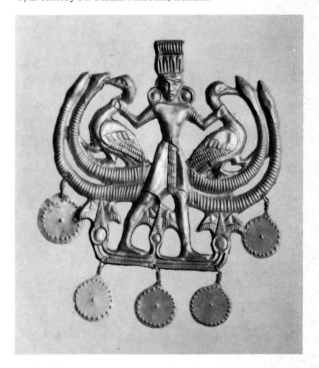

above Gold bracelet with *repoussé* decoration outlined with granulation, from Tharros, Phoenician-Punic, 7th century BC. Museo Archeologico Nazionale, Cagliari.

and oval discs, often quite large and always worked with microscopic precision. Fibulae were made in two main shapes (serpentine and leech) with bow and foot decorated with lions, horses' heads, chimaera or sphinxes.

A real monument to Etruscan jewelry is the fibula from the Regolini-Galassi tomb at Caere now in the Museo Etrusco Gregoriano, Vatican Museums, Rome. Its shape suggests a strange musical instrument and the decorative and plastic materials are skilfully arranged in a harmonious composition.

Unlike in Mesopotamia where naturalistic and sculptural elements took precedence over the decorative, Etruscan work maintained a happy equilibrium between the two, often producing ornaments whose significance as works of art was as great as their decorative value. From the same tomb at Regolini-Galassi is a breastplate made of a gold sheet densely decorated with punched patterns. Here the ornamentation is so elaborate that nothing is discernible and the result is a texture of inferior artistic merit. Bracelets from Vetulonia in the

above Fibula made of double gold sheet decorated with animals in powder granulation, from the Littore tomb, Vetulonia, Etruscan, 7th century BC. Museo Archeologico, Florence.

Large gold fibula decorated with granulation and stamping, from the Regolini-Galassi tomb, Etruscan, 7th century BC. Museo Etrusco Gregoriano, Vatican Museums, Rome.

below Ornament made of long cylindrical granulated pieces supported by winged beasts, sphinxes, chimaeras and lions in stamped and granulated gold, from the Barberini tomb, Etruscan, 7th century BC. Museo Nazionale di Villa Giulia, Rome. Detail on pages 56-7.

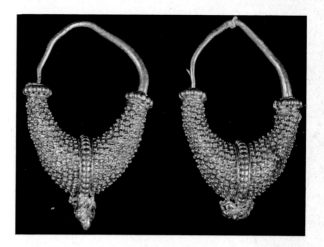

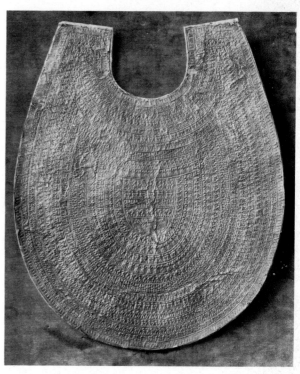

Museo Archeologico, Florence, however, made of parallel bands joined by openwork filigree are designs of exquisite elegance and grace.

One of the few Etruscan necklaces of this period, also from the Regolini-Galassi tomb, consists of two rows of small chains, three spindle-shaped pendants hanging on rings, an amber medallion above and at the bottom leonine bosses with buds. Another characteristic design for necklaces is a chain or band from which hang one or more embossed gold pendants, such as one with repeated embossed women's heads from Vetulonia in the Museo Archeologico, Florence. Generally in finds of this period gold necklaces are scarce, while amber abounds.

After its initial phase of development free from all Greek influences the expansion of the Etruscans towards the north and south gradually brought them into contact with the Greek colonies of Spina and southern Italy. Etruscan art became heavily overlaid with the more severe characteristics of Greek art, although it never completely lost its identity, and greater attention was paid to the plastic content of the components. There is a noticeable difference, for instance, between the plastic characteristics of the heads of the Vetulonian necklace and another 6th-century necklace from Ruvo (Museo Nazionale, Taranto) in which the influences of Ionic art are visible. They are still clearer in a necklace bearing an ornate head of Silenus, also probably from Ruvo (6th to 5th century BC) in the Museo Nazionale, Naples, and a beautiful one from Praeneste with a single

55

above centre Pair of leech-shaped gold earrings decorated with granulation, Greco-Italian, 4th century BC. Museo Nazionale, Taranto.
above Decorated gold breastplate engraved with sixteen different punched patterns, from the Regolini-Galassi tomb, 7th century BC. Museo Etrusco Gregoriano, Vatican Museums, Rome. *Left* Earrings of various styles on busts of women of the Etruscan period. Museo Nazionale di Villa Giulia, Rome.

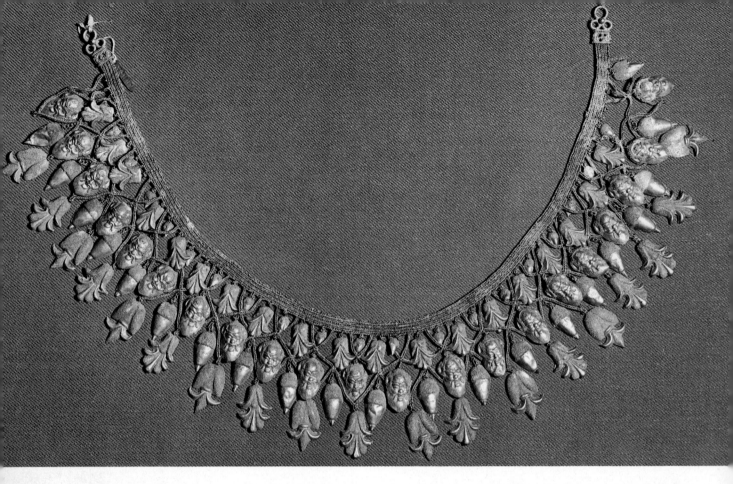

pendant of the head of Achelous of the 4th century BC. Etruscan jewelry now abandoned all stylistic links with its first period, and, though some of its own peculiar characteristics remained, it became closely bound up with the traditions of the Greek colonies in southern Italy and ended by becoming part of them.
Classical Greece In Athens, Attica and the larger islands, after the development of the geometric style, which concentrated on the 8th- and 7th-century linear designs of Crete and Mycenae and which valued the mixing of Mycenean and oriental decorative elements, goldsmiths' interests began to turn increasingly towards the human figure, no longer in summary stylised representations, but with more expressive awareness of reality and proportion. At the beginning of the 6th century BC Attica came to assume the postion of spiritual and artistic centre of the Greek world, and in time other independent artistic centres such as Corinth, Rhodes and the Cyclades were over-

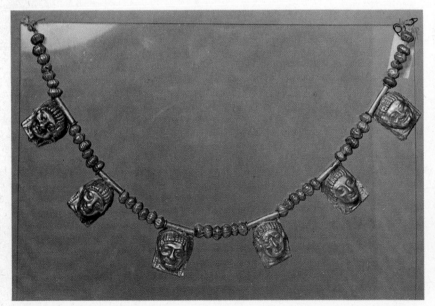

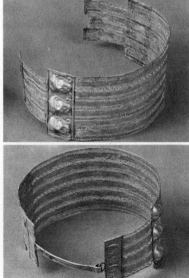

top Strap necklace with pendants and heads of Silenus, from Ruvo, Etruscan, 6th-5th century BC. Museo Nazionale, Naples. *above left* Gold necklace with stamped masks of a woman, from Ruvo, Etruscan, 6th-5th century BC. Museo Nazionale, Naples. *above right* Gold sheet bracelets with openwork, from Vetulonia, Etruscan, 7th century BC. Museo Archeologico, Florence.

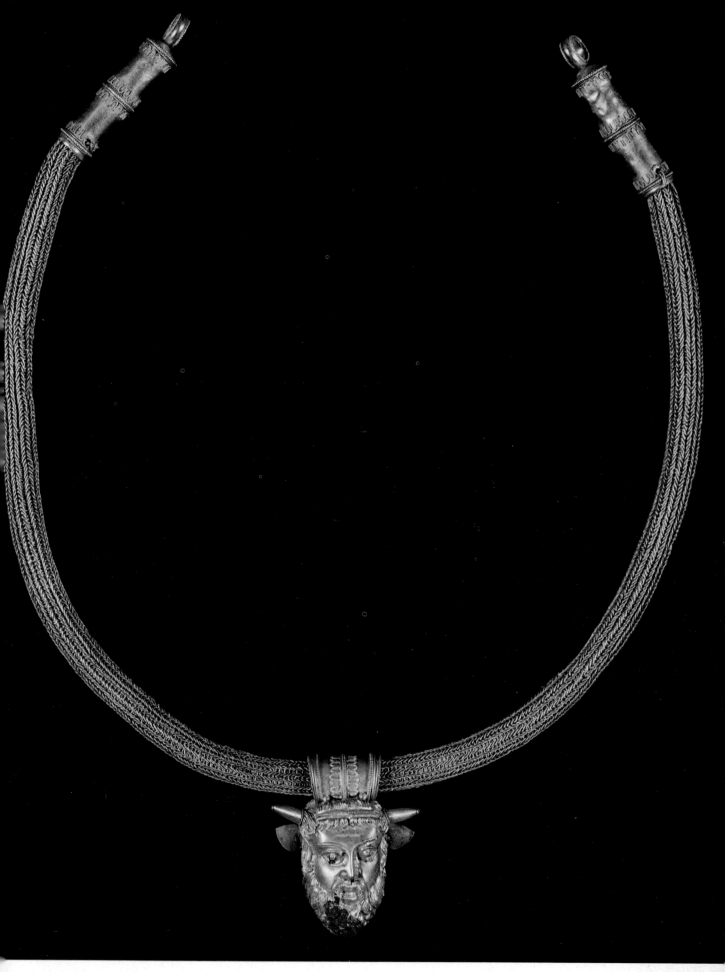

Necklace of thick, tubular-shaped chain meshwork with a head of Achelous, from Praeneste, Etruscan, 4th century BC. Museo Nazionale di Villa Giulia, Rome.

Gold *a baule* earring, Greco-Etruscan, 3rd century BC. Victoria and Albert Museum, London.

jewelry went through its most glorious period in every way. Gold continued to be the sole or almost the sole object for this splendid evolution.

Jewelry and in particular gold ring bezels of the Classical period, inspired by contemporary sculpture, frequently portrayed the human figure either standing or moving; women, bearded men, representations of Silenus, Hermes, Aphrodite, Perseus, Athena, Eros and Nike were part of the repertoire of metalworkers, and there are many examples of quality and finesse. Leech- and disc-shaped earrings continued, while new shapes included anchors, bunches of grapes, upturned pyramids, flower or palmette pendants and hoop earrings with finials decorated with women's heads, rams' skulls or floral motifs. Diadems and decorated headdresses, often of embossed gold with a decorative centrepiece, were worn by men and women over their symmetrically parted hair.

The scarcity of Greek jewelry of this period is partly counterbalanced by literary evidence. We know that Pheidas' great gold and ivory statue of Athena in the Parthenon had enormous gold rosettes, pendant necklaces and huge cluster earrings. Other temple statues were also embellished with gold and must have called for frequent and close cooperation between sculptors and goldsmiths greatly to the advantage of the latter. Some idea of the variety of precious ornaments in use is gained from the inventories of temple treasures; among objects given as offerings were numerous bracelets, anklets, buckles, pins, earrings, rings and necklaces.

Two unique masterpieces of amazing technical skill point to a significant phase in Greek jewelry around the middle of the 5th century BC. They are the Sphinx Pin and the Capital Pin, which were found in a tomb on the west coast of the Peleponese near Patras and are now in the Boston Museum of Fine Arts. The $1\frac{3}{4}$-inch head of the former has an astounding amount of complex decoration which must have called for infinite patience on the part of the goldsmith. A small lobed sphere is surmounted by a bud with eight petals which curl alternately up round the bud and down over the sphere;

whelmed by the incontestable cultural superiority of Athens. Before developing into the brilliant period of the Classical era Greek art had to overcome the somewhat artificial and rigid ideas of the Archaic period. Production of jewelry in this period seemed to be restricted, probably due to a shortage of gold. Although an era of great brilliance and virtuosity stylistically, it tended to fall back on forms derived from old concepts and lacked somewhat in imaginative creativity.

During the Classical period, when sculpture achieved such heights, the minor arts, above all goldwork and jewelry, developed little and were in any case restricted by the many finance laws which were passed at that time. The Greek colonies in southern Italy, however, enlivened by the culture drawn from the mother country, would seem to have been more productive, and many finds have been brought to light. During the succeeding Hellenistic period of expansion with Alexander the Great's fabulous conquests, the plastic arts lost their creative force, while

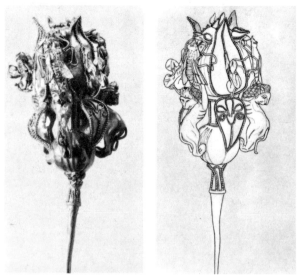

The Sphinx Pin and drawing by Suzanne Chapman, the Peloponese, 5th century BC. Museum of Fine Arts, Boston.

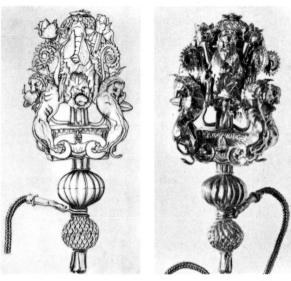

The Capital Pin and drawing by Suzanne Chapman, the Peloponese, 5th century BC. Museum of Fine Arts, Boston.

between the petals are four clinging rampant lions, heads facing outwards, each surmounted by a wasp; above the petals round the bud are arranged four sphinxes. The leaves, the insects and the stem which joins the sphere to the bud are minutely embellished with filigree.

The three-inch head of the second pin is decorated with a similar composition except that the lions rest their hind paws on the scrolls of a capital, beneath which are two spheres one fluted and the other honeycombed; the lions are surmounted by four scrolls which curl outwards and are decorated with a zigzag pattern.

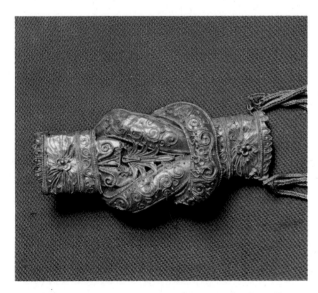

Gold Heracles knot decorated with filigree and floral motifs, from a tomb at Ginosa, Greco-Italian, 4th century BC. Museo Nazionale, Taranto.

Instead of a bud there is a pinecone. These splendid pieces, especially the almost scientific reproduction of the wasps, the heraldic style of the lions and the ornamental richness of the filigree, are fine examples of the naturalistic style. Oriental, Etruscan and Egyptian influences are united in the composition of these pins by the interpretation of a personality of considerable artistic stature.

Hellenistic Greece Efforts to correlate dates of the history of art with political events or with the ends of centuries are useless and, while they may help in orientating oneself, have no effective reference to the facts. This applies to the Hellenistic era which can be said to begin politically with Alexander the Great's accession to the throne in 336 BC rather than with his death in 323 and to end in 31 BC with the Battle of Actium or 87 with the fall of Athens. In art history boundaries are much more fluid, since no king or battle has ever forced stylistic changes overnight.

The 4th century was a period of important development for Greece; the city-states were overwhelmed by greater monarchies, some of which held widely extended territories. This has led some historians to consider the cultural and artistic activities of the various kingdoms separately. In fact, however, Hellenistic art has its solid foundations in Greece as a whole, and

61

the new concepts which countered Classic-ism with human expressivity and naturalism were part of the renovation of ideals of life of a fundamentally civilised people.

Thanks to Alexander the Great's eastern victories large quantities of gold flowed into Greece as the plunder of war and from mineral deposits and mines in the conquered territories. In Macedonia more systematic methods were applied to the extraction of gold, and the re-newed abundance of gold caused a colossal inflation in the Greek economy and provided a great impulse to the production of jewelry. Strong Persian influences are manifest in the first part of this period especially in certain types of jewelry such as bracelets, and many examples have been found in Thrace, Asia Minor, Egypt and Italy. The new taste for luxury, which radiated from the court, was fostered by the many Persian women brought to Greece. This had wide repercussions on jewelry fashions: a noble woman of a certain rank would not dream of being without a vast amount of jewelry, including a diadem, a brace-let, a massive and elaborate belt, rich medallions which would hang from a chain at her throat and lavish earrings.

Towards the end of the 4th century BC semi-precious stones began to appear in Greek jewelry. At first garnets were used in the bezels of rings which were not intended as seals, and then, though very sparingly, in diadems, neck-laces and bracelets. Occasionally emeralds imported from Egypt, cornelians, agates, sar-donyx and rock crystals also appeared. The range of stones became gradually richer until colour was finally the dominant factor. There is no doubt that the taste for polychrome jewelry came with Indo-Persian influence. It is said that the Persian king Sophithes presented himself before Alexander the Great with shoes made of gold and precious stones.

The great quantity of finds indicates that Hellenistic jewelry production flourished, not just in Greece itself, southern Italy and Sicily, but in the many peripheral workshops in the Asian territories, in Thessaly, Macedonia, Asia Minor, central Asia and in southern Russia. Obviously there were local stylistic variations

63

Gold diadem with nine pendants and a Heracles knot in the centre, decorated with garnets, and various kinds of filigree; above the knot is a winged Victory flanked by two sea serpents. From Kerch, southern Russia, Hellenistic, 2nd century BC. J. Loeb collection, Antikensammlungen, Munich.

and preferences, but Hellenistic jewelry was
basically homogeneous throughout this vast
area, and a high average level of quality was
maintained. Since jewelry was easily portable
many exported pieces have been found.

The lavishness and virtuosity of Hellenistic
jewelry reached its zenith in such pieces as the
elaborate earrings from Theodosia (Hermitage,
Leningrad) and another similar pair found in
Asia Minor (Metropolitan Museum, New
York), which has pronounced Indian characteristics of style, or in the Peleponese earrings
in the Boston Museum, which represent a
winged Nike driving a chariot. Other examples
of splendour are the fabulous diadem in the
Loeb collection of the Antikensammlungen,
Munich, and the similar, equally beautiful
examples in a private German collection and the
Benaki Museum, Athens; all these include as
a centrepiece the characteristic Heracles knot
(similar to a reef knot) finished or decorated
with garnets. In addition to these highly exceptional works there are numerous others of
exquisite workmanship, which contribute to
make the jewelry of the Hellenistic era among
the most beautiful ever produced.

An ornament from Taranto, now in a private
Swiss collection, is thought to be a woman's
hair net, although the unconvincing suggestion
has been put forward that it is designed to cover
the breast. It consists of a medallion, with the
head of Medusa in high relief, set in the centre
of a skullcap made of gold wire net festooned
with garnets. The edge of the net cap, which
can be fastened from the back, is finished off
with a decorated gold band and a Heracles knot
in front. A curved medallion in the Rhode
Island Art Museum has nine rings round its
circumference to which a similar net was probably once attached; in the centre is a bust of
Aphrodite in high relief. A third medallion with
the head of Athena as its emblem (Fitzwilliam
Museum, Cambridge) comes from southern
Russia, while a fourth (Count Henri de Clercq-
Boisgelin collection) has a bust of Eros beauti-
fully represented with powerful realism.

Medallions and Heracles knots were also used
in necklaces as pendants or as centrepieces in
necklaces made of gold links. Another popular

Gold leech earring with filigree decoration, Hellenistic, 4th
century BC. Museo Nazionale, Taranto.

Woman's ornament with a medallion of Medusa's head in high relief and a flexible gold net decorated with garnets, from Taranto, Hellenistic, 4th-3rd century BC. Private collection, Switzerland.

design was the strap necklace with small pendants in the form of little jars, pinecones, women's heads or spear-heads, hung either directly or from chains and always delicately decorated with wide use of filigree. In other types of necklace the decorative motif consists solely of two animals' heads suspended on chains, carrying in their mouths the ring and fastening hook of the clasp. Other necklaces are made of tubular elements often entwined with animal forms at the open ends which are linked by a chain. There are also some made of linked

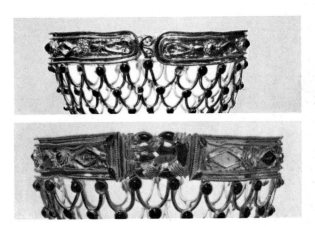

Details of the ornament illustrated above: Heracles knot fastening at the front and clasp at the back.

below Central part of a gold diadem decorated with acanthus and lotus leaves, Hellenistic, 4th century BC. Museo Nazionale, Taranto.

bezel-set semiprecious stones in approximately spherical shapes decorated with filigree.

Pendant earrings with images of Nike, sirens, dancers or cupids hanging from a clasp embellished with a rosette were popular in all the Hellenic areas. Sometimes instead of the rosette there is a little medallion, with a head carved in low relief; some examples have pyramid-shaped pendants with complicated filigree decoration. Hoop earrings of several varieties continued in use, either plain or of coiled wire with heads of lions, goats and many other animals. More unusual are the Negro's head ornaments from Bettona now in the Museo Nazionale di Villa Giulia, Rome.

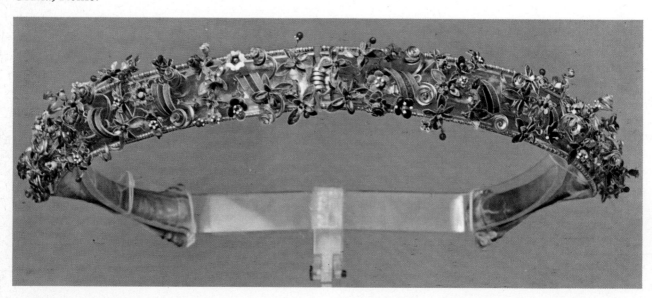

above Gold diadem elaborately decorated with small green, white, red and blue flowers in enamel, from a tomb at Canosa, Hellenistic, 3rd century BC. Museo Nazionale, Taranto. *right* Detail.

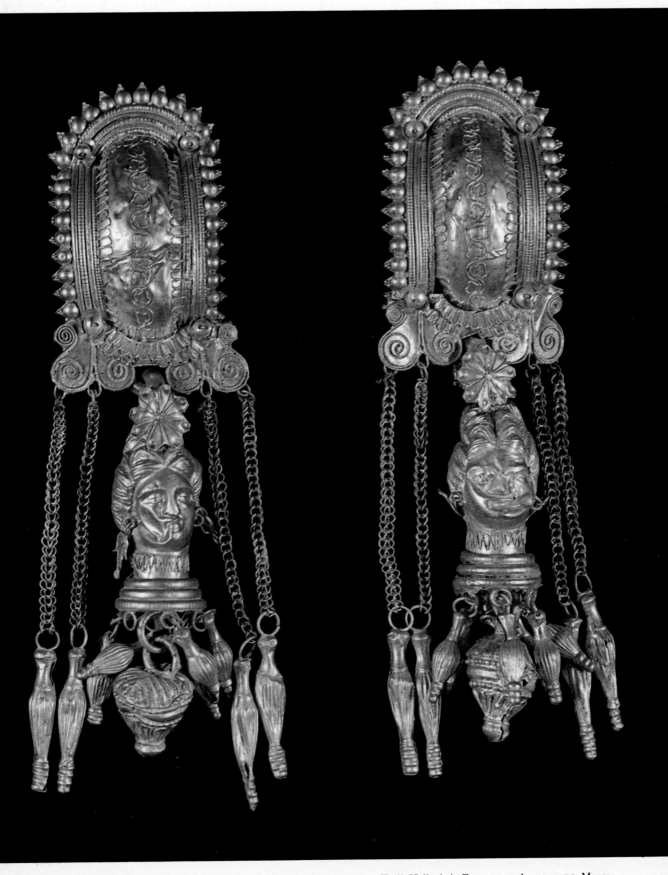

Gold pendant earrings with women's heads and engraved hair, from a tomb at Todi, Hellenistic-Etruscan, 3rd century BC. Museo Nazionale di Villa Giula, Rome.

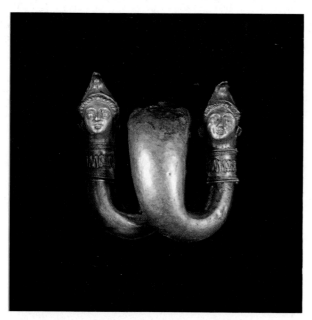

Gold spiral earring with woman's head finials, Greek, 4th century BC. Museo Nazionale, Taranto.

Gold earring showing a fully modelled group of Nike driving a chariot, the Peloponese, 4th century BC. Museum of Fine Arts, Boston.

The large variety of bracelet shapes is further enriched by an inexhaustible repertory of decorative motifs. Some consist of hoops finely wrought with vegetable motifs; those of oriental origin are often of twisted ribbons of gold with animal head finials. A rare example (Ashmolean Museum, Oxford), which comes from Alexandria, consists of a solid gold band, with concave outer surfaces; towards the centre the band broadens and in it is set a medallion with a bust of Isis carved in relief. Spiral bracelets, mostly in the form of snakes, continue from the Classical period and were to have great popularity in the Roman era. They vary from one spiral to as many as six and might be made of

two serpents whose tails formed a Heracles knot as in the one in the Schmuckmuseum at Pforzheim.

There were fibulae in the shape of tubular arches interrupted by dense, minutely detailed decorations, with the terminal part embellished with fully sculptured animal heads and other ornamental forms. One of these from Macedonia is now in the Metropolitan Museum, New York. The leech or boat shape continued, again inventively enriched at the whim of the goldsmith. In others the arch is in the shape of a leaf and the catch-plate is decorated with a terminal sculptured motif. Pins have heads decorated with animals and birds or a figure of

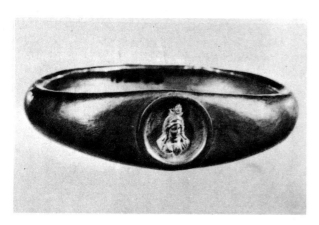

Gold bracelet with a bust of Isis in high relief, from Egypt, Hellenistic, 4th-3rd century BC. Ashmolean Museum, Oxford.

Gold fibula decorated with floral motifs, from Campania, Hellenistic, 4th-3rd century BC. Cleveland Museum of Fine Art.

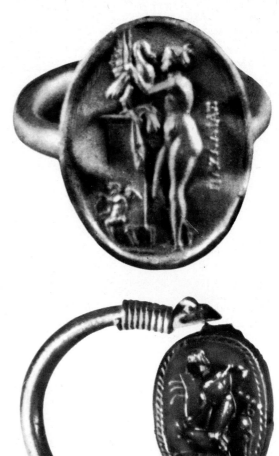

a god on a capital. Gold belts were generally made of intricately woven chains and many have Heracles-knot buckles sometimes further enriched by an animal or human head at the join of the chain.

Stones both plain and engraved were now extremely popular in rings. Those with gold bezels, which are often oval, are stamped for seals or carved in relief with animals, beast fights, profiles of women or images of gods. Compared with those of the Classical period, these carvings have a vitality and realism, which, combined with a disciplined technical quality, constituted the distinctive characteristics of Greek jewelry. Another popular style of ring was a smaller version of a bracelet in the form of a coiled snake.

In the important tumulus at Vix, a village near Châtillon-sur-Seine, a most unusual widely curved torque, thought to be a diadem, was found near a woman's corpse. The finials of the tubular arch, which is gracefully tapered, end in the form of lions paws resting on smooth pear-shaped bullae, the bases of which are exquisitely decorated with a design of concentric circles. On the backs of the paws, between them and the bullae, are two small winged rampant horses resting their hoofs on an elevated oval made of various strands of wavy filigree. The diadem has been dated by archaeologists to the beginning of the 5th century BC, and, although some scholars believe it to originate from Hallstatt, this is the most convincing theory. The various other objects of Greek origin found in the same tomb probably also signify the source of this splendid diadem.

The Celts While Greece was expanding in the 7th century BC, another active centre of civilisation was developing in central Europe east of the Rhine. The famous Austrian cemetery at Hallstatt near Salzburg gives its name to the earliest European iron age culture. During its formative period it was apparently not affected by the cultural influence which was continually radiating from Greece. An export trade in salt, which was plentiful, was the foundation of its economic wealth. Apart from agriculture and commerce, the craft activities of the people of

70

Gold diadem from the Vix treasure, Greco-Scythian, 5th-4th century BC. Musée de Châtillon-sur-Seine.

this civilisation were well developed, especially techniques of working all types of metals from iron to gold. The few pieces of jewelry which have been found indicate a considerable richness in the decoration of women's clothes. Fibulae, bracelets, rings and necklaces were made from gold plates and chains, punched and worked in *repoussé* with highly stylised zoomorphic and geometric motifs.

In the 5th century BC the Celtic culture of La Tène, which originated in western Switzerland, imposed itself on that of Hallstatt, influencing an even wider area for a greater period of time. It extended from Ireland to Asia Minor and preserved homogeneous characteristics in its art forms, with various modifications, until the

Roman conquest, and in the British Isles well into the first millennium AD. The Celtic style expressed itself above all through the working of metals in which the Celts excelled. Its roots were based on local Hallstatt traditions combined with ancient Greco-Etruscan influences and contact with the northern nomads, including the Scythians, which were welded into a style quite distinct from that of the Mediterranean world. Its decorative motifs were complex abstract patterns; fantastic elements exerted an indisputable fascination and the non-representational treatment of animals was applied with imagination and held magical symbolism.

The torque was a characteristic Celtic ornament worn by men. Either solid or in two articulated sections, it could be smooth or twisted with terminals decorated with simple hemispherical forms or by some other more elaborate ornament. In some the front part is worked with relief decoration, with a prominent central group, while the rest is ornamented with vigorous volutes interrupted by other protruding shapes which give rhythm to the composition.

A gold bracelet from Aurillac in the Cabinet des Medailles, Paris, is decorated along its external circumference with an intriguing and complicated plastic composition in high relief which was an absolutely new decorative concept for bracelets. There are, however, many examples of the traditional styles, which usually consisted of solid decorated bands of various widths in the open-ended torque style.

There were new ideas in ring design, too, the decoration of which could be called anti-traditional. Rings generally consisted of bands of various types embellished with reliefs, bordered with small pearls or rough geometric patterns. There was no element which suggested the bezel in any way.

With the conquest of Europe by the Romans, Celtic art moved to other areas, Britain and Ireland, where it was able to continue its long evolution, preserving the original principles which inspired it and enriching them with coloured enamels.

Torque and bracelet with decorated finials, from Rheinheim, Celtic. Landesmuseum, Saarbrücken.

Necklace torque of electrum from Snettisham, Norfolk, Celtic, 75-25 BC. British Museum, London.

73

Gold

The use of gold in Pre-Columbian America

Large gold breastplate in the form of the god of death, Mixteco-Puebla, 14th-15th century. Museo Regional de Oaxaca.

Some regions of Pre-Columbian America can be considered important centres of civilisation and are, therefore, directly relevant to our subject. With no apparent contact with cultures of other continents, the ancient people of the Andes and Central America achieved their own major artistic evolution. The richest gold and mineral deposits in general are in Colombia and are still productive today.

The area between the two parallel Cordillera ranges of the Andes, stretching from the south in the region of Lake Titicaca to as far north as the descent of the mountains into the valleys of Colombia and Ecuador, was the scene of the development of a great civilisation which it is thought reached a high artistic level between 3000 and 7000 BC. The people who formed the Andean culture are thought to have been in part indigenous tribes, who, expanding from the western limits of the Amazon forests, crossed the mountain heights to the coast, and in part foreigners, who came from the north by land or sea.

Opinions about the correct dating of these events have changed, the first estimates placed the period too early; according to more recent studies the Chavin culture of the southern territories is dated to about the 5th century AD and the Mochica and Nasca cultures to the 7th and 8th centuries, followed by the expansion of the Tiahuanaco tribe, which had a highly developed political, social and religious organisation around the 10th century. By the 14th century all these had become part of the Inca empire whose centre and capital was Cuzco. The most beautiful gold of the Andes region came from the centres of Chimu, Chancay and Ica, and especially the first, during the Tiahuanaco and Inca periods. For the Colombian and Ecuadorian regions it has not yet been possible to establish firm dates, but approximate chronology puts the San Augustin area as the oldest, followed by that of Chitcha. In the latter region, the most significant finds were the Quimbaya treasure and the products of the High Cauca.

The civilised regions of Mexican Central America, which is theoretically limited by the Mexican state of Sinaloa to the north and by Honduras and Nicaragua to the south, manifested an artistic development which, together 75

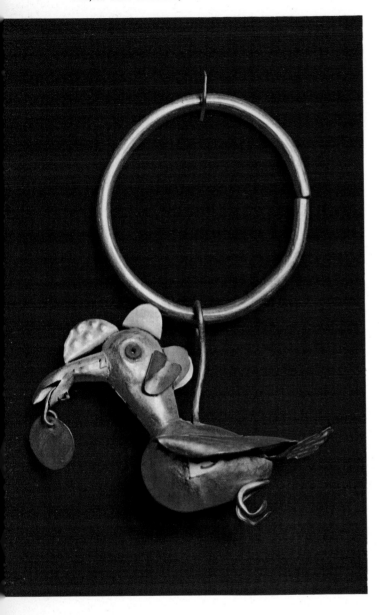

there may have been some link with the Asian
continent. Apart from the gold beating and
repoussé work, the peoples of the Andes, in
particular the northern Chibcha, knew how to
weld and understood the *cire perdue* process,
alloys and copper gilding. A commonly used
alloy was *tumbaga*, which consisted of copper
and gold and was as current among the Andean
cultures as among the Mexican. Copper gilding
was achieved through a process in which plant
saps were mixed with oxalic acid. Pre-Columbian gold ornamental objects, particularly the
earlier ones, probably had religious functions,
as they were often linked with funeral rites.

Great quantities of jewelry and precious
objects have been found at the bottom of sacred
lakes and pools in Colombia. In a description
of the rites of this country chronicles describe
an initiation ceremony for chiefs. The candi-
date, after a period of penitence which rendered
him worthy to be elected, smeared his body with
gold dust, went out on a raft to the middle of the
sacred lake and dived into the water. In addition,
many precious objects were thrown into the
waters ·as offerings to the gods of the lake.

Despite the indiscriminate plundering and
the total spoliation which accompanied the
horrifying massacres of the Spanish conquest,
6700 pieces of Pre-Columbian goldware are
conserved in the Bogota Museum of Gold. To
these one can add a possibly even greater quantity scattered in museums, private collections
and antique markets throughout the world. The
only collection in Peru, that of Miguel Mujica
Gallo, contains above two thousand pieces.

As in Asia, gold was widely used on clothes.
About 13,000 pieces of gold were found sewn
together on a poncho from Chimu. On certain
occasions priests wore tunics made entirely of
strips of gold foil sewn onto cloth. High priests,
nobles and warriors wore a *narriguerra*, a gold
ornament. At its simplest it was disc-shaped;
more complicated ones took the form of an upturned fan with pendants which hooked onto
the nostrils. *Orejeras*, traditional heavy earrings
worn by men, were usually tubular hoops with
openwork ornamental or zoomorphic decorations and a gem in the centre. Two disc-shaped
earrings from the Mujica Gallo collection are
bordered with concentric patterns in pearls,

with that of the Andes, is the most important
of the Pre-Columbian era. This culture was the
work of various peoples who lived at different
periods in large areas of Mexico, Guatemala,
Salvador and in limited areas of Nicaragua and
Honduras.

Mexican craftsmanship in gold developed
about a thousand years after that of the Andes,
partly because the region was poor in gold and
the metal had, therefore, to be imported from
the central southern regions.

Andean Civilisations The techniques known
in the Andes were so advanced that the possi-
bility is suggested that in the pre-Christian era

76

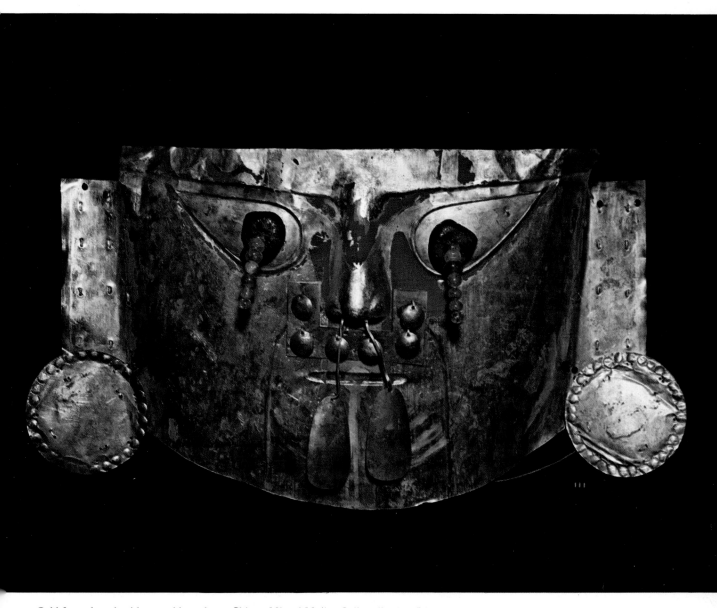

Gold funeral mask with emerald pendants, Chimu. Miguel Mujica Gallo collection, Lima.

while on the disc itself is a fully modelled toucan. Another earring in the same collection consists of a fantastic bird suspended from a plain hoop. Splendidly decorated breastplates in various local styles were in wide use; in addition to anthropological and zoomorphic representations, they were decorated in *repoussé* with the various ornamental motifs often in high relief, which were a feature of Andean culture. A breastplate in the Nationalmuseet in Copenhagen is bordered with embossed stamps of a bird with spread wings and the head, which is very protruding, of a type of cuttlefish. In addition to ornamental motifs of a typically local character we find, perhaps by chance, patterns familiar in the West: the spiral, the Greek key and a version of the running dog. Small ornaments for use on clothing are often embellished with highly realistic reproductions of a large variety of marine fauna.

Among the most remarkable necklaces are those from Chimu (AD 1000-1200). An outstanding example, which was put up for auction at Christie's of London on 21st May 1968, consists of a circlet of granulated gold to which are attached eight similar figures of gods in ritual

Necklace of seven rows of rectangular silver and copper plaques worked in *repoussé* and finished with a row of shells, transition period between the Chimu and the Incas. Museo Arqueológico 'Bruening', Lambayeque.

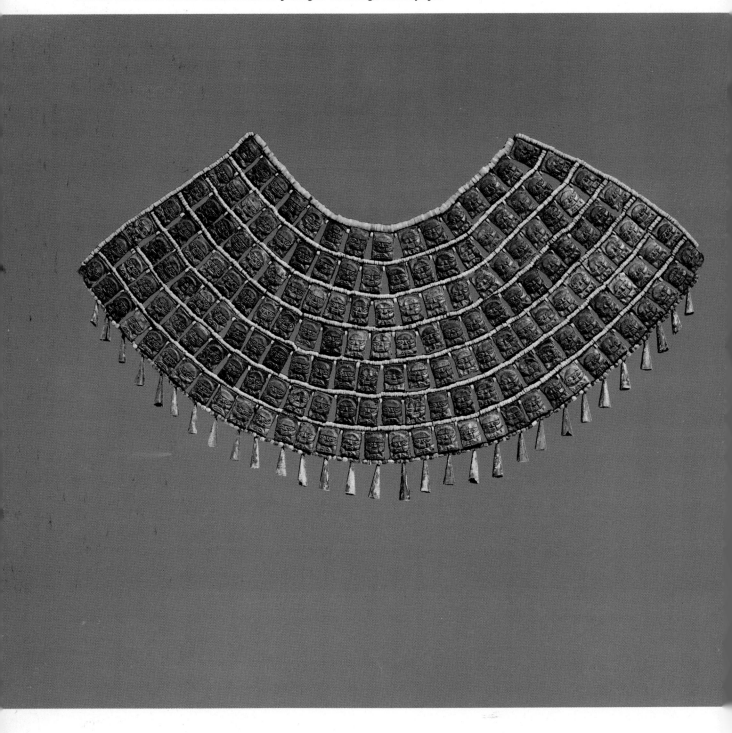

poses worked in *repoussé*; they are alternated with other smaller figures attached to the circlet by two granulated wires. Some other Quimbaya necklaces are made of *tumbaga* pieces in abstract forms of uncertain origin.

Precious stones used in Inca jewelry were rock crystal, emeralds, lapis lazuli, turquoise, pearls and coral. Peruvian skill in making alloys of gold is demonstrated by the remarkable range of different colours, which vary from white to copper-red. Bronze alloy was known to the Andean civilisations later than that of precious metals.

Mexico In the northern region, as well as

78

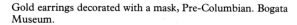

Gold necklace, Chimu, *c.* 1300, British Museum, London.

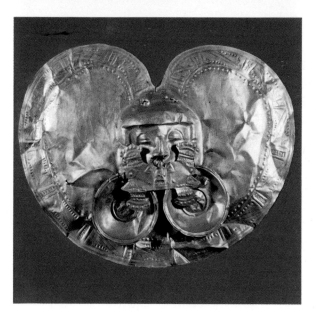

Gold pectoral with a mask, Pre-Columbian. Bogata Museum.

importing gold, goldsmiths were brought in from outside. In the few examples we have, stylistic influence from the Andes can be detected during the Aztec period. The range of ornaments does not differ from that of the southern regions. The stylistic form shows strongly the high expressiveness characteristic of Aztec art which tended to a disciplined plastic interpretation. Of the animals used in decorations, the serpent figures most frequently and in ornamental motifs the disc, sphere or spheroid and bell-shaped pendants often appear.

In the southern region of the Mexican territory the Maya were specialists in the use and carving of jade. The gold objects found in these areas were mostly imported from the southern regions or had been handed down from the ancient Toltec culture. Under Aztec domination things did not change: goldsmiths were still of Andean origin, and, though their formal themes underwent some variations, the basic style remained invariable.

The Spanish conquest put an end to the Pre-Columbian artistic activities. In the centres where the richness of the deposits allowed, what remained of indigenous handicrafts were adapted for works which, with the introduction of Spanish elements, evolved into a hybrid style completely lacking any interest.

79

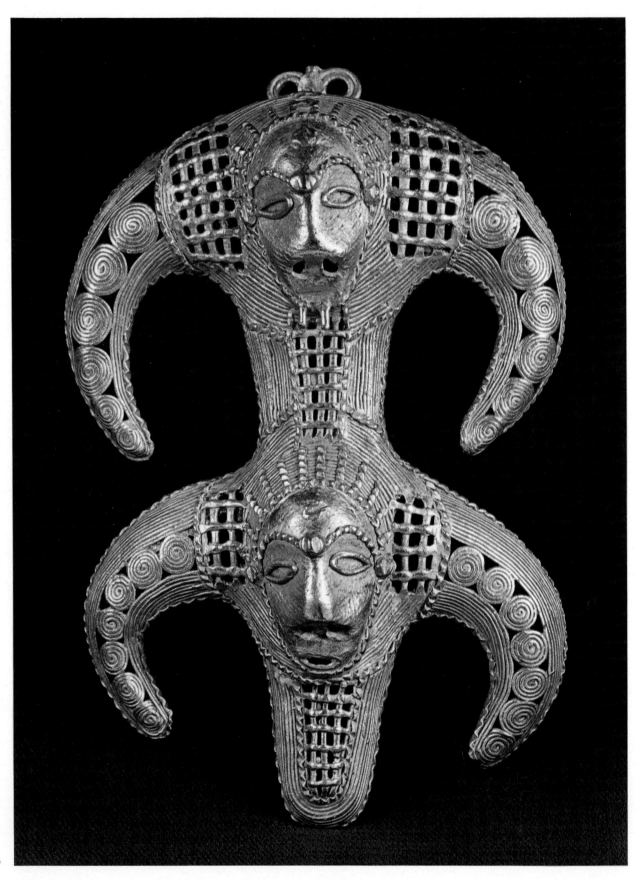

Gold

The use of gold in Africa

Among the most highly developed tribes in Africa those which came into contact, even if only briefly, with more advanced cultures show a certain level of refinement in their personal ornamentation. In general new ideas were carried to various areas by the Arabs and then adapted to local tastes. The influence of higher cultures was mostly felt in the north of the continent, in Ethiopia, through Egyptian and Nubian contacts. These regions were visited by the Mediterranean peoples, in particular the Phoenicians, who carried new artistic ideas wherever they went, and, provided the right conditions prevailed, the seeds of these ideas took root and flourished. Besides the Phoenicians, Armenians, Arabs and Indians also contributed to the diffusion of jewelry styles and technical knowledge.

The ability to be able to prepare the metals in order to make jewelry was one of the main conditions. Another essential was the availability of gold and silver in the particular territory. The prosperity of the areas where a tradition in metallurgy developed was generally based on the extraction and trading of gold. Naturally, the most interesting ornaments were worn by and belonged to members of the ruling classes or religious chiefs, who formed a limited élite in the society, while the use of gold was reserved almost exclusively for the sovereign and the nobles. This was the case in the Sudan, in Ghana, Mali and the Guinea coast, and among the Yoruba peoples, who greatly influenced the Benin culture, the Ashanti and the Baule of the Ivory Coast.

Nigerian Tribes Nigerian sculptures from Ife, Benin and Esie show magnificent headdresses worn by women, which must have been made of gold. There are tiered towers, cupolas surmounted by cylindrical elements and smooth cones decorated with rich borders of embossed metal, with pendants which hang on the centre of the forehead, or with pieces of *repoussé* metal or a net to contain piled-up hair and to which are attached a series of pendants encircling the head. An ancient ivory mask from Benin has a mesh helmet surmounted by a halo-like arc of carved bearded heads. The collar which completed the mask must have been made of the same mesh which covered the head; it was slung

Gold pendant with stylised rams' heads, Baule. Musée de l'Institut Français de l'Afrique Noire, Dakar.

81

Ornament decorated with gold, Ashanti. British Museum, London.

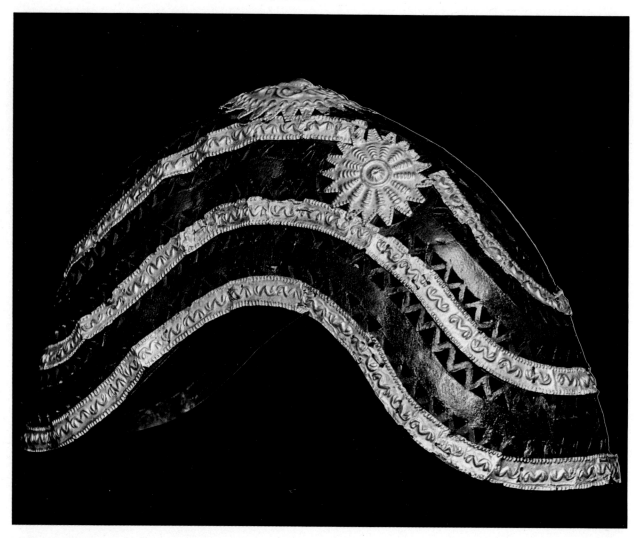

Gold ring with a lion, Ashanti. British Museum, London.

under the chin from ear to ear by a broad band containing a plait of really impeccable workmanship.

A bronze bust of an Ife king (see page 16) shows in great detail the richness of the precious ornaments worn by the sovereigns. In the middle of the forehead, suspended from the helmet is a sumptuous jewel on a lobed support consisting of a large stylised flower, with a protruding gem in the middle; under this is an ornamental boss in high relief, which seems to

Gold ornaments, Ashanti. British Museum, London.

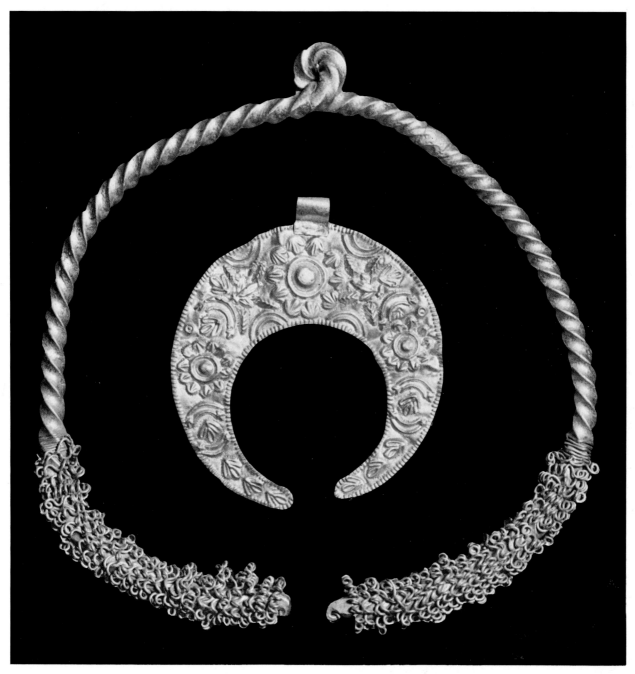

have a stone at its summit. The neck and chest are covered with heavy necklaces of carved beads from which hang other pieces; in addition, an even longer necklace hangs over the bust. The quality of these ornaments rises above folk art to become the expression of a superior culture, which attained particular heights in sculpture. Besides the production for the royal courts, there must certainly have existed a popular art not less interesting, though less valuable materials would have been used. The same standards of quality apply to the Ashanti of Ghana, a territory rich in auriferous minerals. **Ghana** Every local chief had his little court and a workshop for gold and jewelry, but the most fabulous court between the 18th and 19th centuries was that of King Asantehene of Kumasi. Many examples have been found of the emblem of the 'bearer of souls', a decorated disc which, together with other insignia, was worn by the king's pages. The backs of these discs had a little tube through which a cord ran to attach

Disc depicting the 'bearer of souls', Ashanti. British Museum, London.

it to more discs. They were decorated with various *repoussé* concentric designs. The design of these motifs bears no relation to African art, but is reminiscent rather of elements of Classical art juxtaposed in a somewhat unorthodox manner. Hemispheres, stylised flowers, metal bosses of various shapes and sizes, woven patterns, done in *repoussé* or engraved with exceptional technical ability, enrich these discs and in none of them is the same design repeated. Others have pierced designs or are in the shape of stars.

The shapes of the beads used in the necklaces are also very varied. Since no two ever appear alike or even similar, the search for new ideas must have been constant. Bracelets could be made of gold pieces, engraved with the signs of the zodiac linked by short mesh chains. Zodiac signs are sometimes also to be found on the bezels of massive rings. Hairpins are elaborately embellished with high-relief plant or animal forms cast in the *cire perdue* process. The popular works in all regions were mostly in silver and combined oriental and Classical styles, but local taste is also to be found which more often than not consists of a great abundance of pendants of various shapes which aim at maximum gaudiness with minimum effort. There is always a lot of filigree and semiprecious stones and coins were used too.

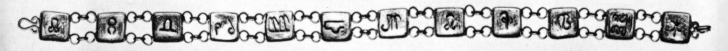

Bracelet with the signs of the zodiac, Ashanti. British Museum, London.

Large gold pectoral decorated with *repoussé* and filigree, Senegal. Musée de l'Institut Français de l'Afrique Noire, Dakar.

86

II
Coloured stones in jewelry

India

In its first phase of development jewelry was made entirely of gold. Even though coloured stones were used at different times in various parts of the world to make necklaces and bracelets, when gold was discovered it soon became the sole element used in the making of important jewelry, and coloured stones were relegated to popular creations. There are some rare examples of the use of coloured stones in the jewelry from the Royal Tombs of Ur, but these were only in ring bezels and necklaces; gem stones are occasionally found in necklaces during the oriental phase of the Etruscans. In Iran polychromy began with the use of glazed composition and inlay as in the Oxus treasure, and then during the Hellenistic period stones and emeralds began to be used in jewelry. These were naturally not used in seals but were mounted in rings.

The taste for colour in jewelry had its greatest manifestation in the lands of south-east Asia, among the civilisations of the Indus. Large quantities of a wide variety of precious and valuable stones abound in India and in the neighbouring countries of Thailand, Burma and Ceylon. Sculptures and paintings of men and women adorned with jewels testify to their use, as does recent work which in quality and taste points to the inheritance of a very ancient tradition. To the rich variety of stones was added the widespread use of pearls (pearl fishing has been carried on since early times) and of enamels and vitreous pastes, which were very popular in jewelry in east Asia.

In Harappa, one of the most ancient centres of the Indus civilisation, a belt has been found of the type which Indian women since the end of the 3rd millennium BC have worn next to their naked bodies encircling their waist and between their legs. The beads which make up this belt are mainly red cornelians, green steatite, agate, jasper, amazonstone from Gujerat, jade from central Asia or Burma, lapis lazuli from Afghanistan and a sort of maiolica. The variety of this assortment gives some idea of the important place already assigned to colour in ancient jewelry. The quantity of gold or other metals used was negligible. The proportion of coloured stones to metal used in jewelry of this huge area corresponds perhaps to the amount of minerals

Detail of a Bodhisattva with a tall diadem encrusted with precious stones and necklaces and bracelets of pearls and stones, from a fresco in the first grotto at Ajanta, Indian, 5th-6th century.

87

extracted from the alluvial deposits in the area compared to the quantity of metal. There are, in fact, far more precious stones to be found in the area than precious metals. Metals were, therefore, used for mounting the stones in various designs to display them to the best possible advantage.

Depending on general conditions, the variety of jewelry was fairly large, from turban ornaments, diadems and headdresses, to rings for the fingers and toes. The techniques of setting, polishing and piercing precious stones developed rapidly in these regions, but cutting was only accepted much later. In the East right up to modern times, it has always been considered preferable to leave the stone as much as possible in its natural state.

The Ruby One of the most precious gems, the ruby, is found in great quantities in the deposits and mines of south-east Asia, the chief producers being Burma, Thailand and Ceylon. The city of Amarapura in Burma is nicknamed the City of Precious Stones. To the north, along the beds of the Irawadi, Oschindwin and Hukong rivers are layers in secondary clay deposits or between calcareous dolomite marbles in which rubies, tourmalines, amber, jadeite and other stones are found. The rubies, highly valued for the vivid richness and intensity of their red colour, come from Mogok, north of Amarapura; those from Burma tend to be a more muted yellow-brown colour and are less prized, while those of Ceylonese origin are slightly violet in colour. They are also found in Afghanistan, Madagascar, Australia, and the United States (Montana and North Carolina). It is very likely that the Indian carbuncle which Pliny mentions, was the ruby, which is among the most rare and precious of gems. The ruby is nine on Mohs' scale of hardness. The mineralogical name for the ruby is corundum, which comes from the old Sanskrit word *kuruvinda*.

Other Precious Stones In the chronological order of the use of precious stones the cornelian comes first. Apart from India, the cornelian is found in central-western Asia, Arabia and Egypt, and more recently deposits have been discovered in Brazil, Siberia, Japan and Germany. Indian cornelians are never their beautiful vivid red colour when they are first extracted;

the colour improves after they have been left a while in the sun. Like cornelian, agate is a variety of chalcedony. Its structure consists of layers which may be opaque or translucent and are various colours. Agate is also found in India and was often used for jewelry on account of the stripes of contrasting colours. Other deposits were in Asia Minor, Madagascar and China and today, above all, in Brazil. Another chalcedony is jasper, of which there are at least twenty varieties. It is found in many localities: Asia Minor, Sicily, Australia, Switzerland, Russia, China, the United States, France, Australia, Madagascar, Germany and Algeria. The East Indian varieties are mottled red with clear grey flecks.

Lapis lazuli has been used in Asiatic jewelry since the 3rd millennium BC. It was also used for cylinder seals. It is a dark blue stone, usually marked with flecks of gold caused by the presence of grains of pyrite. The oldest and most important deposits are those of Afghanistan, Russia, Persia, China and Tibet. Some of these places, however, only exported the stone, and did not use it themselves in jewelry. Less precious is the lapis lazuli from the Chilean Andes and that found in Italy, in Campania and Lazio in small quantities.

The amazonstone, a recent and erroneous name for a variety of feldspar dating from a time when it was believed to come from the Rio region of the Amazon, was evidently found in antiquity in India. Its green colour seems to be caused by the inclusion of oxidised copper. Today it is found in the United States, Russia, Madagascar and South Africa.

Steatite is the Greek name for soapstone, a variety of soft opaque talc with a pearly lustre which is greyish-green in colour. It is a stone of little value, often used in ancient jewelry. In recent times it has been found in Germany, Bohemia, Hungary, the Tyrol, the United States and various regions of Turkestan.

The most important deposits of nephrite and jade are in central Asia (Turkestan) and China. They are not always uniform in colour and vary from grey to grey-green to light, grass and emerald green, and from yellowish-brown to reddish. As an ornamental stone it has been in use from the earliest times until today.

Ruby.

Ruby in its rough state.

Agate.

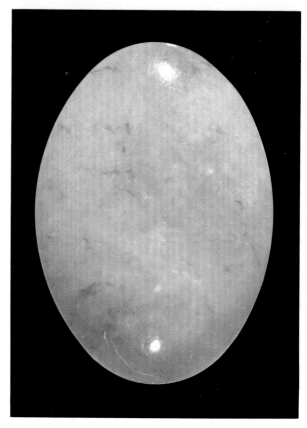

Jade.

89

Jeweled figure of a dancer, detail of a bas-relief at Angkor-Vat, Indian, 12th century.

The Development of Indian Jewelry

After the Aryan invasion of India, to judge from archaeological finds, strong Achemenean stylistic influences from Iran entered the country, followed by Greco-Buddhist and finally Muslim influence. Basically, however, external influences left no profound effects on the traditional and fundamental characteristics of eastern Asian jewelry, with its preference for an ostentatious richness of colour, brilliant, intricate and detailed, aimed above all at stupefying the world rather than expressing the personality of the wearer. Indian and south-east Asian jewelry quickly rose to a remarkable level in the hands of skilled craftsmen, with resourceful and inventive techniques. Original forms, transmitted for the most part by the Sumerian and Akkadian civilisations, were fused with elements of local character which finally resulted in the fabulous appearance of Indian jewelry. This richness of colour was made possible by the presence of huge deposits of precious and semiprecious stones and the abundance of pearls. The gold settings of the stones were embellished with a wide use of filigree, engraving, openwork, *repoussé* and enamelling in complex ornamental forms, which contributed, along with the play of reflected light on the jewel, to its brilliance. Evidence from statues and wall paintings shows how widespread in the most developed areas was the passion for self-adornment with jewelry.

The Harappa culture takes its name from an important centre in the Indus valley around which it developed in the 3rd millennium BC. This culture survived until the 16th century BC, and its artistic tradition survived long after, because during the period of its greatest prosperity it had established such deep roots that, at least as far as jewelry was concerned, a lasting and lively tradition had been created.

A torso (carved in sandstone) from the end of the 3rd millennium BC shows a man with his hair gathered up by a band from which a round ornament dangles onto his forehead; a bracelet on the half-broken arm and a projecting trilobate decoration on the upper border of his garment indicate that personal ornamentation was already considered very important. A terracotta figure of a woman has, in addition to necklaces and bracelets, a belt very similar to

The consecration of Mahavira from a manuscript miniature, Indian, *c.* 1400. British Museum, London.

Woman with ornaments, ivory, 1st century. Kabul Museum.

Bust of Aspara with jewelled turban, earrings and necklace, detail of a fresco at Ajanta, Indian, 6th century.

one which has actually been found in excavations. It consists of six strings of cornelian beads interrupted at equal distances by an element surrounded by small spherical beads; the ends are embellished by round and triangular plates of copper, gold, steatite and maiolica which hang from them.

The beads of the necklaces, armbands, bracelets and belts which adorned the scanty clothing of the women were of a great variety of shapes and materials. A very characteristic type is a gold disc with a tube through the diameter. The discovery of similar discs at Ur and Troy indicates that there was some form of contact between the two areas and that even in those ancient times journeys must have been made over long distances. Necklaces were enriched with numerous rows of stones, gold and carved coral, and often longer ones were fastened with rich clasps which hung down the back.

The paintings of Ajanta (4th-5th century AD) show men and women wearing more jewels than clothes. The size and complexity of earrings, bracelets, armbands, belts, headdresses, diadems, leg bracelets and rings, which adorn these masterpieces of pictorial art, reflect the fantastic splendour that was India.

At Taxila, where Hellenistic influences have been found, excavations have brought to light jewelry with Classical elements to their design but pervaded by the characteristic Indian taste for embellishment. Every available inch of surface on medallions is engraved with flowers, elephants and peacocks; pendants on earrings and necklaces are numerous; and large gold bracelets are decorated with *repoussé* motifs and small stones. A particular element of fantasy manifests itself in the designs of necklaces, which are almost always in several rows, each with beads of a different shape, colour or material alternating on one row, and often with a little gold disc or ring dangling from the bottom.

Types of Jewelry This almost fanatical pre-

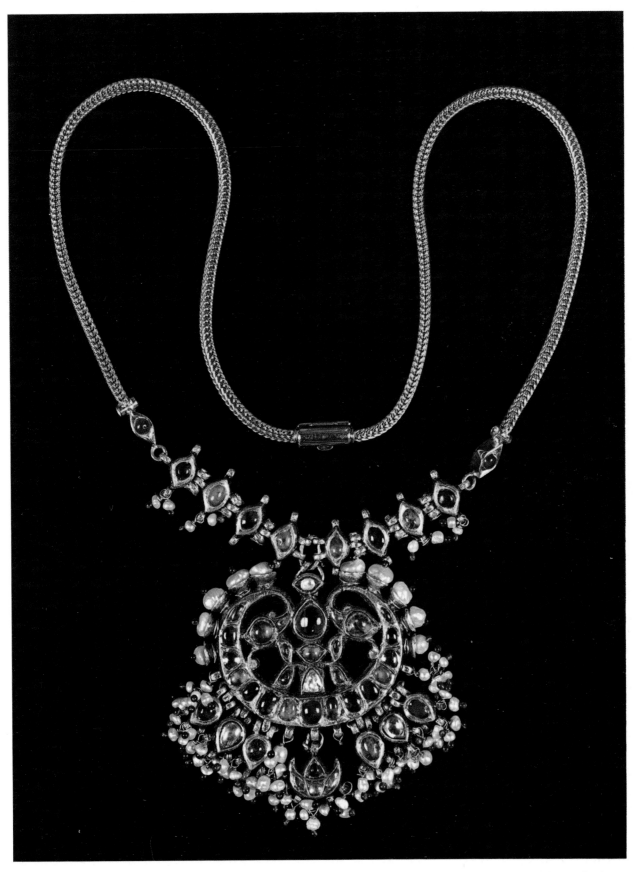

93

Necklace of gold chains with a pendant of gold, emeralds, rubies, diamonds and pearls, Indian, end of 18th century. Private collection, Rome.

94

Necklace of pearls, emeralds and other precious stones, 19th century, Indian. Victoria and Albert Museum, London.

dilection for adorning the body with jewelry continued uninterrupted through the centuries in India, and the craftsmen, whose inventiveness was always in great demand, developed an enormous variety of forms and achieved great heights of technical ability. The sculpture of ancient times has preserved for us a mass of evidence of the jewelry in this huge area. Naturally as time passed the quantity of jewelry accumulated and the amounts still preserved are bigger.

Men's headdresses, turbans or caps were elaborately embellished with jewelry usually with one dominant element placed in the centre or to one side; this might be the plume of a rare bird or perhaps a feather created in gold, enamels and tiny pearls. Princes also wore jewelry in their hair; frequently they had earrings and always rich necklaces and bracelets.

Steatite, agate, cornelian, jasper, Gujerat amazonstone, jade from central Asia and Burma, lapis lazuli from Afghanistan, in addition to ceramics and pearls and, in important pieces, emeralds and rubies, formed with gold and silver the sumptuous palette of Indian jewelry.

Compared with the jewelry which adorned the rajahs, the precious ornaments worn by women were even more numerous. Each had its own name and particular purpose. For the hair alone, there were imitation wreaths of flowers in gold, pins, plaits made of three strips of gold foil embellished with gems with a star in the centre, plaits arranged along the parting of the hair, rows of pearls entwined in the hair, gold bands across the forehead, wreaths of little leaves of beaten gold which tinkled at every movement, imitation lotus leaves made of gold or a bunch of little gold flowers at the nape of the neck. Each of these jewels had a traditional position on the head.

Among the many types of earrings were rows of pearls joined by gold wire, gold hoops with pearls on each side and a gem or cluster of pearls in the middle, studs of pearls and precious stones with a diamond in the centre, tiers of sculptured flowers or palm leaves, gold chains, gems for placing behind the ears and discs of gold with stones in the centre.

Arms were adorned with armbands either of the torque type, with animal head terminals, or

made of beads of various shapes or of square pieces of gold with gems; they could be worn three or four at a time. Bracelets could be made of rows of beads shaped like mice teeth or seeds, of plain strips of gold with decorated borders or decorated all over, or of square metal bosses mounted on strips of silk. Another type of gold bracelet was like a long sleeve made of rows of linked chains; others were tubes with beads inside which rattled when the arm moved, or hoops with pendants dangling from them which also jingled harmoniously; another type was tubular with five links which were attached to the rings on each finger. Then there were bracelets composed of broad bands of many rows of chains or pearls, supporting little gold

Filigree earring with pearls and stones, Indian, 19th century. Victoria and Albert Museum, London.

95

bars decorated with gems, or gold circlets elaborated in various ways.

Rings were either simple bands or could be set with natural gems of various shapes and colours. Often several rings would be worn spaced out on the same finger. The number and variety of belts was comparable with necklaces. They were worn between the legs and fastened across the stomach, with long ends falling away from the knot in the front. Chains with jingling pendants or tubular rings filled with beads, just like the bracelets, were worn round the ankles; some were composed of a series of chains fastened with a clasp set with a jewel. These anklets worn one on top of the other sometimes reached halfway up the leg; often they would be attached to an elaborate network of chains across the foot, with a medallion in the centre and rings on the toes.

In addition to all the items described above, rich and beautiful Indian women wore – and some still do today – a jewel, particularly a diamond, in the skin in the centre of the forehead or in the left nostril. Both men and women pierced their nostrils or the central cartilage of the nose in order to insert large rings embellished with jewels or with pearl pendants. Some of these jewels had little chains which were fixed to the hair. Another custom was to insert a little boss of gold or silver in one or more of the incisor teeth.

In antiquity diadems were sometimes like miniature monuments, with central niches into which were placed statuettes of Buddha. The composition of these headdresses, executed with meticulous use of quantities of coloured elements, became so elaborate that they developed into highly original compositions of fabulous appearance.

A traditional and very ancient Hindu amulet, called *nauratan*, consisted of a gold plate set with nine different precious stones. The *nauratan* was often used in necklaces too.

South-East Asia The influence of Indian culture lasted in Indonesia, together with that of the sacred art of the great religions, Buddhism and Hinduism, until about the beginning of the 17th century. The jewelry styles of these regions also embraced local traditional elements and achieved a notable level of development. It began to decline in the 15th and 16th centuries with the introduction of Islam. From that time on the ancient traditions began to disappear, and the aesthetic appearance of the products was increasingly influenced by indigenous folk art. At the beginning of the 18th century, with the Dutch conquest of Java, the East Indies almost entirely accepted the customs of western civilisation. Only in Bali were the cults and legends of Hinduism handed down with all the ancient ceremonies, rituals and traditional costumes.

right Maharajah Gulab Singh wearing jewelled turban, earrings, necklace, rings and bracelets, 19th century, Indian. Victoria and Albert Museum, London.

Silver-gilt ring with opal-set bezel, 18th century, Indian. Museo Poldi-Pezzoli, Milan.

Coloured stones in jewelry

Pearls

An important and ancient element of colour in oriental jewelry is the pearl. The fascination of pearls, the product of a living organism's defence mechanism, is well known and has given rise to many legends and stories. Most of these are pure invention and some belong to Greek and Roman mythology. The pearl was also attributed with magic or medicinal powers.

The principle producers of pearls are the *Eulamellibranchia* (perliferous) and marine molluscs of the *Meleagrina* genus, which is not really an edible oyster but belongs to the *Aviculidae* family. There are four principle species of the *Meleagrina*: the *Margaritifera* or *Pinctada*, the *Martensii*, the *Vulgaris* or *Fucata*, also called the Ceylon or Californian *Meleagrina*, and the *Radiata*.

The first is the largest (up to seven inches in diameter) and is found in the seas off New Guinea, New Caledonia, Australia and more rarely, the Persian Gulf and Ceylon; the second is found off Japan and has a thinner coating of mother-of-pearl than the former; the third, which is larger than the second (about four inches in diameter), abounds in the Indian Ocean, the coastal waters of Japan, the Red Sea and the Persian Gulf; the fourth, of medium dimensions, lives in the seas off Central America. Theoretically, all molluscs, whether salt or freshwater, can produce pearls, since pearl nacre is formed in the same way as the mother-of-pearl with which the inside of the shell is lined. The *Meleagrina* has the property of being able to fix itself onto a foreign body by means of two organs (feet and byssus), while the oyster attaches itself by the suction of the convex valve of the shell during its early stages of development; if, for some reason, it is later dislodged it cannot fix itself again elsewhere.

Natural beds of molluscs are generally found at a depth of about forty feet. In addition to the *Meleagrina*, many other types of molluscs, including the freshwater or *Unionidae*, produce pearls of various colours, but their iridescence, lustre and sheen are very much inferior to that of the four types mentioned above, and they are therefore seldom used in good jewelry.

The mollusc is provided with all the organs necessary to its underwater existence. Its body is enveloped in a mantle lined with an epithel-

Alessandro Allori, *The Pearl Fisher*. Palazzo Vecchio, Florence.

99

ium which secretes the substances which harden to form the mother-of-pearl on all the internal surfaces of the shell. This nacreous substance is secreted in very thin, transparent, calcareous layers which are held together by a network of organic matter called *conchiolin*.

The pearl is caused by the accidental introduction into the mollusc of some foreign matter. If a grain of sand or a parasite gets lodged between the mantle and the epithelium inside the shell, perhaps while the mollusc opens its valves to feed, it becomes coated with the secretion and gradually forms a pearl. This can be produced in various shapes, the most common being round, pear, button and the irregular or baroque. More than one pearl can form in one mollusc, but it is more likely that there will be none at all, for only one in a thousand molluscs fished up contains a pearl. The button pearl or half pearl is produced when the pearl-sac starts forming near the shell and becomes attached to it, so that a hemispherical pearl is formed.

Pearls take their colour from the pigments contained in the *conchiolin*, which is the organic component of the mother-of-pearl shell lining, and each species has its characteristic colour. Apart from black pearls, there are extremely rare pink pearls (found in the great conch or fountain shell of the West Indies: *Strombus gigas*), and also those of bronze, green, greenish-blue and shades of lavender. The so-called blue pearls show on X-ray examination a large nucleus with a thin nacreous covering.

In many areas pearl fishing is still carried on by native men and women divers working with traditional methods. Each dive lasts about eighty seconds, though a record dive of five minutes has been made. Each fisherman makes about thirty to forty dives in a day and is subject to many dangers and hazards; pearl divers tend to be a short-lived race. Their equipment consists of a rope weighted with a stone along which they descend to the sea bed, a sort of clothes-peg device to keep the nostrils closed, leather finger-stalls to protect the fingers while the molluscs are gathered and a basket in which to put them. In one dive a fisherman can collect about forty to fifty oysters. The best divers are the Arabs. In Japan pearl fishing is carried on exclusively by the young 'daughters of the sea'

100

left and right Exceptionally large baroque pearls mounted with brillian[t] Private collection, London.

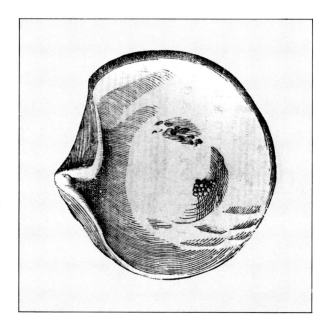

who use somewhat more up-to-date methods in their difficult work. In Central America diving suits are used by pearl fishers, which means that the work is less tiring and the divers can take their time over choosing only the largest oysters so as not to impoverish the bank, without being hampered by lack of oxygen.

The *Meleagrina* have enemies which are capable of destroying whole banks of them. Among the most rapacious are sea urchins, rays, mullets and gasteropodes. Other enemies are certain worms, coelenterates, sponges and protozoa.

There are various ways of extracting the pearls from the molluscs. In the best organised fisheries the molluscs, after being assembled in the workshop, are opened in a search for pearls after which the mother-of-pearl shell is examined for any button pearls which may be embedded in it. Sometimes the molluscs are laid out in the sun so that they decompose. Then the animal is extracted by its valve, washed and sieved. Scientific X-ray techniques are used today in some places to see if the shells contain a pearl. If not, they are thrown back into the sea. When they are removed from the shell pearls are covered with a sort of light greenish coating which is easily removed by washing in a solution of alcohol or ether. Those intended for mounting are only partially perforated while those to be used in necklaces are drilled right through. Irregularly shaped pearls can be reduced to regular forms by means of partially removing some of the outer layers; however, this delicate operation can result in unfortunate surprises if the stratification is not uniform.

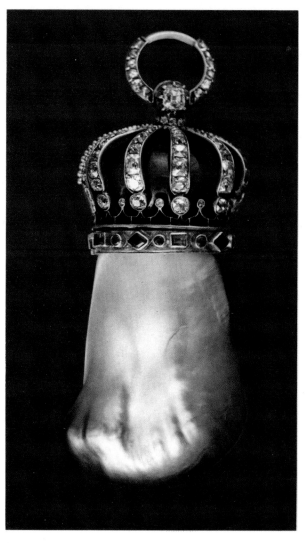

Coloured stones in jewelry

Precious stones in ancient Egypt

The arts of metallurgy and gem cutting and the use of colour in jewelry were from the beginning used with more restraint by the peoples of the Nile civilisation than by those of south-east Asia. Although they were influenced in the earliest stages by Mesapotamian motifs, they later developed characteristics and expressed themselves in forms and rhythms which were entirely their own, bound up with their ceremonies and emblems of dynastic pomp and religious and magical beliefs. The succession of dynasties lasting for centuries in Egypt allowed expressive forms to develop and consolidate, producing sumptuous and spectacular works of art in every field on a level which had never been attained before and still amazes the world today. At the court of the pharaohs the god-king was surrounded by a profusion of gold, gems, colours and precious materials in a dazzling and exciting atmosphere of stupefying splendour.

Bracelets and amulet figures found in tombs of the Thinite era (3007-2780 BC) near Abydos and Nagada give us some idea of the already high level of workmanship and stylistic motifs in gold and jewels. The bracelets are composed in turn of amethysts, lapis lazuli and turquoises, and the working of the metal was clearly considered of equal importance as the value of the gems.

The wearing of jewelry in those times was entirely restricted to the pharaohs and their families, the priests and other functionaries within the circle of the court. The Egyptians knew of gold before silver, which at first they called white gold. The metal of the sun, the planet personified by their chief deity, Aton, was the favourite. Unfortunately few tombs of kings and dignitaries have not been plundered, despite the special devices to foil thieves with which they were built. Some tombs have survived intact, however, and together with coloured statuary and mural paintings form the most valuable sources of our knowledge of the forms and techniques used in the making of precious ornaments in ancient Egypt.

A rare find from the epoch of the Old Kingdom, which lasted from the 1st to the 8th dynasty (3200-2260 BC), was the tomb of Queen Hetepheres I, wife of Senefru, complete with funerary objects. It was thought necessary to

Princess Nofri with coloured diadem and necklace, detail of a carved limestone group of Prince Rahopt and his wife, Egyptian, beginning of the 4th dynasty. Egyptian Museum, Cairo.

103

provide for the comfort of the deceased in the afterlife by supplying surroundings worthy of his lineage. The bed, the throne and a litter are extensively embellished with solid gold *repoussé* work and gold leaf encrusted with precious stones. Among the jewelry there were silver bracelets, with butterfly motifs composed of turquoises, lapis lazuli and cornelians.

The Use of Gold In this period gold was so much more plentiful than silver, which had to be imported, that the latter assumed a superior value to gold. A silver belt which belonged to a prince has been found and is now in the Egyptian Museum in Cairo. It consists partly of a broad band decorated with pearls and beads of red and black stone set in rhomboid patterns and partly of a panel carved with hawks, symbols in openwork and two seated figures on either side. Of the same period are the painted stone statues of Prince Rahopt and his wife Nofri, conserved in the same museum, which show the bridal pair bedecked with necklaces and diadems encrusted with semiprecious stones.

With the expansionist activities of the 12th dynasty (the Middle Kingdom) new territory was conquered in the upper reaches of the Nile valley above the Second Cataract. This brought the gold mines of Nubia within the grasp of the Egyptians, and the resulting increase in wealth naturally led to an increase in the creation of gold objects and jewelry. By the second millennium BC the skills and techniques of the craftsmen in these fields had reached a level of artistic achievement which was amongst the highest ever attained by an Egyptian civilisation.

The pectoral of King Sesostris III, found at Dashur with those of Senusret II and Amenemhet III and conserved in the Egyptian Museum in Cairo, is in its balance, rhythmic composition and harmonious use of colour one of the most beautiful works that has ever been created. It has a characteristically Egyptian design of a frame containing a scene depicting apes with hawks' heads trampling on the vanquished, which symbolises the pharaoh's victory over his enemies. It is in gold openwork, outlined in semiprecious stones, arranged and set in strict symmetry around the central symbol which is surmounted by a vulture with outstretched wings. The beauty of the piece is skilfully en-

hanced by the use of various shades of blue and red and by the yellow of the gold. The necklace from which the pendant hangs is made of round and oblong beads of gold and cornelian. The other two pendants, executed in the same style and with the same skill, are decorated with symbolic animals, hieroglyphics and other emblems and human figures vividly portrayed.

During this period of cultural development relations between Egypt and the Cretan-Mycenaean world were established and stabilised, resulting in a noticeable influence on the jewelry of the pharaohs. However, motifs inspired by the Minoan gold craft, while benefiting the Egyptian techniques, were soon absorbed into the native tradition so that one cannot detect any alteration in the chromatic and structural components which constitute the fundamental character of Egyptian products.

The New Kingdom During the invasion and ensuing domination of the foreign kings, the Hyksos, there was a decline in the arts and in the standard of life in general. The 18th dynasty, with which the New Kingdom (1555-1085) began, initiated one of the most brilliant periods in the history of Egypt. Prosperity returned and with it precious ornaments, many of which fortunately for us followed their owners into their tombs. The most amazing example of the richness of the funerary objects, which it was

Gold pectoral with semiprecious stones belonging to King Sesostris III, Egyptian, 12th dynasty. Egyptian Museum, Cairo.

Gold gorget with cornelians and faience depicting the culture god Nekhbet, from Tutenkhamen's treasure, Egyptian, 18th dynasty. Egyptian Museum, Cairo.

customary to place with a dead pharaoh, was found in Tutenkhamen's tomb discovered in 1922 by H. Carter. The young king had died at the age of eighteen and had already ruled for nine years. It is thought that work on his tomb and the preparation of all it contained was probably begun as soon as he ascended the throne or soon afterwards. It was like a small museum, full of exquisite objects demonstrating the high standard of craftsmanship of the period, and the most complete record of all the contemporary goldsmiths' and jewelers' techniques, from the cutting and moulding of semiprecious stones to enamelling on gold or maiolica, from damascening to filigree.

The motifs used in Egyptian jewelry are mostly either figures of gods, planets (most often the sun) or symbolic abstract forms. Other figures are personifications of animals, which indicates the totemic and fundamentally magical origins of the religion. The hawk, vulture and cobra appear most frequently on the ornamental objects appertaining to a king or queen. The form of a cobra usually rises from the centre of the pharaoh's mitre, while a gold vulture encrusted with gems would cover a queen's headdress with its broad wings, its head above the centre of her forehead. The sun disc and the symbol of life in the shape of a T, with an

Gold and faience plaque depicting the god Nut, from Tutenkhamen's treasure, Egyptian, 18th dynasty. Egyptian Museum, Cairo.

oval knot at the point where the bars cross, are emblems which constantly recur in necklaces, bracelets and pendants. To add colour lapis lazuli, turquoises and cornelians were widely used, as well as glazed enamels.

Earrings began to be worn in Egypt after the 12th dynasty and were generally simple in shape: hoops or round discs or sometimes in the form of bullae. On a bas-relief, found in the Valley of the Queens at Thebes and now in the Metropolitan Museum, New York, the figure of Queen Nefertari wears earrings in the form of battle-axes and band bracelets of black and white interlocking rectangles with borders of dark pearls. The clothes shown on the relief are adorned with pieces of gold and even the pharaoh's footwear is made of gold and gems. The style of necklace most commonly worn by both men and women consisted of a semicircle of parallel strips, compact and many-coloured, fastened at the base of the neck. Some were also made of rows of tiny beads of various shapes using rock crystal, amethyst, green feldspar, garnet, onyx, obsidian and sardonyx, in addition to the popular turquoise, lapis lazuli and cornelian. Beads made of precious stones were nearly always interspersed with gold ones.

Precious Stones Many of these gems were found within Egyptian territory or in lands they had colonised. Turquoise was brought from the Sinai peninsula or from Arabia; rock crystal and amethyst, which is a purple variety of quartz, are found in geodes (cavities formed in volcanic rocks) in the mountains of southern Arabia, while obsidian, which is a volcanic glass of various intense colours, is found in Ethiopia.

Detail of necklace shown on opposite page.

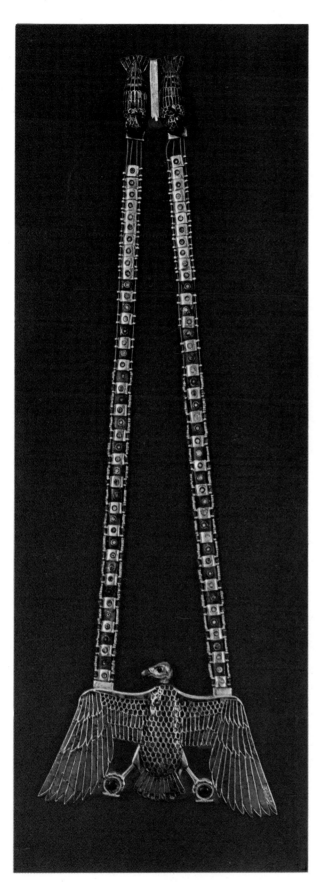

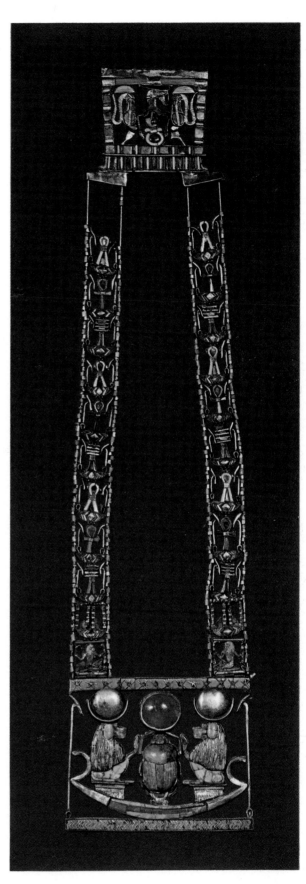

Necklace with a pendant depicting the symbol of the god Nekhbet, from Tutenkhamen's treasure, Egyptian, 18th dynasty. Egyptian Museum, Cairo.

Large collar with pectoral in gold, faience and cornelian, from Tutenkhamen's treasure, Egyptian, 18th dynasty. Egyptian Museum, Cairo.

A wife of Tut-moses III wearing earrings and headdress in gold, turquoises, faience and cornelians, from the tomb of the Three Ladies, Thebes, Egyptian, 18th dynasty. The Huntley Bequest, Metropolitan Museum of Art, New York.

A faience substance made of powdered quartz, lime and soda (natron) and covered with an alkaline glaze was used for making beads for necklaces or to provide coloured bezels in gold jewelry. The colours usually imitated those of lapis lazuli and turquoise and therefore varied from dark blue to a light blue-green; the colouring agents were cobalt and copper respectively. Objects of this glazed composition such as amulets and scarabs were usually cast from clay moulds.

Gold, precious and semiprecious gems, and coral and maiolica in particular, were used to make the sacred scarabs. Scarabs were used as seals and ring bezels and as amulets, with an inscription or magic sign on the smooth part of the abdomen. They were also incorporated in many other kinds of jewelry. Later the scarab became widespread through the whole Mediterranean region.

The emerald, which was already known and

below and below centre Amulet rings with inscriptions and engraved decoration, Egyptian, 18th dynasty (?). Victoria and Albert Museum, London.

Earrings in faience and cornelians set in gold, from Tutenkhamen's treasure, Egyptian, 18th dynasty. Egyptian Museum, Cairo.

Bracelet in gold and faience depicting a winged divinity, from the Meroe pyramid, Nubia, 25-10 BC. Antikensammlungen, Munich.

used in the time of Sesostris in the 19th century BC, appeared in limited quantities in Egypt. It is rarely found in Egyptian jewelry from tombs, although a small number has been found on mummies. The sole source of the precious gem in that period was Upper Egypt. During the Alexandrian era the mines were worked by the Greeks, and later mining received fresh impetus under Cleopatra. As has been noted, emeralds are the most valuable of the beryl species and

one of the most important precious stones. Despite their extreme hardness (7·5 on Mohs' scale), the ancient Egyptians and the Greeks managed to engrave them for use as ring stones. **Decline** The New Kingdom was followed by a long period of stagnation. Nothing new was contributed in the field of the decorative arts, in fact if anything, activity in this sphere was reduced. The situation grew still worse in the so-called Dark Ages which followed. A suc-

Pectoral in gold and faience depicting a large scarab, from Saqqara, Egyptian, 19th dynasty. Louvre, Paris.

cession of Ethiopian and Persian rulers each brought with him his own decadent style. The domination of the Ptolemies finally extinguished all the creative impulses in Egyptian art. Hellenistic concepts and forms were introduced and spread rapidly particularly in Lower Egypt where Alexandria now became the centre of an expanding school of Greek art. Jewels continued to be created into the 26th dynasty and even later, but by then the steady decline of the kings, the source of inspiration as well as the actual patrons of the splendid works of the past, failed to inspire works of interest.

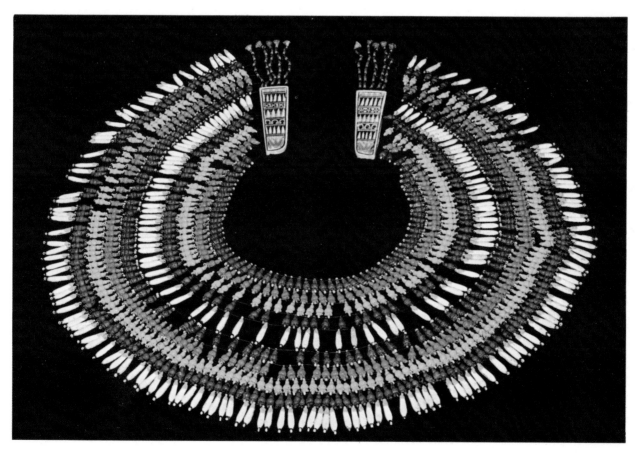

113

Polychrome necklace from Tutenkhamen's treasure, Egyptian, 18th dynasty. Egyptian Museum, Cairo.

Coloured stones in jewelry

Precious stones in Greece and Rome

During the period of Hellenistic expansion Greek jewelry imprinted many of its forms and styles on Eastern and Egyptian jewelry. Now in its turn Hellenistic jewelry began to absorb the taste for colour. By the 4th-3rd century BC cornelians, turquoises, garnets and malachites were being used in Hellenistic diadems for the first time. These were gradually followed by amethysts, rock crystals and plasma, a type of chalcedony of various shades of green which was fairly common.

Amber, known since very ancient times, was now often employed. Amber is not in fact a truc mineral but a fossilised resin which used to be called electrum because of its property of generating electricity when rubbed and magnetising light objects. It varies in colour from deep yellow to red, and from pale wine yellow to brown.

Engraved Gemstones The art of engraving gemstones is an important technique which has lasted with varying degrees of popularity almost to the present day. Until the Hellenistic period gems were nearly always engraved in intaglio for use as seals which would imprint a relief mould on some soft material such as clay or wax. The same period saw the introduction of the engraving of gems in relief (cameo) and, thereafter, certain stones such as agate or sardonyx were chosen for their particular structure which enabled colour effects of great attractiveness to be obtained.

The skill of the Greek technique of stone cutting, for which small stones were generally used, is amazing: the scale of the work was minute and the kinds of tools available were primitive. Before the iron age tools were of bronze or copper, and before that of stone, laboriously shaped, harder than those to be cut. What a tool lacked in efficiency was made up for with the patience of the craftsman. It is believed that a primitive form of drill was among the most ancient tools to be used for gem cutting. Engraved stones were originally employed only as seals, their first use in jewelry being when they were set in rings, and then only those which were precious stones were regarded as jewels. Later they were also used as pendants, medallions and in bracelets and earrings. The art of engraving is particularly interesting when one

Gold ring set with an engraved agate, Greco-Roman, 2nd century BC. Victoria and Albert Museum, London.

Engraved stone from a gold ring, Roman. Museo Poldi-Pezzoli, Milan.

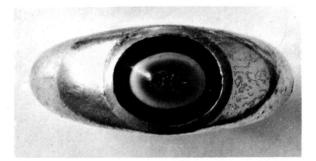

considers that the figures carved complement, both in form and content, the sculpture of the various epochs. Another aspect is their importance to archaeologists in helping to date sites where they are found; for instance, the city of Ur in Mesopotamia was identified by the inscription on a cylinder seal found on the site prior to excavation.

The art of engraving reached a high level of development in Egypt too. Right up to the Greco-Roman era the most widely used type of engraved stone was the seal amulet in the form of a scarab. The portrait of a sovereign or prince appeared for the first time on engraved gems during the Hellenistic era. There were numerous other motifs as well, linked to religious or

Gold necklace with semiprecious stones engraved with scarabs, from Vulci, Etruscan, 4th-3rd century BC. British Museum, London.

mythological concepts, and all executed with rare skill. During the Roman era this art continued to flourish, and some real masterpieces were produced often, with the increasing popularity of colour, for use in jewelry. In China engraving was also practiced, particularly on jade and coral pendants, buttons and diadems.

Later Hellenistic jewelry, in addition to its influence in southern Italy, was diffused throughout the Roman provinces without undergoing any notable stylistic modifications at first.

The Roman Empire Rome during the republican period was comparable to pre-Hellenistic Greece. Little jewelry or valuable plate was made owing to laws passed to limit the amount of gold to be used. Again, as had happened in Greece, the new conquests in southern Italy, Macedonia, Greece, Asia and Africa reversed the situation, bringing a wave of prosperity and removing all restraint on wealth. The wearing of gold rings, which had been a sign of the highest distinction reserved exclusively for nobles, senators and ambassadors, was bestowed on lesser functionaries by the late 3rd century, and towards the end of the republic rings were worn by quite ordinary people. Engraved gems became so popular that wealthy people, including Caesar himself, made collections of them.

During the imperial period, as a result of the increasing wealth flowing into Rome, the city became a centre for goldsmiths' workshops, a development which could only act as an incentive for new ideas. Gradually local and provin-

Cameo with portrait of Julia, daughter of Titus, Roman. The mounting is of much later date. Bibliothéque Nationale, Cabinet des Médailles, Paris.

cial production acquired a homogeneity of style. In addition to gold, pearls and exotic precious stones were also coming onto the Roman markets in large numbers, and the influx resulted in an increasing use of colour in Roman jewelry. There is evidence to show that the many goldsmiths and lapidaries who were attracted to Rome to supply the growing demands came from Greece and the oriental provinces. This helps to explain the predominance of Hellenistic influences in Roman jewelry until the first imperial period.

The shape of a spiral serpent, sometimes with precious stones for the eyes, was popular for bracelets and rings. From the Etruscans the Romans took the curious form of the bulla, originally a lens-shaped pendant suspended from a broad loop and later worn as an amulet. As the Roman version of the *Etruscum aurum* (an ornament worn by the Etruscan kings), it was either decorated with filigree and adapted for use in necklaces as a pendant, or completely plain and hemispherical and attached to bracelets. An example is the bracelet found at Pompeii made of thirteen pairs of hemispheres attached to a beaded wire. The clasp is decorated with a widely used motif: the ivy leaf.

In Pompeii and Rome jewelry began to acquire Italian characteristics, but in the outlying parts of the empire it came under local influences. Thus in Taranto Hellenistic motifs were somewhat wearily perpetuated; in Gaul Roman products were influenced by Celtic traditions, in north Africa by Egyptian ones, and in Syria, where the Palmyra sculptures show women adorned with Roman jewelry, by Iranian.

With the liberation of Roman jewelry from the Hellenistic tradition, three new techniques were developed. The first was the technique of pierced work, known as *opus interassile*; second was the indiscriminate use of masses of coloured stones with a minimum of setting or none at all; and third was the use of niello (a method of decorating engraved metals with a black compound of silver and copper). Although used occasionally in the Hellenistic period, niello does not occur in Roman jewelry before the 4th century when it was used in brooches and rings.

118

centre right Gold serpentine ring, Hellenistic. Schmuckmuseum, Pforzheim.

above Gold ring with an engraved stone, from the House of Menander, Pompeii, 1st century BC-1st century AD. Museo Nazionale, Naples.

Funerary statue with a necklace, earrings, bracelets and a diadem, Palmyra. British Museum, London.

All these techniques continued without interruption into the Early Christian and Byzantine periods.

Opus interassile consists of working out a design on a metal sheet, after which all the unwanted parts are removed with a chisel. It was used in bracelets, rings, parts of necklaces and the borders of medallions. A bracelet of the 4th century AD (Staatliche Museen, Berlin), found at Tartus in Syria, consists of a broad band, the outer edge of which forms a curving hexagon decorated with *opus interassile* so minutely executed that it has the appearance of gold lace. From the same period is a ring, the bezel of which is surrounded by a wide border of openwork scrolls and tracery (Museo di Antichità, Parma). A Syrian necklace from Tortosa (British Museum, London) consists of cut-out Heracles knots interspersed with elongated plasma stones, and at Pavia (Museo Civico) there is a necklace with a pendant consisting of a coin showing Emperor Theodosius framed by a rich openwork border.

In Roman jewelry stones are often set in a broad frame indented with parallel grooves. They were usually cut oval or square with

Pearl cluster earrings from the House of Menander, Pompeii, Roman, 1st century BC-1st century AD. Museo Nazionale, Naples.

Gold bracelet with sections decorated with *opus interassile*, from Tartus, Syria, Roman, 4th century. Staatliche Museen, Berlin.

Gold mesh necklace with emeralds and mother-of-pearl, from Pompeii, Roman, 1st century BC. Museo Nazionale, Naples.

Polychrome necklace, Roman, 2nd-3rd century. Victoria and Albert Museum, London.

convex, simply polished surfaces. More unusual are the almond, round, cylindrical or prismatic shaped stones. Frequently stones are mounted without a setting, secured by a hinge threaded through them. Pearls mounted in earrings and bracelets are fastened by thick gold hinges.

An earring which appeared in the Roman period is one made up of clusters of little plasma stones, garnets or pearls. Also common was the ball type of earring (a hemisphere of plain gold), and hoops either plain or embellished with one or more pendants, pearls or gold bosses.

In necklaces and bracelets gold was from now on relegated to the background as a mount for gems. However, it was still used prominently in the rich variety of chain necklaces which often consisted of highly intricate meshwork. A bracelet of the 2nd century AD (Benaki Museum, Athens) consists of a series of gold ivy leaves each set with three green plasma stones. In a necklace made of garnets from a tomb at Montemesola (Museo Nazionale, Taranto), the stones are threaded on a gold wire which forms an eye on either side of the stone. The violet of the amethyst, the green of the emerald and plasma, the lustre of the pearl and the yellow of gold, often grouped together in one jewel to create a spectacular chromatic effect, were to become the typical colours used in Roman jewelry when it developed its own characteristic style after about the 2nd century BC.

Outside Influences In the various products of the metropolis and the provinces it is possible to detect forms which reveal their oriental or western origins. As we have noted, Hellenistic motifs or forms of Etruscan derivation such as the bulla, to which Roman goldsmiths gave new shapes such as spheres or hemispheres, or sparingly decorated in earrings, bracelets, pendants or necklaces, were used early on. Polychromy was learned from the oriental provinces, while from Gaul came Celtic motifs of ornamentation. New symbols such as the wheel, the half-moon, ivy and laurel leaves were discreetly used in necklaces, bracelets and pendants. The use of plain or framed coins as pendants was introduced and became popular; pins were decorated in the same way.

The ever-growing taste for colour led to the use of a wider variety of precious stones. Blue or pink topaz was considered more precious than yellow in the Roman era. In antiquity it was extracted, like the emerald, from mines in Upper Egypt. Notwithstanding its great hardness (eight on Mohs' scale), it is a very fragile stone and is easily shattered if dropped or knocked. Its usual colouring is honey or golden yellow, while colourless or clear crystals are not uncommon. The blue, greenish-blue and pink varieties are rare. Like the deposits in Germany, those of Upper Egypt have long since been abandoned.

Gold earring set with stones, Roman, 2nd-3rd century. National Museum, Bucharest.

123

Ornament of gold and engraved stones, Roman, 3rd century. Victoria and Albert Museum, London.

Coloured stones in jewelry

Archaeological discoveries

As more and more archaeological finds permit the reconstruction of the history of art in its various phases of development, so our interest in and knowledge of past civilisations increases.

The term treasure in art and archaeology does not just apply to accumulations of objects made of precious materials, but includes almost anything which is found on ancient sites, including architectural remains. This book will only discuss certain important archaeological finds with regard to the jewelry or goldware they contained, even if the only value of the objects is aesthetic.

Interest in archaeology, which goes back as far as the late Middle Ages, increased greatly during the Renaissance period. It was with the discovery of Herculaneum and Pompeii in the 18th century that the most intense and spectacular phase began. In addition to influencing contemporary artistic taste, especially in the field of the decorative arts, these discoveries gave an incentive for renewed research into ancient Greece in the first decades of the 19th century, which witnessed vast activity and results. In addition to the new enthusiasm, the methods of archaeological exploration had by then become better organised. Following the Napoleonic campaigns Egypt also became the object of vast, if at first disorganised, researches. Later, qualified specialists from museums and famous archaeologists undertook excavations in Egypt, Iran, Pre-Columbian America, Russia, Greece, Asia Minor and Italy, finding an immense amount of material. Texts and inscriptions, when deciphered, facilitated the correct dating of historical facts and naming of the protagonists, so that our ideas about the proto-history and pre-history of many areas were completely changed by these new discoveries. The frontiers of time were pushed further and further back, as if a mist had lifted to reveal a fascinating panorama. Archaeological research is today a science widely and actively pursued everywhere, making exciting discoveries of great importance and revealing the fascinating secrets of the past.

The Discovery of Troy The name of Heinrich Schliemann will always be linked with the so-called treasure of Priam and the discovery of Troy. Schliemann (born in Neu Buckow, Ger-

top far left Heinrich Schliemann in about 1860.

top left Heinrich Schliemann's wife, Sophia Engastromenos, wearing the diadem and ornaments thought to have belonged to Helen of Troy.

left Troy during the excavations on the hill of Hissarlik.

many, in 1822) was forced as a boy to abandon his studies because of lack of money. Making his way via being a grocer's apprentice, a cabin-boy, a clerk and a student of languages to become a successful businessman, he went to America where he again took up his study of Greek and in particular of Homer. He could never erase from his mind the Homeric poems of the *Iliad*, which had impressed him so profoundly as a boy that they were to determine the course of his future life. In 1863, after a rapid and successful career in commerce, he wound up all his business affairs. The profits brought him an income of 200,000 francs a year, half of which he spent on his great passion, archaeological excavations. In 1858 he made his first journey round Europe, Egypt and the Middle East, and the next year he went to Turkey and Greece. Between 1864 and 1866 he visited North Africa, Asia and Central America, and he spent the years 1866-68 in Paris. Now, with a vast knowledge of foreign languages, he began his archaeological activities which he was to continue without interruption until his death in 1890 in Naples.

In 1873, after three exciting years of research in Turkey, this passionate amateur archaeologist claimed to have identified the true location of Homer's Troy. The generally accepted opinion of the scholars was that the village of Bunarbashi was the site, but Schliemann, after his first reasearches there, soon became convinced that the location of the place bore no resemblance to that described by Homer in the *Iliad*. He was attracted by the little hill of Hissarlik (from the Turkish for palace and fortress), which was situated at the confluence of the ancient rivers Scamander and Simoenta, whose situation corresponded to Homer's description. The hill, which was about three hundred metres long and two hundred metres wide and was at that time covered in ruined walls, had been identified as the Hellenic-Roman city of Ilion. In 1868 part of it belonged to the American consul, Calvert, who was also an amateur archaeologist.

Schliemann began his excavations in 1871 and was to have fantastic success. He found the treasure on 17th June 1873 on the north-west side of the hill at a depth of about nine metres,

near the encircling wall of an edifice which he was convinced was the palace of Priam. There were some gold and silver plates, a silver vase containing two splendid gold diadems and a third of exceptional workmanship, and four gold earrings 'worked with the highest artistry'; in addition there were fifty-six earrings, 8750 little rings, six bracelets, and prisms, buttons and other little pieces, all of gold.

In his memoirs Schliemann gives an interesting account from his firsthand knowledge of the facts of the excavations and of the perils with which the workmen were sometimes faced. It is also interesting to know that the men, whose pay was two francs a day, dug from five in the morning until six in the evening, 'however with half an hour at nine in the morning and an hour at one-thirty to eat and smoke'. This habit of smoking caused a sort of mutiny among the workers when Schliemann prohibited it during working hours; on 25th April 1872 they struck in protest. But Schliemann won the day--because, during the night, his overseer was able to replace the striking workmen with others hired from neighbouring villages, and in fact found more new workmen than he had had before. According to Schliemann's calculations, each workman should be able to dig four cubic metres per day. In a little more than three months, therefore, he should dig four hundred; as there were about a hundred workmen hired, they must have been able to move about four thousand cubic metres of earth during that time.

Schliemann also made important finds at Mycenae, capital of ancient Argolid, in 1876 and at Ithaca in 1878, and in 1888 his archaeological interest extended also to Crete, but Hissarlik remained his chief interest. From 1882 he had as a collaborator the archaeologist Wilhelm Dörpfeld. Later nine layers of the remains of human habitation, superimposed one on top of the other, were identified in the hill of Hissarlik dating from 3000 BC to the 4th century AD. The layer which Schliemann identified as the rock of Pergamos of Troy and Priam's palace belongs in fact to a city of the 2nd millennium BC, before the beginning of the Creto-Mycenian civilisation. It has now been ascertained that Homer's Troy is to be found between the sixth and seventh layers.

The Turkish Government had agreed to allow Schliemann to keep for himself a third of whatever he found; but because of the continual obstruction and unhelpfulness of the Turks over his work, he eventually smuggled the whole treasure out of Turkey and presented it to the Berlin Museum. During the war the treasure was dispersed for safety's sake and, tragically, some of the pottery was smashed by villagers during festivities, and part of the jewelry was destroyed during bombing raids or lost.

The Royal Tombs of Ur The Royal Tombs at Ur in Mesopotamia (3rd millennium BC) have already been mentioned. In addition to Queen Shubad's jewels, the tomb contained many other extraordinary objects such as harps, sacred animals, and horses' harnesses, either of solid gold or plated with gold *repoussé* work.

The Tomb of Tutenkhamen Since the Napoleonic era archaeological excavations had proceeded chaotically in Egypt until, in the 1920s, Howard Carter, chief inspector of the antiquities service of the Egyptian government, reorganised it on a scientific basis. It was he who made the famous discovery in 1922 of the tomb, with all its treasure intact, of Tutenkhamen, a pharaoh of the 18th dynasty (14th century BC), who died when he was eighteen. Tutenkhamen's actual tomb was still under construction when he died prematurely, and he was interred in the more modest tomb which the priest Eje, who had acquired the right of succession to the throne, had built for himself in the Valley of Kings.

In the antechamber of the tomb Carter found all kinds of furniture decorated with *repoussé*, gold plate, a gold and enamelled throne, chariots, alabaster vases and chests inlaid with ivory containing precious objects and vestments. In the burial chamber itself the sarcophagus was concealed inside four gilded wooden shrines. Inside it were three more coffins in effigy form, one inside the other. The first is covered in gold and inlaid with dipped enamel in feathered motifs, the second is gilded and decorated wood and the third, containing the mummy, is solid gold weighing ninety kilograms set with precious gems. The king's mummy had a gold mask decorated with gems and enamel and was adorned with a diadem, necklaces, breastplate, rings and earrings and gold sandals decorated with inlaid colours. The four shrines, the gold coffin and the wooden one, the gold mask and the jewels were taken to the Egyptian Museum in Cairo, while the sarcophagus and the third coffin have until now been left in their original place in the burial chamber. The sandals are in the Metropolitan Museum, New York.

Aegina On the Greek island of Aegina in the Gulf of Aegina, about equidistant from Attica, Corinth and Argos, was found a treasure consisting of bracelets, rings, pendants and a gold goblet. Some archaeologists think it dates back to the 17th century BC, while others believe it is more recent. The island, which has a rich history full of important events, was in close contact with the civilisations of the Aegean, Asia Minor and Egypt, and the jewelry shows strong influences of art from Egypt and Asia Minor. The treasure is conserved in the British Museum, London.

Olbia Olbia was an ancient Greco-Scythian colony of the 7th century BC on the north-west coast of the Black Sea and an important commercial and cultural centre. In the 4th- to 3rd-century tumulus tombs discovered in 1851 at the necropolis of Alexandropol, now known as Solokha, necklaces, bracelets and other jewels and gold objects were found, all bearing strong Greek stylistic influence.

The Oxus Treasure This treasure takes its name from the modern name of the ancient Amu Darya river in central south-east Asia, the sands of which were rich with gold. The find was made in 1877, but exactly where is not known, and it arrived, after having suffered some losses, at the British Museum. It is made up of bronzes, gold and silver plate and jewelry. The stylistic form of most of the pieces is 4th-century BC Achaemenid, and it displays a discipline and balance of composition which cannot be other than Greek.

The Ziwiye Treasure The Ziwiye treasure, discovered in 1947 and collected in 1949, is discussed on page 42. In addition to the jewels, dagger sheaths, little animal figures in beaten gold and plaques of carved ivory, horse brasses and a silver plate were found.

III
The Middle Ages

Byzantium

In Europe the use of colour in jewelry, introduced by the Hellenistic epoch, gradually increased until by the Roman epoch the taste for using coloured stones and enamels was so widespread that the work of the metalworkers was overshadowed. In some jewelry, gold was used merely as a setting for the precious stones or for enamelled surfaces. In fact the Roman period saw the beginning of a decline in the art of the great master jewelers of Asia, Egypt and Greece, not only from the point of view of style, but of creativity. Indeed by the late Roman period the wide use of coins in jewelry, which was to continue in the early Byzantine era, indicates an attempt to speed up the manufacture of necklaces and bracelets.

The Byzantine World The desire of the Byzantine court to maintain the hegemony of the Roman empire in the field of the arts soon had to give way to the passage of time. It evolved a style more nearly related to the Near East, just as in religious affairs it acquired a new spirit which reflected its own characteristic appearance and development. Jewelry became essentially ornate in appearance and composition, and the techniques most used were filigree and enamelling, in addition to the copious application of precious stones and pearls. Among the Roman traditions passed on to the new Byzantine workshops was a heritage of various forms of jewelry, the techniques of pierced work and the use of coins.

Two bracelets of the 6th century in the Archaeological Museum in Istanbul are smooth tubular hoops with the decoration concentrated at the terminals. Their form clearly derives from Iranian styles, but the decoration of an ornamental geometric design worked in granulation is distinctly Byzantine in character. In the same museum are some earrings of the 6th-7th century which demonstrate two different styles. The earliest part consists of a ring-shaped hook from which hang two successive clusters of stones. The first cluster is a ring of six stones around a centre gem. The second cluster, which is suspended from the first, is a square with a large centre stone, surrounded by eight smaller and one very small stone in each corner. All the settings are embellished with granulation. Three larger stones are attached to the 129

The Empress Theodora wearing a diadem, necklaces, earrings and brooches, from a 6th-century Byzantine mosaic. San Vitale, Ravenna.

Earrings of gold, pearls and precious stones, Byzantine, 11th-12th century. Archaeological Museum, Athens.

Gold filigree earring, Byzantine, 11th century. Archaeological Museum, Athens.

lower side of the square, also copiously embellished with granulation, and from them hang five small pendants, each consisting of a rock crystal with two pearls on each side.

To this type of design, which is reminiscent of a Roman insignia, can be added another inspired by the same stylistic trend. Suspended from its elaborate clasp is an ornament composed of two arches joined together like an inverted w from which hang several pendants. In a pair of earrings of this type, in the British Museum, London, the arch is made of two scrolls which meet at the centre and divide on top to form another two scrolls, each enclosing a bezel setting with another in the centre. Along the base of the arch are three more stones and from this hang three pendants each containing one round and one square bezel setting, separated by three little gold granules. Each pendant ends in two drops of rock crystal separated by a cylindrical element. A similar pair is in the Campana collection, Louvre, Paris. In these the heightened arch is decorated with little filigree scrolls; in the centre is a large garnet and the three pendants each carry two pearls, one larger than the other. To complete this summary of the Roman types, one must mention a more simple version consisting of a ring from which hang three long chains ending in little bell

Earring of gold and rock crystal, Byzantine, 2nd-3rd century. British Museum, London.

Earring of gold pearls and stones, Byzantine, *c.* 3rd century. Archaeological Museum, Istanbul.

An empress wearing a Byzantine-style crown and earrings, from a Greek miniature, 13th century. Bodleian Library, Oxford.

Gold earring with three plaited chain pendants terminating in spherical stones, Byzantine. Thyssen collection, Lugano.

shapes or knots from which are suspended round stones; there are examples in the Thyssen collection, Lugano, Switzerland, and in the British Museum.

Essentially Byzantine are the crescent moon earrings which enjoyed a long period of popularity. There are some depicting bird's heads in pierced work in the Museum of Archaeology, Istanbul; others worked in subtle filigree tracery are basket-shaped or take the form of enamel birds on a crescent moon of gold. The use of medallions as pendants was widespread. Many are decorated with filigree tracery, openwork or enamel on a gold background, often completed with stones or pearls in bezel or coronet settings. Others are square and bordered with mock granulation.

A 12th-century oval medallion from Aosta cathedral treasury is a tribute to the enduring qualities of the distinctive stylistic character of Byzantine jewelry. It is in fact a reframed Roman agate cameo showing the bust of a goddess in profile. The frame consists of three bands of filigree scrolls differently arranged in concentric patterns. In the first the scrolls are embellished with little cabochon gems and the third with pearls.

132 **The Court at Ravenna** Court jewels (those

Gold earring with a bird depicted in enamel, Byzantine. British Museum, London.

Agate cameo mounted in a filigree and pearl frame, Roman, 12th century. Cathedral treasury, Aosta.

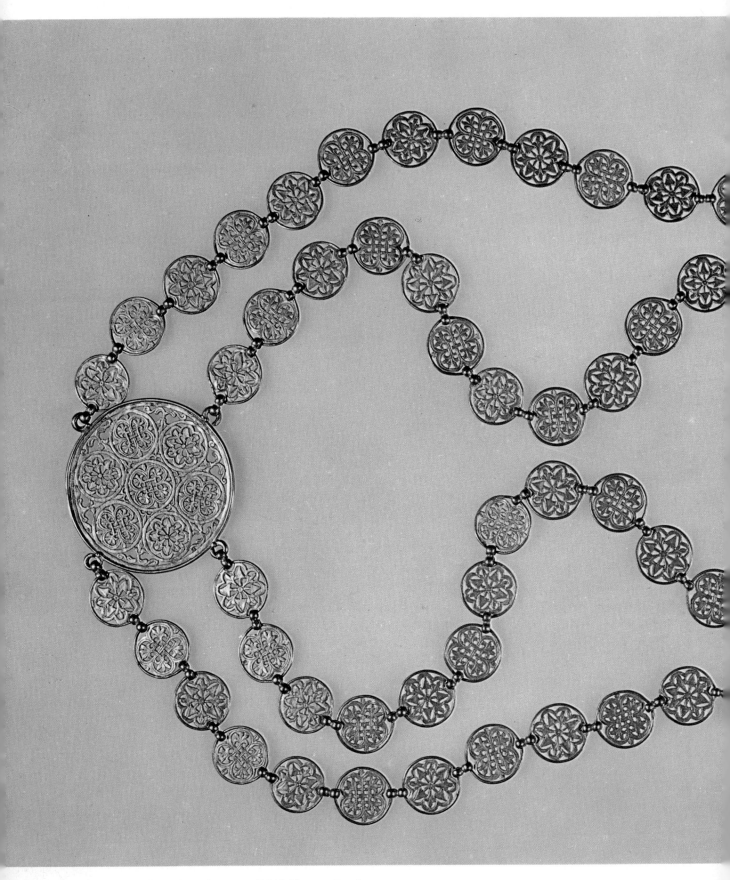

Gold necklace, Byzantine, 9th century. British Museum, London.

Cone-shaped bracelet decorated with enamel, 9th century. Archaeological Museum, Salonika.

Gold earrings of the Christian era, 5th-6th century. British Museum, London.

Silver bracelet with a figure on a medallion, 6th-7th century. Kunsthistorisches Museum, Vienna.

in the Museo di Ravenna, Italy, are representative) must have been of staggering magnificence. The mosaics in San Vitale, Ravenna, clearly show the jewelry worn by Justinian and Theodora and members of their court. The fibula which fastened the emperor's cloak is a huge flower made of gems with long pearl pendants. The empress wears, in addition to a valuable crown, a headdress and earrings with innumerable precious pendants. Some of the court ladies are adorned with jewels, earrings, bracelets and rings, which, though they were functional, give clear evidence of a splendid world appropriate to the enormous power of these people. Plain fabrics are sumptuously embellished with gold, precious stones and pearls, while the famous and valuable embroideries were sufficiently ornate on their own and would be left free of jewels.

Necklaces might be made entirely of pearls or rows of variously shaped precious and semi-precious stones interspersed with plaited gold chains or gold elements such as beads, cylinders or little medallions. Bracelets often consisted of enamelled funnel-shaped gold bands with the surface divided into a square pattern with filigree.

Byzantine Influences The spiritual concepts of Byzantine art established a new aesthetic order throughout the Christian world, and its vast sphere of influence, extending from the Balkan peninsula and Russia to parts of Italy and Egypt, endured for a length of time unrivalled by any other preceding stylistic period. Goldsmiths' work was of prime importance, and Constantinople was the first place where a method of marking silver was used which makes it possible to date the pieces. Although culture was widely diffused, most of the workshops and the best goldsmiths were certainly in the capital, the enormously wealthy centre of commerce between East and West.

The conquest and sacking of Constantinople in 1204 during the crusades effectively put an end to its artistic activity. Goldware and jewelry suffered terrible and irreparable damage: the soldiers appreciated only the intrinsic value of the objects and melted them down without the slightest regard for their aesthetic or historical worth.

Necklace of round and oblong beads of variegated faience and coins bordered with filigree beads (one stamped with Anastasius I, five with Justinian I, and one with Tiberius Constantine II) from Castel Trosino, 7th century. Museo dell' Alto Medioevo, Rome.

The Middle Ages
Early medieval Europe

While new and individual forms of expression were evolving and developing in the Byzantine world, powerful groups of people were exerting their influence further West during and following the dissolution of the Roman empire. These were the northern tribes who between the 4th and 8th centuries were actively expanding by invading large parts of southern Europe from the Danube to Spain and, above all, the Italian peninsula. The most significant remains left by these people are the metal objects in which they excelled. The enormous quantity of finds in the various areas constitutes a broader basis for study than the scanty written records. Nevertheless, it is difficult to coordinate because of the vastness of the area in question and the frequent displacement of the various ethnic groups, which comprised Ostrogoths, Visigoths, Franks, Burgundians, Anglo-Saxons, Germans and Lombards. Although the works of these tribes, who were closely related to each other, are referred to collectively as Barbarian art, many technical and stylistic differences are discernible. Oriental and Celtic influences in differing quantities are mixed with the local characteristics of the various regions.

Colour is the factor dominating most Barbarian jewelry: precious stones, faience and enamels often cover the entire jewel, giving it the appearance of a miniature stained-glass window with gold supports instead of lead. Filigree was also extensively used. To these techniques must be added a consummate skill in the art of relief work (in all its varieties: punching, piercing, casting and welding), although some pieces are rather clumsily made.

Barbarian Jewelry Forms The brooch (fibula) was the most widely used form of jewelry. One of the largest from Petrossa in Rumania is in the shape of a bird measuring thirty-five centimetres; at the other end of the scale there are tiny brooches measuring only a few centimetres. The brooches most often recurring are the tiny so-called buckler variety with fan heads, arched bridges and a flat or moulded foot. This type of fibula is often voluptuously embellished with anthropomorphic or zoomorphic motifs. There are also round and s-shaped brooches. Some necklaces are made of elements hanging from a chain; others are like

Brooch of gold, silver and enamel, from Wittislingen on the Danube, Barbarian, 7th century. Bayerisches Nationalmuseum, Munich.

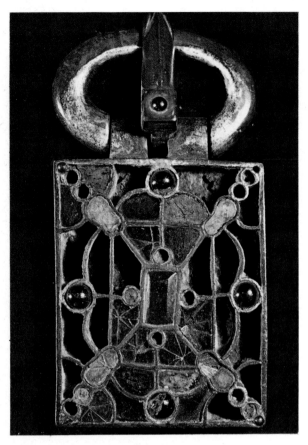

Merovingian buckle from Tressan, St Germain.

Earring of gold and stones, from Castel Trosino, Barbarian, 7th century. Museo Nazionale Romano, Rome.

torques, made of one or more solid tubes which fasten with a hinge at the back.

Other types of jewelry are rare. An earring found at Castel Trosino, Italy, is reminiscent of the Roman style. On the hook is a small disc decorated with a hemisphere surrounded by granulated filigree (filigree made of little grains); suspended from the disc is a triangular shape of three small hemispheres, and from this hangs two gold drops and another larger triangular piece decorated with four bezels, one in the centre and one at each angle, decorated with filigree. Another three pendants hang from the bottom of this pendant, the central one of amber, and those on either side of gold decorated with filigree.

Two medallions bear the heads of kings rendered in a purely descriptive rather than volumetric manner and show largely Roman influence. They come from excavations in Sweden and were probably made there between the 5th and 6th centuries. These medallions

show that similar stylistic influences were current at about the same period in Italy as well as in the Scandinavian countries, except that in the latter, as we shall see, the use of colour was more restrained than elsewhere.

Another two pairs of earrings from Castel Trosino are interesting; the first are discs concentrically decorated with filigree from which hang hinges for a gem (missing), while the second pair are spheres covered in a complicated pierced work pattern. Filigree is also used on a disc brooch from the same source, which has a bezel-set stone in the centre framed by gold braid. The rest of the surface is concentrically divided by two more plaited braids; the area enclosed by the first is full of little filigree rings arranged at random and the second with filigree scrolls in the shape of question marks, facing and diverging according to the radius of the disc. Only the central plaited bezel is higher than the raised braids separating these decorations. In addition to this simple type of disc

Gold disc brooch decorated with beaded filigree and stones, from Wittislingen, Barbarian, mid 7th century. Bayerisches National-museum, Munich.

Polychrome s-shaped fibula, Barbarian. Museo Civico, Cividale del Friuli.

brooch, there was another of more complex design which has in the centre and on the external band hemispheres of equal size decorated with little rings of filigree granules. The characteristic feature of this type was the semi-tubular concentric division also embellished with rings of filigree granules.

Returning once more to Sweden to Alleberg, we find a splendid necklace collar of the same period, which is twenty-one centimetres long.

Gold disc-shaped boss with decorations of Byzantine derivation, from Castel Trosino, Lombard, 7th century. Museo dell' Alto Medioevo, Rome.

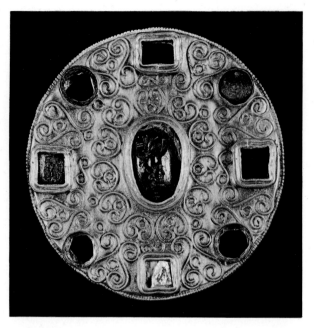

Gold disc brooch set with stones with an engraved stone in the centre, Barbarian, 7th century. Museo dell' Alto Medioevo, Rome.

It consists of three solid tubular elements linked together and widening slightly at the front; they are hinged at the back, and the clasp in the front is made of three long teeth which, following the curve, fit into the hollow part of the corresponding tubes. The basic shape of the three tubes, which appear to have been turned on a lathe, is embellished at short regular distances with variously fashioned rings. The whole composition is minutely decorated with filigree tracery, studded or in double scrolls interlaced with fillet mouldings. The hinge clasps are also elaborately decorated, and in the centre of the necklace are two human heads and a little figure seen from the back leaning against the curve of a ring. In the ridges where the tubes join are fantastic crouching animals, masks and human figures. The style and the quality of the technique of this necklace belong to one of the periods when goldsmiths' work was at its height. The richness and variety of this and other examples makes them comparable to the greatest of the Etruscan fibulae in the oriental period.

The pieces described above constitute some of the most noble examples of Barbarian work which have come down to us and particularly illustrate the distinguished level of the goldsmiths' art of this period in certain areas. An-

Gold necklace from Alleberg, Västergötland, Sweden, Barbarian, 6th century. National Museum of Antiquities, Stockholm. Detail on page 144-5.

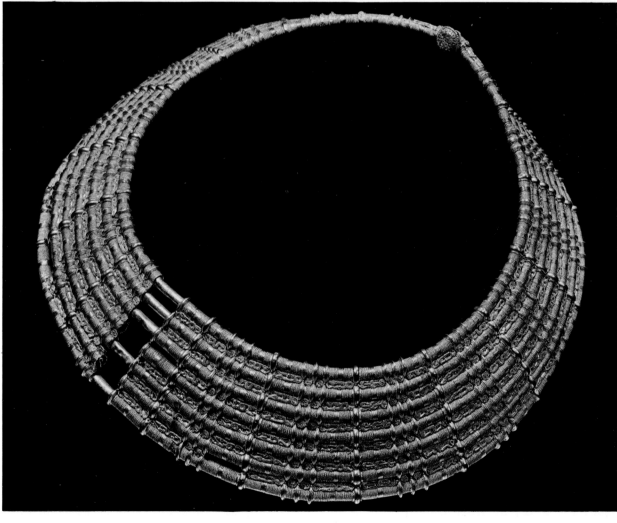

Gold necklace from Färjestaden, Oland, Sweden, Barbarian, 6th century. National Museum of Antiquities, Stockholm.

other form, which in the Scandinavian countries shows Mediterranean influences, is the torque necklace, typically Celtic in design, but often decorated with a taste that relates more to the spirit of Etruscan jewelry.

We shall now examine, through other examples, the most typical characteristics of Barbarian art. The fibula from Gummersmark in the Nationalmuseet, Copenhagen, is one of the most significant examples of an enigmatic mode of expression developed within the limits of a mould which is both traditional and functional. The foot of the fibula looks like an amphora with scroll handles from which rise two horses' heads interpreted very subjectively so that the mouth of the vase might be a mane which breaks off to meet, within angular divisions, other obscure but finely modelled shapes. All round the supposed vase are other zoomorphic figures of fantastic form, which end in three closed scrolls, two together and one lower down in the centre. The head of the fibula is rectangular and framed by a row of close-set triangular crenellations rising from a disc with a central hemisphere. In the centre, at the angles and at the base, the crenellations take on the form of freely interpreted human and animal heads. Parts of the rectangular head and the bridge are embellished with elaborate traceries of scrolls, while some of the margins are decorated with pierced work which accentuates its plastic quality.

From this type, where decorative intricacy attains a high level, we pass to others of a less plastic quality but modelled with more fantasy and decorated with complicated patterns, which frequently recall anthropomorphic or zoomorphic forms, usually heads but sometimes single arms. The technical skill of these examples is notable; stamping, casting, punching and relief work are all employed and show a precise stylistic and aesthetic discipline of a high order. The curved, dynamic lines, the rigid disjointedness, the fine tracery and the many uses in ornamentation of vegetable, human and animal forms indicate the wide interests and varied sources of the craftsmen, but are abstractly expressed or invented from fantasy, rarely adhering to nature. In the fibulae described above we find aesthetic concepts of ancient Celtic art, but even in those which reveal

Gold brooch worked in *repoussé* from near Hon, Norway, Barbarian, possibly 9th century. Universitetets Oldsaksamling, Oslo.

oriental, Byzantine or Roman stylistic influence, there is a general tendency to shun the imitation of nature, and forms and shapes are violated, distorted and altered in order to excite greater emotion. Apart from the many Nordic jewels, evidence of this spirit has been found in Lombard pieces found in Italy at Friuli, Castel Trosino and Nocera Umbra. Almost identical are two more fibulae from Lingotto (Museo di Antichità, Trieste) and Nocera Umbra (Museo dell'Alto Medioevo, Rome).

Distances appear to have counted for relatively little in the Barbarian world, to judge from the wide use of the same materials and the affinity of stylistic forms. The stone most frequently used was the almandine, a wine-coloured variety of garnet, found in many European countries as well as in India. The oldest and most significant examples of Barbarian jewelry in which colour plays a predominant role were found in the Petrossa treasure discovered in Rumania in 1837. The most spectacular piece is a fibula, fashioned like a bird (an eagle?) from a sheet of gold. The lower part of the creature is divided longitudi-

nally to coincide with the curve of the wings, while the neck and the head rise up fully modelled. The whole of its body is covered with precious stones, some of them quite large, while from the bottom four oval quartzes are suspended on gold wires. Most of the pieces found are fibulae, but there is also a necklace made of hinged pieces of solid plate fastening at the back. The surface is densely covered in pierced work hollow motifs, using ivy leaves in threes (one growing out of the other) and various other ornamental motifs.

The bird-shaped type of fibula, with certain simplifications and variations, is found in Italy and Spain until the 6th century. Those of the Petrossa treasure probably date from the second half of the 4th century, which means that this form was popular for about two centuries. Round and shield-shaped brooches, buckles and pieces of necklaces, covered with super-

Brooch in the shape of a bird modelled from gold sheet, from the Petrossa treasure, Barbarian, 4th century. National Museum of History, Bucharest.

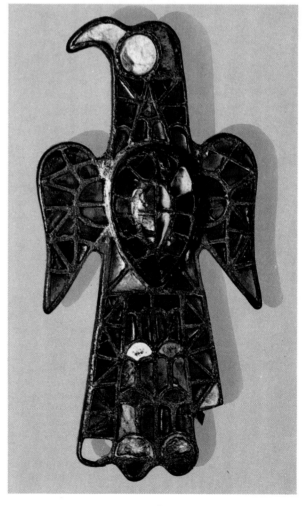

147

Polychrome bird-shaped brooch from Saragossa, Barbarian, c. 585-620. Museo Arqueológico Nacional, Madrid.

Large shoulder brooch decorated with *cloisonné* enamel, from the Sutton Hoo ship burial, Anglo-Saxon, 7th century. British Museum, London.

imposed hollows or cut out geometric designs, have been found in Scandinavia, Germany, France and Spain. Some use mixed techniques, part metal with enamel or filigree embellishments.

The Sutton Hoo Ship Burial The most masterly examples of the use of polychromy were found in 1939 in the ship burial of Sutton Hoo, England. During excavation work prior to the building of the Ipswich Museum, Suffolk, east of the river Deben, a complete funeral ship containing the richest treasure ever found in England was discovered in a barrow. There were no human remains, and it is thought that the ship was a cenotaph or memorial to a 7th-century East Anglian king. The splendid jewels which constitute the treasure are rare examples of the skill of the Anglo-Saxon goldsmiths, particularly in the art of enamelling. This can be seen in the huge shoulder pin composed of two hinged elements, with curved smooth surfaces decorated with *cloisonné* enamel geometric chessboard designs bordered with a tracery of zoomorphic shapes, and with moulded ends. A

unique piece is an ivory purse, with enamelled gold plaques decorated with human zoomorphic and ornamental motifs executed with the greatest virtuosity, refinement and aesthetic taste. The style which is Celtic in derivation relates to Irish manuscript painting. Apart from the colourful jeweled pieces, there are some other gold objects, such as a triangular fibula which has a smooth hemisphere embellished with filigree in each corner, while the rest of its surface, including its buckle-shaped head, is covered with a finely worked tracery of niello, a technique often used in Anglo-Saxon jewelry. A ring with the hoop decorated in small filigree volutes and set with a huge murky agate is very similar to Roman examples. The treasure, which also includes thirty-seven gold coins extremely valuable in assessing the date, can now be seen in the British Museum.

Another example of polychromy is a ring in the Museo Civico at Reggio Emilia; its thin band, which has cylindrical markings, supports a bezel in the shape of a hexahedron, with a gold framework set with precious stones.

148

Gold buckle from the Sutton Hoo ship burial, Anglo-Saxon, 7th century. British Museum, London.

The Carolingian and Ottonian Periods

The Carolingian and Ottonian periods witnessed a great expansion in the production of religious objects in the abbey and court workshops of Germany. Numerous crosses, reliquaries, monstrances, gospel covers, complete altars and sceptres, crowns and other royal insignia were made by skilled goldsmiths. The application of jewelry techniques is discernible in the use of refined filigree work and precious stones in crosses, shrines and gospel covers. As a result of the spread of Christianity one observes, in addition to traces of Byzantine influences above all in the enamelling, a return to the major forms of Classical Rome.

Christian burial rites, by then in general use, put an end to the tradition of burying the dead with all their wealth and jewels. From the beginning of the 8th century, therefore, the most interesting products of goldware which have come down to us are almost exclusively important pieces which were preserved in cathedral, abbey or royal treasuries. Jewels surviving from the end of the first millennium are very rare, since funeral ornaments so widespread in the past are completely lacking. The scant written information is also of a religious nature and therefore includes little about jewelry.

Royal Jewels A very important find amongst the few secular survivals from this period are the rings of Ethelwulf, king of Wessex (839-58), and Ethelswith, queen of Mercia (855-89), found at Laverstock, England, in 1870 and preserved in the British Museum. The two rings are worked in niello. The king's is in the form of a bishop's mitre, with his name engraved around the brim, flanked by two Greek crosses.

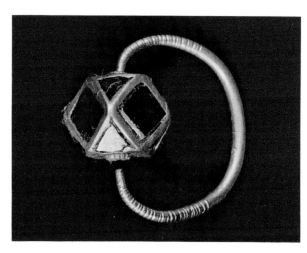

149

Gold ring with a hexahedron-shaped bezel, Barbarian. Museo Civico, Reggio Emilia.

The upper part is decorated with a design of two swans facing each other across a central triangular motif surmounted by a rose, from which a vertical stem ends in a second flower. The workmanship is not particularly refined and foreshadows the almost unpleasant Romanesque modes. The central ornament of the queen's ring is a hemisphere shape bordered by seed pearls. The disc is decorated with a fantastic animal, a chimaera within a four-lobed circle. The various spaces in between are filled with simple ornamentation.

The famous iron crown in the cathedral treasury at Monza is a diadem composed of six curved gold plates, each bearing a large cabochon stone set in the centre surrounded by four gold *repoussé* rosettes, with the background filled in with *cloisonné* enamel. The crown is backed with an iron hoop which, it is said, is one of the nails of the Cross. The crown is traditionally thought to have been a present from Pope Gregory the Great to Queen Theodolinda, who died in 626, but most scholars agree in dating it to the 9th century.

The holy Roman emperor's crown (Schatzkammer, Kunsthistorisches Museum, Vienna) is an example of skilful use of colour at its highest level. The crown has eight arched panels hinged together; the front and back panels are rather higher and the four intermediate panels slightly higher than the two side ones. The bridge and the cross were added to the crown in the 11th century, and various precious stones were put on at other times. The four intermediate panels are jewel-framed gold plates bearing scenes of biblical and holy subjects worked in enamel, symbolising humility, long life, justice and wisdom. The other panels are encrusted with valuable precious stones and pearls, their settings embellished with filigree and held with gold chickens' claws. The filigree mountings are considerably raised from the base of the plate in order to give prominence to the gems. The crown is believed to have been made in the workshops of Reichenau Abbey in the 10th century, and the prevailing stylistic influences are Sicilian and Byzantine.

With rare exceptions the services of goldsmiths were completely monopolised by the Church and, therefore, hardly any jewelry was made for the laity, although there is an 11th-century account of certain shops on the Grand-Pont in Paris, where necklaces, pins and clasps were made *à l'usage des barons et des nobles dames*.

The pieces of this period tend to be a mixture of Barbaric, Byzantine and Classical stylistic elements, which are often clumsily worked. As in architecture, in which elements derived from Roman buildings were incorporated, so in jewelry, gems engraved in the old way were often used, and it is not uncommon to find a bishop's ring set with a gem engraved with a pagan subject, in strong contrast to Catholic principles. Enamel, filigree pearls and irregularly shaped polished precious stones continued

top right The Iron Crown of Lombardy, 9th century. Cathedral treasury, Monza.

right Crown said to be that of the holy Roman emperor, 10th century. Attributed to the workshop of the abbey of Reichenau. Kunsthistorisches Museum, Vienna.

Stucco saint wearing a crown, necklace and decorated robes c. 762-776. Tempietto, Santa Maria in Valle, Cividale del Friuli.

Gold ring with granulated filigree and engraved stone of Classical origin, 5th century. British Museum, London.

to be the dominant decorative elements, while the composition alternates between severe simplicity and costly richness.

Even in north-central Europe the famous monastery workshops dedicated to the production of sacred objects often reflect marked Byzantine influence in the richness of decoration and wide use of filigree and enamels.

Pictures and sculptures of this period give scant illustration of jewelry. One of the few exceptions is found in two stucco figures of saints in the tempietto of Santa Maria in Valle, at Cividale del Friuli. The young women, dressed in Byzantine fashion, wear crowns which seem to be decorated with pearls; their necklaces consist of several elements which together make a broad band. Their robes are richly bordered with pearls and precious stones sewn on in a lozenge arrangement composed into stylised flowers or geometric patterns.

Italy The best Italian workshops were in Venice, Milan and Palermo. The Norman court in Sicily favoured the decoration of ceremonial costumes of kings and other dignitaries with splendid jewels, for which skilled oriental craftsmen were employed. The cuffs and hems of the silk robes of Roger II and William II were sumptuously embroidered with pearls, gold thread, gems and enamel. These fabulous robes can be seen today in the Schatzkammer at the Kunsthistorisches Museum in Vienna. There

Crown of Queen Constanza of Aragon, late 12th century. Cathedral treasury, Palermo.

are also Frederick II's gloves made of precious woven silk encrusted with little pearls, pieces of finely enamelled gold and gems.

The *tiraz* or workshop of Palermo, with its Muslim, Greek and local craftsmen, produced exquisite works for the court, the styles of which consisted of a mixture of local characteristics, superimposed on basic Byzantine models, attaining a quality and technical perfection which place them amongst the greatest European achievements of the period. The crown of about 1130 which belonged to Queen Constanza of Aragon, wife of Frederick II, is preserved in the cathedral treasury of Palermo. This precious royal ceremonial headdress clearly shows mixed Byzantine and oriental influences in the style of its composition. It is in the shape of a skullcap of heavy woven gold. Rising from the band which encircles the lower part of the cap are two arches which cross each other creating four divisions. Gold four-lobed motifs decorated with enamel from which protrude coronet-set cabochon gems, with a large pearl between each, are the chief recurring pattern on the arches and the band. The remaining spaces between the motifs are filled with pieces of moulded and enamelled gold, while the edges of the two arches, the band and every patterned piece on them are emphasised by being outlined by a double row of seed pearls. Spaced out along the edge of the cap there are sixteen finely punched gold stylised lilies in the oriental manner, each with a little turquoise in the centre. The four spaces between the arches each contain seven gems, a central one surrounded by three small and large ones alternately set. On top of the cap where the two arches cross each other is an oval stone surrounded by pearls. Two long gold pendants, finely decorated in enamel, hang from superimposed rings on each side of the crown. They consist of a triangular network of links horizontally crossed by three crescent-shaped and three rhomboid bars alternately; from the base of each triangle hang three gold pendants, a drop-shaped one with a spherical one on each side.

Brooches and Rings Among people of high rank brooches were the most frequently used

Brooch, Swedish, 8th century. Victoria and Albert Museum, London.

Ring with a prominent cone-shaped bezel, 12th century. Museo Poldi-Pezzoli, Milan.

ornament after rings. They were usually round, often with protruding cone-shaped surfaces decorated with concentric patterns; others were set with cabochon stones on prominent bezels. A popular motif was an eagle inside a decorated circle in pierced work embellished with enamel. Other motifs used were stars and stylised flowers, encrusted with gems, pearls and filigree. Often an old cameo was reset in a rich filigree frame with pearls and precious stones.

Rings were widely worn and were increasingly attributed with religious or superstitious value; they were used for ceremonial purposes and, as always, as seals. It was around this time that the ring given as a promise of marriage became known as a betrothal ring.

155

above centre Solid gold ring, 13th century. Victoria and Albert Museum, London.

above Gold ring with an inscription in runes, 9th–10th century. British Museum, London.

The Middle Ages

*Superstition,
amulets and talismans*

Ancient Egypt In ancient Egypt boomerang-shaped ivory amulets engraved with magic words and symbols gave way to the widespread use of the scarab, which represented Phtah, creator of the universe, and was linked to the sun cult. It was also the symbol of the future and an important part of the death rites; during embalming a stone scarab bearing magic formulae would be placed on the heart of the corpse to propitiate him with Osiris. Towards the end of the 16th dynasty the flat part of the scarab was engraved with words to bring good luck. From the beginning of the 9th century BC scarabs bore the names of the kings and have, therefore, been very important in the study of the chronology of the pharaohs. The scarab was widely used throughout the Mediterranean area and imitated by the Greeks, the Phoenicians and the Etruscans until the 5th-4th century BC. Cornelians, agates, crystals, sardonyx, faience, enamelled terracotta and coral were all used to make scarabs.

Another important Egyptian symbol used on amulets was the eye of Horus, the first born god, whose symbol was the falcon. These were usually made of enamelled terracotta or similar material, but in some exceptional cases enamelled gold was used. A rich variety of shapes was used for amulets: Isis knots, head rests, sceptres, stairs, squares, fingers, crosses, handles, feathers, frogs and hearts. Most of these amulets and talismans were used in jewelry as ornaments in necklaces, bracelets, earrings and crescent-shaped pendants. The sphinx, which in Egypt had a lion's body and a king's head, while in Greece and elsewhere it had a woman's head, was attributed with magic powers. In Greece amulets were made like griffons, sirens, gorgon's heads, phallic symbols, satyrs, sphinxes and animals, both fierce and tame.

Superstition in the Middle Ages As Christianity spread throughout the world despite great opposition and persecution, paganism was gradually abandoned, although belief in magic and many superstitions persisted for a long time. Often aspects of the supernatural, the prediction of the future and magical practises were incorporated into Christianity.

The transmission of magic powers was thought to occur through contact with certain

Roman bronze hand. Museo Etrusco Gregoriano, Vatican Museums, Rome.

157

special objects. In the beginning these were stones; white ones were thought to favour breast feeding, while striped agates vaguely resembling an eye were thought to ward off the evil eye. Amulets were believed to give protection from misfortunes and danger and to be good auguries, while possession of a talisman was thought to endow positive magic powers (Aladdin's lamp, Aaron's rod, etc.).

During the High Middle Ages magic symbols lost prestige, but, with the rediscovery of magic texts and Greek and Arabic astrology, occult practices again flourished in the later Middle Ages and in the Renaissance, becoming subjects for study even for famous scholars and writers. The statutes of the hospital of Troyes, France, of 1263 declare that no nun may wear rings or precious stones except in case of illness. Precious stones were also thought to prevent contagion. In an inventory of 1380 of Charles V of France a stone is mentioned called the Holy Stone which helped any woman wearing it to have children; another had the power to cure gout.

Medieval magic was closely linked with alchemy, which was more concerned with natural phenomena and considered to be a science or a higher form of knowledge. The word, which is of Arabic origin and refers to the philosopher's stone, is the name given to the still undiscovered process which would transform base metals into gold. The practice of alchemy, which is the precursor of modern chemistry, began in Hellenistic Egypt in the 1st century AD and reached its peak in the 15th and 16th centuries.

The Powers of Particular Stones Fine and precious stones, apart from being prized for their beauty and value in ancient times, were also thought to have the power of protecting men from poison or of curing illnesses if touched or even swallowed; these are beliefs which have persisted right up to relatively recent times. Writing in his *Septenaire Chronology* on the death of Philip II (1598), Palma Cayet says: 'Two days before his death, the doctors gave him a beverage containing dregs of precious stones (zircon), and when he took it he said that his mother, the empress, had drunk a similar concoction a year before her death.'

Diamonds were thought to make one merry,

Charlemagne's talisman. Cathedral treasury, Rheims.

prevent fear of darkness, guarantee marital happiness and neutralise bad spells and contagion from the worst diseases. In heraldry they were the symbols of power, constancy and loyalty.

Among the many virtues attributed to the ruby, possession of it was thought to make men good, to prevent effervescence in water, to help in acquiring lands and titles, to soothe temper and protect from seduction; but its powers were rendered negative if it was worn on the right-hand side.

The sapphire, a stone much prized by the ancients, was thought to be protection from scorpion bites and to cure internal sores if held in the mouth. It was also thought to be an aid to those who took a vow of chastity, to ward off the evil eye, to cure dysentery and to have the power to arrest a haemorrhage.

The emerald, according to various old beliefs, speeded up or held back childbirth if tied to the thigh or placed on the womb of a pregnant woman; it was believed to be a good antidote for any illness caused by poison. According to some it was a symbol of chastity and shattered at the moment of contact between a man and a woman, but according to others it was an aphrodisiac.

The aquamarine was thought to ensure happy marriage, to be the best remedy for liver complaints or toothache, and taken in a pulverised form was believed to cure sore eyes. The zircon was held to be a symbol of prudence and sentiment, the red one being an expression of fury and the violet one of great elevation of mind. In the Middle Ages it was believed that a mixture of powdered quartz and honey was the best thing for stimulating lactation in wet-nurses. Other varieties of quartz were thought to preserve one from drunkenness.

As correct adornment for the Jewish high priest, Moses prescribed an ornament containing twelve stones which symbolised the twelve attributes of God; seven of these were varieties of quartz stones: sardonyx (king), topaz (benefactor), jasper (the living God), cornelian (omnipotent God), agate (strength), amethyst (spirit) and onyx (Lord).

Rock crystal was the symbol of virginity, innocence and chastity; the amethyst had the power to protect the fields from tempests and locusts and to ward off evil spirits. Jasper stopped haemorrhages in wounded people and appeased faithless love. Topaz relieved melancholy and quenched thirst if held in the mouth. Agate inspired eloquence. Turquoise warded off the damnation of the fallen, and heliotrope prolonged life. Carbuncle (a name for red stones) made men gallant. Onyx ensured health of body and spirit and together with coral cured epilepsy. Many stones, for example opal, were believed in antiquity to provide protection against poisoned food, and, since the practice of poisoning one's enemies was so widespread, it was considered essential to always carry some such stone. Thus men deceived themselves that they were protected from death.

Charlemagne's Talisman One of the most famous talisman jewels belonged to Charlemagne. It consists of two enormous oval cabochon sapphires, mounted back to back with a piece of wood from the True Cross between them, in a richly set round frame shaped like a pilgrim's flask. The neck of the flask, a rectangular shape, possibly contained relics of the Virgin's hair and was flanked on each side by the figures of two kneeling women supporting it with their hands. The bezel is surrounded with pearls and richly embellished with filigree volutes, the rest of the frame is studded with ten square and oval semiprecious stones and pearls, and the rectangular neck is set with a rhomboid gem. To judge from its stylistic characteristics, it is possible that the jewel was made in Asia Minor and that the two little female figures were added later.

The talisman was buried with the emperor in 814 at Aachen, exhumed by Otto III in 1000 and conserved in the cathedral treasury. In 1804 the canons presented it to the empress Josephine to wear at her coronation ceremony. It later passed to Napoleon III, whose widow presented it to the archbishop of Rheims before she died in 1920, as a contribution to the cathedral for the damage suffered from bombing during the First World War.

The Middle Ages

The Gothic era

Jewelry in Europe at the beginning of the 11th century underwent a gradual blending of various artistic currents. In some places strong Byzantine characteristics were integrated with Classical elements and lacked vitality, while in others the old Barbarian style was taken as a foundation and became refined and in some aspects elevated. This uncertainty of direction was gradually crystallised by the reawakening of the long dormant interest of the educated layman in learning and the arts encouraged by new conditions of prosperity. This resurgence gradually affected the whole of the western world and prepared the way for the wonderful flowering of the Renaissance.

The Increasing Use of Jewelry The new prosperity inevitably led to an increased demand for jewelry in Europe, and soon the jewelers began to liberate themselves from the patronage of the Church to serve the numerous courts and other rich masters. In the largest centres they organised themselves into guilds, and the growth of the guild system brought the craft to a high degree of technical achievement. A rigorous apprenticeship and high standards of workmanship were insisted upon, and, to avoid deception, it was laid down that the alloys used in goldware and jewelry should be richer than those used for gold and silver coins. Various rules prohibited the mounting of freshwater pearls together with sea pearls in the same piece of jewelry, the imitation of gems by using vitreous pastes or the backing of precious and semiprecious stones with foils in order to enhance their brightness. Guilds became very powerful in some countries, and their attempts to organise these laws of prohibition often brought them into conflict with other local authorities.

We have noted that between the Barbarian and Romanesque periods jewelry underwent great stylistic changes, we have also seen that during the Romanesque period little jewelry was produced. The beginning of the Gothic era appears to have seen such an increase in jewelry production that by the 14th century it was considered necessary in England and Spain to pass new laws regulating according to social standing the quality and quantity of jewelry which citizens might wear.

A goldsmith, from Taddeo Gaddi, *St Eligius as a Goldsmith*, 14th century. Prado, Madrid.

Justice wearing a diadem and robes decorated with pearls and precious stones, from Ambrogio Lorenzetti, *Allegory of Good Government*, 1337-40. Palazzo Pubblico, Siena.

St Agnes wearing a diadem and a brooch, from Simone Martini, *The Pisa Polyptych*. Museo Nazionale, Pisa.

Gothic Jewelry in Art While in the Romanesque period pictures or sculptures rarely reveal any information on contemporary jewelry, with the beginning of the Gothic era jewelry appears again; even religious pictures reflected worldly fashions, and as time went on they greatly increased. Some angels painted by Duccio da Buoninsegna (about 1255/60-1318/19) wear gold fillets with in the centre a gold disc set with a gem surrounded by little pearls. Other saints in Duccio's *Maestà* wear even more elaborate diadems. In a polyptych by Simone Martini (about 1284-1344) in the Museo Nazionale, Pisa, St Agnes is wearing a diadem embellished with a lily, bordered by rows of pearls. In the centre of the rich upper hem of the saint's tunic is a round clasp with a large central gem surrounded by eight enormous pearls. In the same altarpiece St Catherine's veil is held in place by a crown consisting of a fine band decorated with precious stones in lozenge and oval shapes bordered by pearls. These were certainly not figments of the artist's imagination but must have been the type of

jewel which he saw adorning the rich Siennese ladies. Nor are they isolated examples. In Pietro Lorenzetti's altarpiece (first half of the 14th century) for San Pietro a Ovile, Siena, a large round decorated clasp fastens the Madonna's mantle on her breast, while Ambrogio Lorenzetti adorns the figure of Justice, in the Palazzo Pubblico, Siena, with a large diadem and with precious stones and pearls along the hems of her robes. A diadem in the British Museum displays noticeable similarities to the one in Simone Martini's painting. It consists of a band bordered with pearls and a raised central element in a shape somewhat like a shamrock, with a large pearl in the middle. The base of the support is a tracery of gold wires; the band and the extreme parts of the central element are set with irregularly shaped stones.

Brooches One of the most frequently worn precious ornaments at this time was the brooch, which was used both functionally or purely ornamentally. The most common were round, star-shaped, pentagonal and, more rarely, lozenge-shaped. There were also ring brooches

Brooch, English, 14th century. British Museum, London.

St. Agnes wearing a diadem, from Duccio di Buoninsegna, *The Maestà*. Museo dell' Opera del Duomo, Siena.

which were usually smaller and were also round, pentagonal, lobed, star, wheel or heart-shaped, or in the form of a monogram. The decoration of the first type was largely arrangements of gems and pearls on a gold base often embellished with filigree. The bezels were often raised and encrusted with filigree, with claws to hold the stones in place. A most beautiful lozenge-shaped clasp is the Fleur-de-Lys Brooch, among the French crown jewels conserved in the Louvre, Paris. On a background of enamel patterned all over with stylised fleurs-de-lys is a large gold lily, set with precious and semi-precious cabochon stones of various sizes and shapes. The brooch is framed by a band set with thirty-two stones, each in a different setting. In this brooch, as in other types of jewelry, stones are used without much regard for symmetry (a circle in a square), shape or size, which shows how little progress had been made in stone cutting during the preceding Romanesque period.

More refined results were obtained in ring brooches, which continued to be popular in the

163

above centre Brooch of gold and precious stones, French, 13th-14th century. Victoria and Albert Museum, London.

above The Fleur-de-Lys Brooch in gold and precious stones, 14th century. Louvre, Paris.

Brooch, French, 14th century. Victoria and Albert Museum, London.

The Founders Jewel, English or French, *c.* 1400. New College, Oxford.

following century. The gold ring might be worked in *repoussé* with stylised animals, foliage or tracery and was often set with small precious stones which heightened the colourful effect. Little inscriptions were engraved behind these decorations or, more rarely, in front of them, and the Gothic lettering made them highly ornamental. The inscriptions could be of a religious, friendly or amorous nature, appropriate to the chivalrous spirit of the age.

Monogram brooches found more frequently

in the northern countries are very ingenious. In a splendid example called the Founder's Jewel, bequeathed in 1404 to New College, Oxford, by its founder William of Wykeham, the two spaces formed by the arches of the letter M have been made into two Gothic niches framed with pierced work. On the left is the figure of the Angel of the Annunciation, and on the right is the Madonna exquisitely modelled and enamelled. There is a vase on the middle stroke of the letter with three lilies, and above them are three

Brooch of pearls and precious stones, northern Italian, mid 14th century. Museo Civico, Verona.

Star-shaped brooch set with pearls and precious stones, northern Italian, mid 14th century. Museo Civico, Verona.

Ring, English, 14th century. Museo Poldi-Pezzoli, Milan.

Ring, 14th century, National Museum of Antiquities, Bucharest.

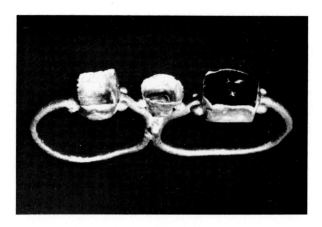

pearls set in a triangular shape. The letter is surmounted by a crown composed of three lilies interspersed with two pearls; the two outer strokes of the letter are each set with three gems. This piece is a very important example of the development of style, for it is among the first medieval objects to show an affinity with the ideas being expressed in contemporary figurative art. As in Hellenistic Greece the collaboration between artist and goldsmith was to give rise to impressive results.

Rings and Necklaces Another increasingly popular jewel in the Gothic period was the ring. Examples frequently had a polygon-shaped hoop instead of a round one, a prominent bezel and inscriptions worked in niello on the outside

above centre Opal and pearl ring, 14th century. National Museum of Antiquities, Bucharest.

above Ring of John the Fearless. Louvre, Paris.

above and above centre Marriage rings, 14th century. National Museum of Antiquities, Bucharest.

or inside. If it was not inscribed or decorated, the outside of the hoop might be moulded with a flower-shaped bezel, the petals being covered with tiny pearls and a half pearl in the centre. On some there were two heraldic lions modelled in full relief, one paw on top of the other, or fantastic animals in similar poses, flanking the bezel, as on the ring of John the Fearless in the Louvre, with its bezel in high relief flanked by two dragons arising out of fleurs-de-lys crowns. Finally, the Classical type, with an oval or round bezel containing an engraved gem persisted, sometimes framed by a gold band inscribed in niello.

Necklaces were infrequently used at this time. There are records of sòme, made of diamonds, rubies and large pearls, in inventories, but these must have been exceptional, since they are usually absent from the numerous paintings and statues of the time. Instead, the fashion for adorning the neckline and sleeves of the robes of nobility with precious stones was continued.

Jeweled Belts Around 1340 it became the fashion to enrich belts with elegantly elaborate buckles and with linked gold elements decorated with enamel. A beautiful Italian example in London's Victoria and Albert Museum shows the great skill and plastic decorative quality of

Central part of a gold diadem of precious stones bordered by pearls, 14th century. British Museum, London.

167

High Gothic. The two sections of the buckle are covered with a rich, skilfully engraved tracery of branches and leaves, which form a background on which rests a coat of arms and a medallion engraved between two half medallions. The whole is bordered by various kinds of plaits. The ring which holds the two fastening pins is two-lobed and bordered with a double plait.

The buckle of a belt discovered in 1881 at Dune in the parish of Dalhem-sur-Gotland is a masterpiece of its kind. It dates from about 1340 and is carved with a scene depicting a man riding towards a lady attended by her page. The ring has an openwork scene showing a seated man with another man kneeling before him surrounded by branches and bunches of grapes. In this beautiful example of Rhenish art, the plastic conception is of high artistic quality and must have been the work of a highly gifted sculptor, able to overcome the great technical difficulties in order to realise the theme. The piece was displayed in Paris at the 1968 Council of Europe exhibition, *L'Europe Gothique XIIe et XIVe siècles*.

Valuable belts were very fashionable for both men and women in this period. There are some worn by women in a mosaic of about 1270 in St Mark's Cathedral, Venice; they consist of a network of alternate red and gold pieces, buckled at the waist with one of the ends falling halfway down the leg.

Other Forms An unusual jewel from the second half of the 14th century is the oval medallion known as the Onyx of Schaffhausen. This is a Roman cameo engraved with an image of Fortune in a jeweled frame. The stones in the frame are rubies and other gems of varying sizes in very prominent close-set bezels, alternating with pearls. The stones are polished and set in their natural irregular shapes which gives a very rich effect to the whole piece.

A rare bracelet in the Bucharest Museum is made of a gold band, the hinged clasp of which is decorated with two lions facing each other

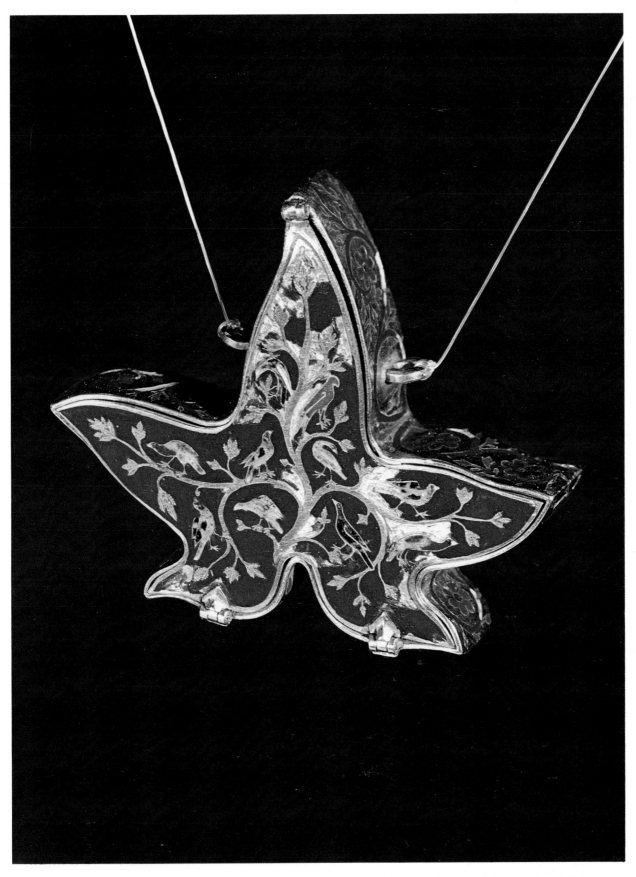

Cover *above* and back *left* of a gold and enamel pendant decorated with ivy leaves, France, 14th century. Museo Civico, Cividale del Friuli.

Crown of Princess Blanche, *c.* 1400 Schatzkammer der Residenz, Munich.

carved in low relief. In this piece oriental influences are clear.

The crown worn by Princess Blanche (Residenz Museum, Munich), daughter of Henry IV of England, on the occasion of her wedding to the elector Ludwig III in 1402, is a typical example of the Gothic style and presents a clear contrast to the types of diadem-style crown belonging to the previous era. Six long stems and six shorter ones rise alternately from the coronet, with Gothic flowers on top. The taller ones are surmounted by three triangularly arranged pearls. Along the stems, which are forked where they join the coronet, little branches with notched leaves project, thus giving this piece a close stylistic affinity with the vertical and branching forms of the contemporary architecture.

Not all Gothic jewelry can be thus obviously compared with the architectural forms, but its design tended to use the pointed arch shape (rather than the Romanesque round arch), and vertical lines draw the eye from the bottom to top where the arch would often be many-lobed. In the northern countries and in Spain this style endured for much longer, while in Italy new ideas and conceptions were evolving.

A valuable pendant in the shape of an ivy leaf which opens (Museo di Cividale, Italy) is decorated with enamels of outstanding fineness. The entire surface of the outside is covered with branches, which follow the line of the veins in the ivy leaf; various birds in lively poses perch on the branches and the side of the pendant is decorated with volutes, flowers and leaves. The back is covered with a chessboard pattern of red and blue rhombuses, containing alternately two pairs of lilies divided by a bar and a two-headed eagle, which are the arms of Charles IV of France and his wife, Blanche de Valois. The workmanship is mid 14th-century French and is probably by a court artist, who was clearly influenced by the miniatures of Jean Pucelle. It is typical of the splendid court art. The symbolic significance attached to the ivy leaf makes it very likely that the pendant was a wedding or anniversary present, although how it would have been used is not clear, since the rings on each side do not seem to be suitable for suspending it.

The Queen of Sheba or Queen Clothilde with a crown and brooch, from a proto-Gothic statue from Nôtre Dame de Corbeil, 1180-90. Louvre, Paris.

171

Detail of a gold mesh belt with a gilt, silver and enamel buckle, Italy, 15th century. Victoria and Albert Museum, London.

IV

The Renaissance

The age of elaborate jewels

Many factors, political, economic, religious, social and cultural, which had already been manifesting themselves since the 13th century, prepared the way in Italy for the artistic and cultural ideas of the Renaissance. Humanism began to invade the field of politics, opposing clericalism, and the power of the Church as an institution began to shrink. Gradually beginning to develop was a middle or bourgeois class which was patriotic, ambitious and desirous of prestige. More rational attitudes towards the social order evolved, and the process of economic development led to the improvement of transport and of technical and commercial organisation. Free enterprise was sanctioned, and in Italy the first banking organisations in Europe were founded. The feudal system disintegrated, and a new order based on wealth arose in its place.

In the field of art the revival of interest in the antique gave rise to new aesthetic standards. During the Gothic era naturalism had partially manifested itself, in the sense that attention was paid to detail, but this had been entirely to the detriment of the vision as a whole. The new tendency, however, was to see the work, no matter how complex in detail, as a fundamental element in an ordered and rational world and as an individual whole. The decorative arts, including jewelry and goldwork, were greatly influenced by these concepts. Although all Renaissance art was permeated by Classical culture, the jewelry had only the slightest connection with that of the Greco-Roman period.

The desire of princes and despots to show their wealth and power led to a great demand for jewelry and, therefore, a great increase in its production. This was fostered in particular by the display of magnificence at the courts of Burgundy and Berry in France; by the families of Este, Gonzaga, Medici, Montefeltro, Sforza and Malatesta in Italy; among the royalty of England and Spain; as well as by the development of a rich bourgeoisie in all countries.

The Artist-Jewelers Some experience in this art came to be regarded as an essential apprenticeship for young men who wished to become artists. Two young goldsmiths, Ghiberti and Brunelleschi, submitted designs for the competition in 1401 for a new baptistry door in

Angel wearing a pearl and coral necklace and a pearl head ornament, from Piero della Francesca, *The Montefeltro Altarpiece*. Brera, Milan.

173

Florence. More than a century later Hans Holbein the Younger designed jewels for the English court. Young artists such as Antonio Pollaiuolo, Francesco Francia, Maso Finiguerra, Caradosso, Ghirlandaio, Michelozzo, Verrocchio and Lorenzo di Credi worked as jewelers, making pendants and *enseigne* (discshaped hat ornaments worn by men). These works are never signed, and the subjects range from portraits to themes of Classical figures. Often they can be judged more as sculpture than jewelry, for virtuosity sometimes predominates over art.

Although the famous sculptor and goldsmith, Benvenuto Cellini, left many writings and descriptions of his work, little material evidence survives, as no jewelry definitely known to have been made by him still exists. A necklace in the Desmoni collection in New York is, however, attributed to him. It is composed of eleven elaborately decorated plates of two alternating types: smaller ones with a large pearl in the centre of each and larger ones with a table-cut gem. The use of colour is very varied and enriched with finely decorated surfaces in enamel. Cellini in his autobiography lists a few pieces of jewelry which he made, most frequent is the *enseigne*, and he also mentions Pope Clement VII's cope button and Pope Paul III's ring. The design with which the pope's button is embellished consists of a large diamond supporting a figure of God the Father. The diamond itself is surrounded by three cherubs in high and half relief.

As this type of decoration developed, the skilled craftsman was able to obtain wonderful results. From an objective point of view one could say that if, as decorative creations bound by the dictates of rhythm, balance of mass, colour and shape, the realistic scenes on jewels were not enriched by a certain imaginative quality, they would definitely be over elaborate. A complex battle scene, for example, modelled in high relief on a medallion three centimetres in diameter was intended apparently to be worn on a hat, but on a jewel it seems to be quite out of place. On the other hand, the art of jewelry in the Renaissance abounds with happy solutions to decorative problems which amaze modern designers.

Piero di Cosimo, portrait of Simonetta Vespucci wearing a pearl headdress. Musée Condé, Chantilly.

Jewelry in general and gems in particular made great progress when new ways were found for cutting diamonds. It was discovered that the reflection of light on the polished surfaces of the crystals greatly enhanced the brilliance of the gem and made possible greater perfection in the workmanship of the jewel.

Headdresses Already from the end of the 14th century styles of women's headdress indicate how thoroughly the craftsmen-goldsmiths planned the line and form of meshwork and the application of pearls and little gems in the gold nets which enveloped all or part of the head. These nets were often very elaborate, as is shown in the portrait of Bianca Maria Sforza by Ambrogio de Predis (National Gallery, Washington). Her net of pearls is a design of stylised flower shapes bordered with precious stones; a large jewel is suspended at ear level and her plait of hair is sheathed in a spiral twist of pearls.

Piero della Francesca liked to adorn the heads of his women with a single jewel suspended on a ribbon in the centre of the forehead, like the one worn by one of the figures in *The Madonna dell'Uovo* (Brera, Milan), or by an angel in *The Montefeltro Altarpiece* (Brera, Milan), or by Battista Sforza in his portrait in the Uffizi. All these jewels consist of a large central gem encircled by stylised petals each with a large pearl. In the portrait of Simonetta Vespucci by Piero di Cosimo (Musée Condé, Chantilly), a jewel of a similar design to those described is suspended from a row of pearls which are knotted into the elaborate twist of a long plait. Simonetta, in a portrait attributed to Botticelli in Frankfurt, also wears a flower-shaped jewel at the nape of her neck, with a very prominent bud holding a cabochon gem. The jewel, like the various rows of pearls which cover her hair, appears to be secured by a sort of cap made of ribbons.

Brooches The fashion for brooches continued in the 15th century. Innumerable Madonnas painted at this time wear robes clasped at the breast by jeweled brooches. An important

175

Brooch in gold, pearls and enamel depicting a man and a woman, Burgundian or Dutch, *c.* 1430-40. Kunsthistorisches Museum, Vienna.

example is on the white tunic of the Madonna of the Annunciation in an altarpiece by Van Eyck in St Bavone in Ghent. There are other examples by Antoniazzo Romano, Fiorenzo di Lorenzo, Domenico Ghirlandaio and Mainardi, as well as on two of the Graces in Botticelli's *Primavera* (Uffizi, Florence), one of whom also wears a jewel at the nape of her neck.

A masterpiece in which the figures realistically make use of the natural shape of gems and pearls in a composition of fairytale enchantment is a brooch in the Kunsthistorisches Museum, Vienna. It depicts two boys hand in hand holding a garland of flowers and leaves, standing in a little field of tulips. The pair are surrounded by a country scene with pearls and gems, and the indented gold leaves swayed by the wind which frame the scene make this jewel an accomplished work of art. This brooch is

part of the treasure of the house of Burgundy and was taken to Vienna by Mary of Burgundy when she married the emperor Maximilian I.

Necklaces The fashion for necklaces returned in this period too. A woman in a portrait by Dürer (Kunsthistorisches Museum, Vienna) wears one of rhomboid stones, probably amber, interspaced with four pairs of seed pearls side by side. It is a modest but extremely refined piece. In Baldassare Estense's portrait of Umberto de' Sacrati and his family (Alte Pinakothek, Munich) the lady wears a necklace consisting of rows of little beads spaced out by fine chains, forming the lightest and most elegant of compositions; in the same painting the boy's skullcap has an *aigrette* (a plume usually fashioned in silver and sometimes in gold) clasped by a beautiful jewel with a rectangular stone set in gold and three pearls, the lower one being drop-

Baldassare Estense, detail from *The Family of Umberto de' Sacrati*. Alte Pinakothek, Munich.

Albrecht Dürer, portrait of a young Venetian woman wearing a necklace of garnets and pearls, 1505. Kunsthistorisches Museum, Vienna.

Barthel Behan, portrait of Ursula Eudolphin Stüpf wearing a chain necklace with pendant, 1528. Thyssen collection, Lugano.

shaped. In the portrait of a young girl by Petrus Christus (Staatliche Museum, Berlin) a necklace composed of three rows of little gold bars, linked by pearls, gives her a most elegant distinction.

Necklaces of gold chains of a great variety of size and shape were worn by both men and women and were particularly popular in Germany. In a portrait by Barthel Behan (Thyssen collection, Lugano) the lady wears, together with numerous other jewels, two very large chain necklaces; Jacopo Strada by Titian (Kunsthistorisches Museum, Vienna) wears round his neck several such necklaces. The chain construction could be simple, double or multiple, and could have a jewel suspended from it as on the figure by Piero della Francesca mentioned previously in the *Madonna dell' Uovo*, or a medallion like that in the portrait of Bia, daughter of Cosimo de'Medici, painted by Bronzino (Uffizi, Florence).

As time went on elaborate necklaces became

Bernhard Strigel, portrait of Sybilla von Freyberg. Alte Pinakothek, Munich.

Detail of the portrait of Sybilla von Freyberg showing the jewelry. Alte Pinakothek, Munich.

178

Agnolo Bronzino, portrait of a Medici princess wearing earrings, a pearl necklace, a belt and a gold chain with a pendant. Uffizi, Florence.

Agnolo Bronzino, portrait of Lucrezia Panciatichi, *c.* 1540.
Uffizi, Florence. Details showing the jewelry.

increasingly important in the adornment of rich Italian women. In *The Portinari Altarpiece* (Uffizi, Florence) Hugo van der Goes portrays one of the daughters of a Florentine banker wearing a necklace of two rows of pearls, with a gem between every pair of pearls, and a lily-shaped jeweled pendant with a large drop-shaped pearl suspended from it. Like the princess painted by Bronzino, this rich heiress wears a very wide belt which is not functional and is probably fastened by a thong at the back. The belt in the portrait of Bia is a mesh of chain links, slightly larger than those of the necklace, and one of the ends hangs free. The one in Van der Goes' picture is made of little gold plates hinged together, decorated with *repoussé* geometric motifs, and is interrupted in front by two metal bosses linked by a chain which hangs down from the centre.

The Unrestrained Use of Jewels From contemporary portraits, it would seem that in the richest European countries all sense of proportion was gradually lost. The passion for jewelry, particularly at the English court and

Hans Maler, portrait of Queen Anne of Hungary. Thyssen collection, Lugano.

Joos van Cleve, portrait of Eleanor of Austria, 16th century. Museu Nacional di Arte Antiga, Lisbon.

among the rich German burghers, was indulged with so little restraint that balance and good taste were sacrificed.

Eleanora of France, Charles V's sister and wife of Francis I, was supposed to have led a secluded life away from court. To judge from a portrait of her by the Fleming Joss van Cleve, this did not prevent her from being very vain and adorning herself lavishly with jewels. In this portrait (Museu Nacional de Arte Antiga, Lisbon), she wears a soft hat with a brim encrusted with pearls and precious stones. On the side of her head, revealed by the tilt of the hat, there is a jeweled gold band from which hangs a circular pendant containing a large bezel set with a valuable stone; from this a drop-shaped gem is suspended. The hair style covers her ear, but it does not hide a huge elliptical earring from which hangs three drop-shaped pearls. A necklace made of the most elaborate gold and enamel medallions, each containing alternately a pearl or a ruby, stretches from shoulder to shoulder, while on her bosom below the neckline of the dress is pinned a huge jewel with a

drop pendant from which another necklace of pearls, which disappears behind her shoulder, is suspended. Two more jewels pin the pleats of the fastening of the sleeves. Not content with such ostentation the royal lady holds, clearly displayed between her finger and thumb, a beautiful ring.

A little more restrained but in the same spirit, Giovanna Tornabuoni, in her portrait by Ghirlandaio (Thyssen collection, Lugano), wears only one important jewel, but beside her is an equally impressive piece of jewelry, and a necklace hangs on the wall. Queen Anne of Hungary's hat in the portrait by Hans Maler (Thyssen collection, Lugano) is as rich as the one worn by Eleanora of France. An Italianate jewel, oval in shape and decorated with enamel and gems, supporting a minute sculpture of a nude woman waving a long scarf, with three large pearls hanging from the base, is pinned to the sumptuously pearl-embellished brim. The queen wears no earrings or rings, but a large jewel composed of two oval elements in succession with moulded, indented borders hangs from a 183

Necklace of linked segments of amethyst, gold, agate, emerald, rock crystal and pearl, probably Nuremberg, c. 1530. Germanisches Nationalmuseum, Nuremberg.

gold band round her neck. The indentations are repeated at the base of the two bezels which hold the two four-lobed gems.

From the above descriptions and from those which follow it is clear that between the 15th and 16th centuries jewelry was widely produced in Europe. The many surviving examples help to give some idea of the quality of the production, while evidence of the impressive quantity is shown in the works of painters from every country. In addition to revealing the vanity of the men and women, they help us to appreciate the craftsmanship of the goldsmiths, lapidaries, enamellers and other unknown craftsmen who, under pressure from the constant demand, acquired great skill and continually perfected their knowledge.

In addition to what was being done in Italy where, as has been noted, famous artists also made designs for goldsmiths and jewelers, engravers and designers in France, Germany and England produced engravings of decorative motifs and jewelry designs, especially pendants. Although this encouraged the diffusion of the Italian Renaissance forms throughout Europe by means of borrowing or as a result of the work or the craftsmen themselves being exported, the individual characteristics of each country were not completely eliminated. If, for example, we were to compare a Spanish jewel with a German one, the rich embellishment of the former and the greater elaboration of detail of the latter would always, or almost always, be distinguishable, even if the maker of the first happened to be Flemish and the second a Venetian. However, much more difficult is the identification of certain types of pendants which were produced over a wide area of Europe during the Renaissance. These elaborate objects were gold, coloured with enamels and precious stones, and frequent use was made of baroque pearls especially chosen so that their shapes would form an integral part of the composition. They depict mythological or biblical scenes or persons, monsters, seahorses, dragons, reptiles, birds, symbolic figures, sailing ships, portraits and so on. The production of this type of jewel continued until the beginning of the 17th century.

Intaglio Cutting Another art which became

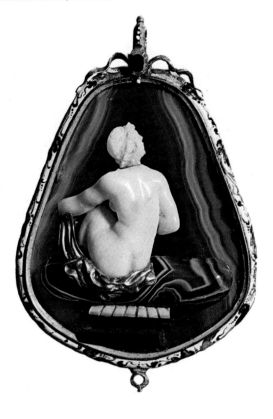

Nymph of Hellenistic derivation on a pendant of onyx and chalcedony, 16th century. Compare with the Canosa disc. British Museum, London.

Nereid on a partially silver-gilt disc with *repousé* work, from Canosa, 3rd century BC. Museo Nazionale, Taranto.

very popular at this period, which also harked back to Classical models, was the art of intaglio cutting on cameos and gems. On an agate intaglio in the British Museum a seated nude female figure is portrayed from the back in a pose which is certainly inspired by a silver disc from Canosa (Museo Nazionale, Taranto). Another gem engraved in the antique Hellenic style shows a man, a woman and a child doing a Bacchic dance, their movement being depicted with uninhibited dynamism.

Italian Renaissance lapidaries were also highly skilled in their art. First Florence and Rome, and later Venice, were centres in which this art was greatly cultivated. The collections of Pope Paul II and Lorenzo the Magnificent were famous, and the work of engravers was highly appreciated. For a cornelian engraved in 1471 with a portrait of Pope Paul II Giuliano del Scipione received at least two hundred ducats in payment. Giovanni delle Corniuole of Pisa, one of the most famous engravers, made two portraits on cameos, one of Savonarola and the other of Lorenzo the Magnificent. A famous emerald seal engraved with the figure of Hercules, which from the technical point of view

186

presented almost insurmountable difficulties, is attributed to Pietro Maria Seobaldi, and dated 1532. Matteo Massaro, a Veronese lapidary, went to work at the court of Francis I of France in 1515, and the Milanese, Alessandro Masnago, was in the service of Rudolph II of Austria; other Italian engravers dispersed in various European centres spread the style and technique of this difficult art. The fame of Valerio Belli (1468-1546) was international, but as with other artists in this field, the only objects defi-

Ring with a Classical subject, 16th century. British Museum, London.

Diana on an onyx cameo in a gold and enamel frame, 16th century. Kunsthistorisches Museum, Vienna.

Ottavio Miseroni, pendant cameo in chalcedony, gold and enamel, 16th century. Kunsthistorisches Museum, Vienna.

nitely known to be his are some splendid pieces of gold, most notably several inlaid with rock crystal. Towards the end of the century Milan became one of the most active centres for the production of cameos and engraved gems, with numerous splendidly executed examples of portraiture or mythological figures and scenes.

When medallions were first framed for use in jewelry they were plain or simply decorated with engraving or enamel. Later the frames became increasingly elaborate, the medallion

itself smaller, and the figures were depicted with more colour and ever greater boldness. A particular feature of these pendants is the decoration on the flat reverse side, which varies from modest engraved arabesque patterns to coloured figurations in translucent enamel. They were also inscribed with mottoes or dedications. The frames gradually became so elaborate, with traceries of scrolls, cartouches, name plates in openwork, that finally they swallowed up the medallion altogether, and the composi-

Gold, enamel and chalcedony brooch, traditionally attributed to Benvenuto Cellini, 1550-1600. Kunsthistorisches Museum, Vienna.

The Rape of Europa on a mid 16th-century chalcedony cameo mounted in a 17th-century gold and enamel frame. Kunsthistorisches Museum, Vienna.

Charity on a pendant of gold, enamel and precious stones. Thyssen collection, Lugano.

Gold, pearl and enamel pendant in the shape of a man. Museo degli Argenti, Florence.

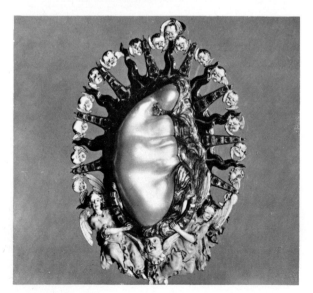

above centre Gold and pearl pendant, 16th century. Victoria and Albert Museum, London.

above Pendant with a large pearl in the centre mounted in a star-shaped frame with gold and enamel cherubims' heads between each point. Kunsthistorisches Museum, Vienna.

above centre Pendant of gold enamel and precious stones in the form of a ship, 16th century. Museo Poldi-Pezzoli, Milan.

above Pendant in the form of a cluster of pearls, rubies, gold and enamel, late 16th century. Kunsthistorisches Museum, Vienna.

The Canning Jewel, a pendant of gold, enamel, precious stones and baroque pearls (the torso is made of a single pearl), late 16th century. Victoria and Albert Museum, London.

Man and woman on a cameo made of a snail's shell, French, 16th century; frame, 17th century. Museo Nazionale, Florence.

above centre Prudence on a pendant of gold, enamel and precious stones. Wallace Collection, London.

above Venus and Cupid on a pendant in gold, enamel and chalcedony, Italian, 16th century; frame, 17th century. Kunsthistorisches Museum, Vienna.

tion became entirely decorative, rich with colour and highly animated forms.

Lastly there were pendants, composed of several linked pieces, with subjects modelled in full relief, using gold, enamels, rubies, emeralds, diamonds and baroque pearls, whose curious shapes were often incorporated as parts of birds, dragons or human torsos. Towards the end of the 16th century they reached new heights of elaboration, hitherto unequalled. Entire miniature architectural compositions were composed, with niches for figures or groups of figures fully modelled and adorned with a profusion of volutes, arches, pillars and bosses which foreshadow the decorative opulence of the Baroque era. The technical skill was amazing when one considers the minute dimensions.

The Jewels of Henry VIII An idea of the flamboyance of male adornment, which has never been surpassed, is given by the official portrait of Henry VIII of England painted by Hans Holbein the Younger (Palazzo Barberini, Rome). Men seem to be more sumptuously dressed than women; in the 1540s Henry VIII certainly wore more jewels than any of his six wives. The king had also taken advantage of his power to dispose, as he wished, of the Church's enormous treasure. In this portrait of Henry, as in others of a later date, we note a harmonious consistency of the precious ornaments, for he wears a *parure* (a suite of matching jewelry). The components of a *parure* were not necessarily limited to movable jewelry but could also include pieces which formed an integral part of a suit of clothes, such as jeweled buttons to fasten the doublet and jewels to clasp the slashes of the sleeves. These *parures* (of which the king had more than one) indicate the evolution in taste in the art of personal adornment. Forms and colours had to be in harmonious accord or contrast with the colours of the fabrics. Here the brim of the hat is hemmed with feathers and adorned with two different kinds of jewel: a crescent shape outlined with pearls and a rectangular gem in a decorative setting. Across his imposing broad shoulders is a chain from which hangs a decorated medallion. The chain is the same as one designed by Holbein now in the British Museum, London;

Pierre Woeriot, designs for a pendant, French, 16th century. Victoria and Albert Museum, London.

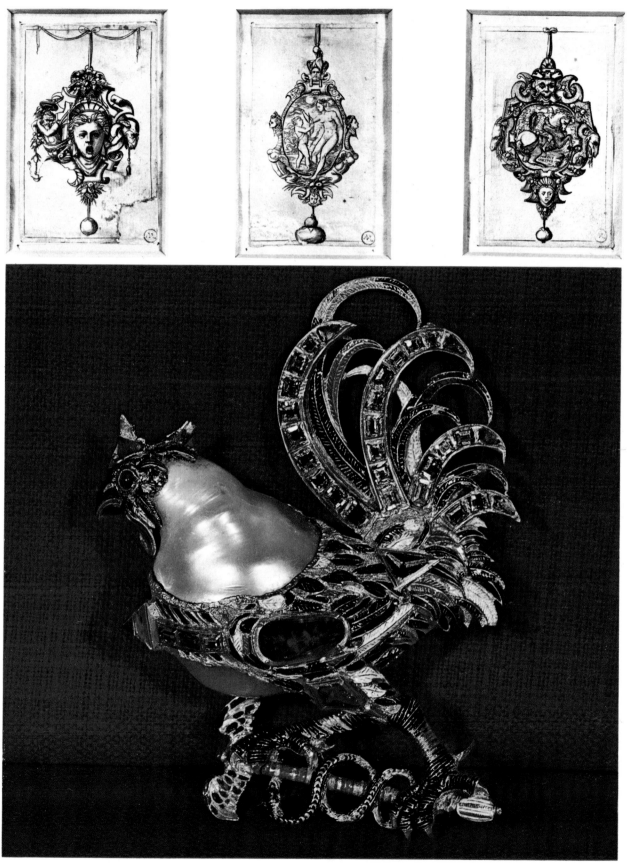

Brooch of gold, enamel, gems and baroque pearls, from the collection of the grand duke of Tuscany, 17th century. Museo degli Argenti, Florence.

Hans Holbein, portrait of Henry VIII. Palazzo Barberini, Rome.

right Portrait of Queen Elizabeth I, English, 16th century. Palazzo Pitti, Florence.

Naturally, Henry VIII's ornaments of about 1540 show only how a king might be adorned. The others, the dignitaries, nobles and rich merchants of England and other European countries, wore necklaces of pearls or gold with elaborate pendants. They embellished their clothes with decorated gold buttons, pinned medallions of varying importance to their hats or berets, or used a jeweled support for their *aigrette*.

Elizabeth I's Passion for Jewels If the numerous portraits of Queen Elizabeth of England are of minimal interest from an artistic point of view, they at least have the merit of making perfectly clear her passion for jewelry. It was so great that in order to have enough pearls to sew onto her dresses, she did not hesitate to buy hundreds of false ones for a penny each. Portraits of this type bring to mind a phrase of Petrarch's criticising the excessive amount of jewelry worn by tyrants 'adorned like altars on festival days'. A glance at one of these court portraits is enough to give some idea of how this queen hoarded pearls and other precious stones. Of her greed, suffice it to say that she had received as a surety the Portuguese crown jewels and could not bear to return them to Henry IV until the day she died.

it consists of knotted elements finely modelled with buds, leaves and scrolls set with large table-cut rubies in embellished mounts. Between each gem are two pearls. Even the bezels of the rings are decorated with designs matching the necklace.

A woman looking at herself in a mirror and a cupid with bow and arrow on each side, belt buckle in gold, enamel and precious stones, late 16th century. Private collection, Paris.

In the portrait in the Palazzo Pitti the queen is portrayed with the stiff expression of a sad child, sheathed in a costume with permanent pleats in which contrasts of excessive minuteness and vastness alternate. It is covered with various jeweled motifs and innumerable pearls in her hair, on veils, on her bosom and neck and, without any break in continuity, on the hems of her skirts and her cloak.

In addition to all this she wears the famous pearl necklace which Pope Clement VII had given to Catherine de' Medici on the occasion of her marriage to the second son of Francis I of France, the future Henry II. Apparently, the pope had set great store by this marriage and, so it is said, had paid all the expenses by pawning the largest diamond in his tiara. The necklace had six rows of pearls with twenty-five drop pearls, known to be among the largest and most beautiful ever seen. Catherine wore it almost constantly. When her son Francis married Mary Queen of Scots the necklace passed to her. In 1559 Francis succeeded his father to the throne, but ruled for only seventeen months, and died aged only sixteen. Mary, who remained a widow until she was eighteen, returned to Scotland with her necklace, where times of happiness, passion, fear, tears and abdication awaited her, and finally her life closed with imprisonment and death. The pearls passed to her son, James, and later were acquired by Queen Elizabeth for £300.

Mary Queen of Scots' son, succeeding Elizabeth as James I, regained possession of the necklace, which he presented in turn to his daughter Elizabeth on her marriage to Frederick of Bohemia. Frederick reigned amidst troubled circumstances, and in 1620 he took refuge in Holland with his family. His daughter Sophia married the elector of Hanover, and it was their son who, as the only Protestant heir, succeeded to the throne of England as George I on the death of Queen Anne. The necklace now passed to George I's wife, Sophia Dorothea of Celle. The marriage was unhappy; the queen, accused of having a love affair with the Count Königsmarck, was thrown into prison in Schloss Ahlden until her death. Her son became George II, and his wife Caroline wore the famous pearls. He was succeeded to the throne by his

grandson, George III and he, in turn, by his son William IV, in whose time the necklace came to be known as the Hanover Pearls. On the death of William, Victoria succeeded to the throne, but, since, under Hanoverian law, women were not admitted to the succession, the two crowns were once again divided. George III's youngest son, Ernest Augustus, became king of Hanover and did not hesitate to demand from London the famous pearls, but received no response. In 1843 the Hanoverian sovereign came to England to press his claims formally (going back to 1837) and initiate a law suit which did not finish until 1858, six years after his death. In the end Hanover recovered the splendid pearl necklace, but it is doubtful whether it was still composed of all or even part of the pearls which had adorned the necks of at least fourteen queens.

Jewelry Forms In the portrait of Isotta Brembati by Giovanni Battista Moroni (Moroni collection, Bergamo), an unusual precious ornament on the pelt of a marten is worn across her shoulders. The animal's head has been replaced by a decorated gold one with gems for eyes. From its muzzle falls a chain which links the fur to the centre of a belt of equal workmanship

School of Bronzino, portrait of a woman wearing a gold and pearl earring. Galleria Palatina, Palazzo Pitti, Florence.

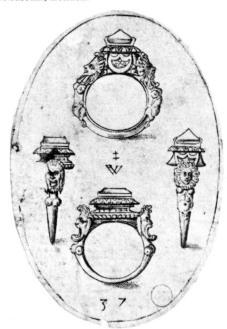

Pierre Woeriot, designs for rings, 16th century. Victoria and Albert Museum, London.

encircling her waist. The fashion for attaching heads of beaten gold to valuable furs was very popular in the second half of the 16th century, and they show the expert mastery of *repoussé* work which the goldsmiths of this period had.

Earrings were not much worn in the 16th century and bracelets still less; in portraits of ladies, who are otherwise lavishly jeweled, these articles of adornment are very often lacking. Earrings frequently consisted of drop-shaped pearls or gems. Occasionally one comes across a more elaborate design in which three pearls are suspended from an ornately decorated gold element set with a gem.

Bracelets, even those made from a meshwork of chains, could have a medallion and decorations of various types inserted, and, if they were made of linked pieces, these would almost always be in the shape of ornamental scrolls surrounding a gem and embellished with pearls.

Rings During the Renaissance era rings achieved a status of primary importance, so naturally there were a great variety of designs. In the 15th century there was a great vogue for engraved gems and gold bezels, either with heraldic devices which could also be used as seals or with Classical subjects. For the devout reliquary rings were made; these contained a small reliquary in the centre of the bezel. In most of them, the box setting was used, and the sides would be delicately decorated. A thin piece of metal foil was often placed under the stone in a box setting in order to enhance its colour. The foil used for this purpose was made of gold, silver and copper alloys, and, according to the proportions of these metals in the alloy, various shades of yellow, red and green could be obtained.

In the 16th century the shoulders of rings were increasingly richly ornamented with punched or pierced work, niello or enamel. There are bezels delicately decorated with enamels on the back as well as the front; others again are linked to the hoop by hinges on which they can be turned round. Many have bezels which open to reveal a miniature portrait or, according to romantic stories, to contain poison. In general, all the rings of this period are decorated with extreme delicacy. A ring in the Museo Poldi-Pezzoli in Milan has a bezel in the shape of a pyramid with a table-cut emerald at the summit and one in each face of the pyramid which is minutely decorated in black and white enamel; each angle is set with three minute rubies. The reverse side of the bezel is just as minutely decorated with enamel and gold embellishments.

A new fashion often employed was to set a pearl with its central pivot placed horizontally between two decorated supports. In another type of ring, instead of a bezel there is a scene carved in full relief and coloured with enamels.

Gold, enamel and pearl ring, 16th century. *right* The same ring with the bezel open. Museo Poldi-Pezzoli, Milan.

Gold, enamel and diamond ring, late 16th century.
Kunsthistorisches Museum, Vienna.

Bishop's ring, late 16th century. Louvre, Paris.

above White and black enamel ring with emeralds and rubies. *right* The back of the bezel decorated in gold and enamel. Museo Poldi-Pezzoli, Milan.

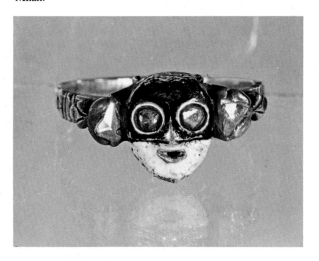

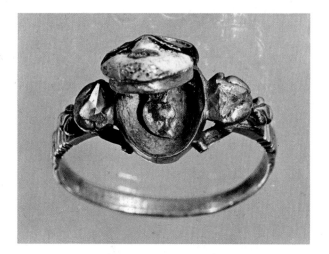

In the Museo Poldi-Pezzoli two like this depict fauns and goats. Another type is the *memento mori* ring with a mask and diamonds for eyes or a skull in place of the bezel.

A popular type of wedding ring in Italy was the *gimmel* ring made of two divisible hoops of plain gold or with motifs of hands painted in enamel; when the two rings were united the two hands interlocked. Many engagement rings had bezels in the shape of hearts set with gems.

European Centres Jewelry produced in Venice and in the Bohemian area under oriental influence have a particular characteristic style. Filigree decoration is dominant and enamels are applied with extremely fine and delicate workmanship. Although they were made in Europe, they are completely unrelated to western stylistic concepts of the time and definitely linked to oriental traditions.

A necklace in the Museo Poldi-Pezzoli is composed of fifty-two spherical beads each

above Wedding ring, late 16th century. Thyssen collection, Lugano.

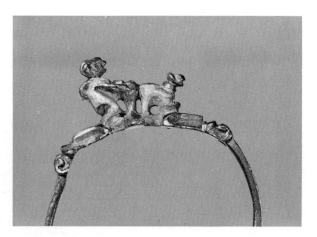

Gold and enamel ring with a faun and a goat, 16th century. Museo Poldi-Pezzoli, Milan.

Gold and enamel ring with figures, 16th century. Museo Poldi-Pezzoli, Milan.

made out of a fine tissue of openwork filigree; at opposite points on each bead there are stylised flowers embellished with volutes and blue and green enamel leaves. The technical difficulty in making these openwork beads is the problem of successively applying and soldering the flowers, volutes, leaves and enamel onto the delicate filigree background, but the technical resources of the craftsmen of that time were infinite. Other similar necklaces were set with gems of various colours framed with complex traceries of filigree.

Italian Renaissance styles were swiftly and enthusiastically accepted by European artists and patrons. In Germany the famous centres of Augsburg and Nuremberg maintained a tradition of artistic metallurgy which was amongst the highest, and during the Renaissance these towns produced some pieces of great value. Skilled artists like Erasmus Hornick, Hans Mülich, Virgilio Solis, Hans Collaert and Théodore de Bry, a Frenchman who migrated from Liège to Frankfurt with his sons and

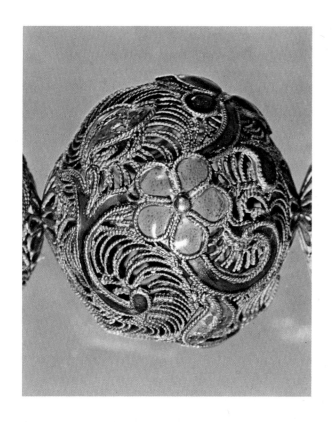

Filigree and enamel necklace with fifty-two spherical beads, Venetian, 16th century. *top* Detail of a bead. Museo Poldi-Pezzoli, Milan.

200

The order of the Knights of St George made of gold, enamels, pearls and precious stones, 1570-75. It belonged to Duke Albert V of Bavaria. Schatzkammer der Residenz, Munich.

published numerous jewelry designs, above all for pendants, often with distinct characteristics. Other centres of notable importance were Munich and Basle. Prague under the patronage of Rudolph II, an enthusiastic collector, had many goldsmiths' shops where highly skilled artists and foreign craftsmen worked; among these was the Italian stonecutter, Miseroni.

Francis I of France was also a noted patron; he surrounded himself with famous Italian artists, among them Leonardo da Vinci and Benvenuto Cellini who, inevitably, were the dominating artistic influences at Fontainebleau. In Paris artists such as Jean Duvet, Etienne Delaune and the Dutchman Abraham de Bruyn were the foremost jewelry designers.

It is Hans Holbein the Younger who can claim the merit of having introduced Renaissance jewelry to England. He found fertile ground in Henry VIII's great passion for jewelry, an obsession which was to manifest itself again later in his daughter Queen Elizabeth. The English court also welcomed a considerable number of French, Italian and Flemish craftsmen and goldsmiths. The jeweled monogram brooch was very popular at the English court. Men, almost more than women, loved

Hans Mülich, drawing on parchment of a bracelet in linked segments with motifs of clasped hands, from the collection of Duke Albert V of Bavaria, *c.* 1550. Bayerisches Nationalmuseum, Munich.

Hans Holbein the Younger, design for a pendant, *c.* 1530.
British Museum, London.

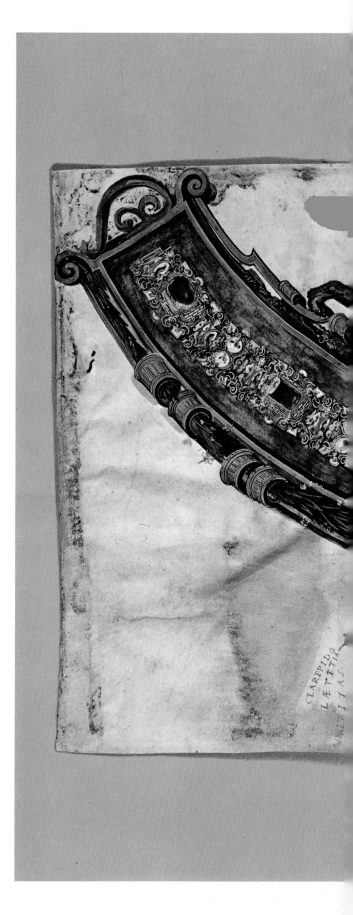

to adorn themselves with earrings. The ship
motif in brooches, pendants and *ensignes* probably spread from England where, as a result of
her supremacy at sea, it had become almost a
national emblem. Rings of the highest workmanship were in wide use; Henry VIII had
hundreds of them.

Spain in the 16th century could be considered
the richest country in the world. Her growing
trade with the orient and the conquest of the
American continent brought to the peninsula
an enormous amount of treasure. The traditional tendency of Spanish taste was towards
rich use of colour, and this was combined with
forms of jewelry derived from the Italian
Renaissance. Earrings lavishly decorated with
long pendants were more popular in Spain than
elsewhere. In addition, religious jewelry, such

202

Hans Mülich, design on parchment for a necklace of pearls and rubies alternating with enamel satyrs and a ruby pendant in the centre. The jewel is bordered by a rich decoration of festoons of leaves, flowers and figures. Bayerisches Nationalmuseum, Munich.

The Nativity, from a gold and enamel pendant, French.

Valentin Sezenius, sketch of the pendant engraved on copper, 1623. Victoria and Albert Museum, London.

as portable reliquaries, crosses and pendants carved with sacred subjects, was widely used. A technique brought to its finest peak by Spanish jewelers was *verre églomisé*, which involved painting the underside of a piece of glass or rock crystal with a design (usually a religious scene or the head of Christ) in colours and gold leaf and mounting it on a decorated frame embellished with gems and gold. Spanish jewelry is also distinguishable for the more intense use of filigree and enamel decoration on the ever-increasing number of gems. Towards the end of the century emeralds coming from deposits in South America became very popular.

Hans Mülich, illuminated drawing on parchment for a ceremonial necklace in the collection of Duke Albert V of Bavaria, 1554. The diamonds and pearls which decorate each element alternate with little enamel satyrs, in the centre are two emeralds. Bayerisches National Museum, Munich.

right Felipe de Liano, portrait of Isabella Clara Eugenia with Magdalena Ruiz. Prado, Madrid.

V

The Baroque period

The age of stone cutting

The trends in style of the Renaissance blended gradually with the manifestations of the Baroque era at the turn of the 16th century.

The stylistic development of jewelry at this period was mainly conditioned by two important factors. The first is of a technical nature and concerns the improvement of methods of cutting precious stones. This had a notable effect, for gems began to take over from gold as the most important part of the jewel. The second was a great vogue for the cultivation of flowers. Floral and vegetable subjects thus became fashionable in jewelry design and were spread throughout Europe by means of prints.

Floral Motifs The unconscious initiator of this fashion was a Parisian, Jean Robin, who at the end of the 16th century set up a greenhouse to cultivate exotic flowers to be copied by embroidery designers. A few years later the greenhouses were bought by Henry IV and became known as the *Jardins du Roi*; they are now in the Paris botanical gardens. This increasing interest in exotic plants was copied in other countries too, encouraged by the intensification of trade with the orient from where the seeds of such plants and flowers were imported. The first tulip was grown in Europe at Augsburg in 1559. The creative interest of jewelry designers was excited and inspired by the wonderful fantasy of nature's forms and colours, which offered infinite possibilities and variations of interpretation, often enriched by the addition of such features as leaves, birds, ribbons or insects.

The important publications, *Livres des Ouvrages d'Orfèvrerie* (1663) and *Livre de Fleurs propre pour Orfèvres et Graveurs* (1680), which set out the new stylistic ideas, contributed greatly to the spreading of the new jewelry styles throughout Europe. These 'inventions', as they are called in the books, are principally inspired by flowers, but also show a noticeable development in the use of openwork knots and ribbons, which give the pieces an appearance of great complexity. The wide use of faceted diamonds and other precious stones covering almost the whole design of the jewels gives an appearance of lightness.

At first floral motifs were particularly used to decorate the backs of bejeweled medallions, 207

Hans Georg Beuerl, gold, enamel, diamond and pearl badge. On the back of the banner is the coat of arms of the house of Bavaria and the motto *Maximilianus Bavariae Dux*; on the back of the shield is the motto *Dominus Virtutum Nobiscum*. Schatzkammer der Residenz, Munich.

Gold, enamel and diamond brooch, French or German, *c.* 1630. Victoria and Albert Museum, London.

208

Gold, emerald and crystal ring from Andalusia, late 16th century to early 17th century. Victoria and Albert Museum, London.

with miniature portraits enclosed by little shutters. The portrait might be enamelled in black and white or in full colour or engraved in low relief. As time went on the Renaissance predilection for richly embellished ornaments lessened, while figures were abandoned altogether, inspiration being sought entirely in floral motifs.

There was a considerable decrease in the number of pieces worn, and it became less fashionable for men to adorn themselves with jewelry. As far as forms were concerned, the use of pendants waned while bracelets, earrings and lavish pins became popular, using an ever-increasing number of gems. Bracelets, necklaces, brooches and *aigrettes* continued to be made of a complex elaboration of linked pieces well into the middle of the 17th century, with scrolls embellished with the fashionable leaf designs set with precious stones mounted in the form of flowers, pearls and enamelled arabesques, mostly in black and white. In a pair of mid The leafy motifs and the ribbons testify to the goldsmith's skill in the execution of this complicated work but are hidden by the enamel. The intention one may presume, therefore, was

Much less jewelry has survived from this and the succeeding epoch than from the preceding period. This was because the material worth of a Renaissance jewel was small compared with its artistic value, and the amount of gold and gems recoverable was insignificant. Pieces of

Diamond necklace and earrings set in silver with the visible ornamental pieces in gold. Museo Poldi-Pezzoli, Milan.

Earrings of pearls, white enamel and light gold, Spanish, mid 17th century. Museo Poldi-Pezzoli, Milan.

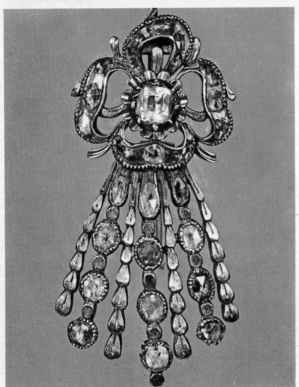

Gold, silver and diamond *aigrette*, late 17th century. Museo Poldi-Pezzoli, Milan.

the Baroque or succeeding periods, however, with their lavish use of precious stones, gave up to 90% of their value when broken up.

The Popularity of Diamonds In the 17th century the diamond, which had previously been little used partly because of the difficulty of cutting, came into its own. This was due above all to the market being flooded with diamonds from the newly discovered South American deposits. The chief form of diamond cut used till then was the pyramid or *pointe naive*, sometimes called the writing diamond from the fact that its point was so sharp that it could write quite smoothly on glass. This shape generally corresponded with the natural octahedron form of the crystal. However, table, square or rectangular cuts were also used. The situation underwent a radical change in 1640 thanks to Cardinal Mazarin's patronage, which enabled lapidaries to experiment. A new cut with thirty-two facets more than the table cut was discovered and was called after the cardinal.

Gold, enamel and gem necklace, 17th century. Museo Poldi-Pezzoli, Milan.

Necklace of gold and enamel with a pendant of rock crystal, French, mid 17th century. Victoria and Albert Museum, London.

From then on the diamond assumed the first place amongst gems, and it became the most fashionable stone. This period also saw great fluctuations in the prices as a result of the market being flooded with Brazilian diamonds.

Thus in the 17th century a great change occurred in jewelry: from the second half of the century onwards, precious personal ornaments were dominated by faceted gems, and it became inconceivable to mount cabochon stones. The use of enamel decorations also gradually declined, and even gold assumed a secondary role, acting merely as an ornamental link, in the form of branches, leaves or flower petals, between the numerous gems. The principal place in the design was given to precious stones cut in various shapes and sizes.

This period also saw the beginning of a fashion, which lasted until the 19th century, for a necklace consisting of a black velvet ribbon with a pendant pinned to it. An alternative to this was to wear an important jewel at the centre of the décolleté. There was also a development in coral work which began to be used in jewels and particularly in necklaces.

Gilles Légaré, design for rings seen from the front and the side, *c.* 1640. Victoria and Albert Museum, London. Gilles Légaré, design for a brooch, *c.* 1640. Victoria and Albert Museum, London.

The Age of Louis XIV The new expansion and development in the field of decorative arts in France in the last quarter of the 17th century was due to above all Louis XIV. The work of his indefatigable minister Colbert, and the collaboration of the court painter Le Brun to satisfy his grandiose visions resulted in forms which differed completely from past styles. The most skilled Italian, Dutch, French and German craftsmen worked in the Louvre workshops, producing the highest quality tapestries, lace, furniture, metalware and sculpture with which to furnish the palace of Versailles, the most

213

bombastic expression of the Sun King's ideas, summed up in the phrase: *L'Etat c'est moi*.

In jewelry, too, France became the *arbiter elegantiarum* to Europe. The court led the fashion, although attention was paid not so much to Queen Marie Thérèse as to the ladies who succeeded to the king's favour. Although it was no longer so fashionable for men to adorn themselves with jewels, many court nobles, and above all the king himself, wore spectacular jewelry on festive occasions at Versailles and elsewhere. Louis XIV possessed among other things two complete suites of matching jewelry to adorn his jerkin and his entire costume. One comprised 123 buttons, 300 eyelets and 90 frog-fastenings for the jerkin, in addition to 48 buttons and 96 eyelets for his suit; the other consisted of 168 buttons and double the number of eyelets, another 19 *fleurons* for the jerkin and 48 buttons with the corresponding number of

eyelets for the suit. Both these *parures*, as matching sets were called, included a knot in which to fold the brim of the hat, garters, the Cross of the Holy Spirit and a sword hilt. Jewelled buckles for shoes were among the few ornaments which were widely worn by men outside court circles, and those who could not afford real gems turned instead to false ones.

Imitation Diamonds The earliest imitation diamonds came from England; George Ravenscroft is said to have been the first to produce them, having probably learned the process from an Italian, Da Costa. But in 1657 Villiers in his *Journal d'un Voyageur à Paris* had already mentioned a certain Monsieur d'Arre who, in the Temple district of Paris, had made himself rich by meeting the huge demand for counterfeit diamonds, emeralds, topazes and rubies.

Ravenscroft's 'flint glass' was obtained from a compound based on lead oxide from which

Medallion with a miniature of a woman, 18th century. Schmuckmuseum, Pforzheim.

Baroque bow brooch of gold and emeralds. Schmuckmuseum, Pforzheim.

Pendant in the shape of a woman, made of gold, pearls and precious stones, Italy, late 17th century. Kunsthistorisches Museum, Vienna.

bright glass suitable for faceting with a high refractive index was created. Cut like a rose-cut diamond, it looks like a real gem, especially by candlelight, so it was particularly suitable for evening wear and, indeed, was widely used even in important pieces in the following period. At the beginning of the 18th century, Josef Strass or Strasser gave his name to a type of paste now commonly known as strass, which was a compound glass based on lead oxide (32% quartz, 11% potash, 3% borax, 54% red lead and traces of anhydride arsenic). Plain, it was very suitable for imitating diamonds, and with the addition of coloured metallic oxides it looked like other precious stones.

Towards the end of the 17th century European jewelry still preserved a certain density of matter, although it was brightened by the glitter of the numerous gems, and, thanks to the activity of skilful designers, it kept up with the fashionable trends. In fact, one could say that the craze for frequent changes of fashion, although not comparable to that of our own times, helped to create variations which anticipated the capricious and unstable forms of the Rococo.

216

Amethyst pendant with hair-like inclusions, Spain, 17th century. Kunsthistoristisches Museum, Vienna.

Bodice ornament with emeralds and enamel flowers, from the treasure of the Virgin of Pilar, Spanish, mid 17th century. Victoria and Albert Museum, London.

The Baroque period

The diamond

From the end of the 17th century the diamond began its career as the dominant factor in jewelry.

Structure The explanations given by the scholars of the formation of this precious crystal are varied, but they practically all agree that it is formed deep down in the earth's crust by enormous pressures and high temperatures exerted on carbon and magma gases in the rocks. The mineral thus formed is gradually brought to the surface by eruptions and vertical alluvial movements. It tends always to be associated with accumulations of granite sand, whose particularly recognisable characteristics render the geological sites of diamond deposits relatively easily identifiable.

The diamond is pure carbon, one of the principle elements of which organic and inorganic bodies are composed; plants, animals, the air we breathe, food, clothes and about a fifth of the human body contain carbon. It appears in its pure state only in diamonds and graphite and in a relatively pure state in coal and lignite, which are fossilised vegetable matter. Although they are composed of the same substance, the enormous physical differences between diamond and graphite are due to the difference in the arrangement of their atoms: diamond crystals are arranged cubically (monometric), while in graphite they are rhomboid (trigonometric). As a result, the diamond is the hardest of all the minerals, number ten on Mohs' scale of hardness, while the index of graphite is only one.

Although the diamond is the hardest mineral, being much harder than steel, it is not the heaviest. It is usually found in octahedral or hexahedral shapes, often with protruding points and slightly convex facets pitted or marked by corrosion. Sometimes two octahedral shapes may be united into 'twin' crystals. Less common are the cube crystals and rhombic dodecahedrons. The ease with which they can be cut relates to the structure of the crystals in the octahedron. Thus a clever swindler could, by knowing how to shatter the stone at one blow, deceive the ignorant into believing that his stone was not a real diamond and so acquire the precious fragments at little cost.

The diamond has both high refractive and

Maso da San Friano, *Diamond Mining*. Studiolo di Francesco I de' Medici, Palazzo Vecchio, Florence.

dispersive levels, and, when skilfully cut, these give it the characteristic fire due to the lively play of colours and its extraordinary brilliance. It cannot be harmed by the strongest acids. It will burn at about 850° in oxygen or air, but in the absence of oxidising agents it can be raised to a much higher temperature. It will leave a minute amount of ash according to whether there are any impurities in the stone. At a certain temperature it is converted into graphite, but no one has yet succeeded in transforming graphite into diamonds.

In addition to colourless diamonds, which are clear (white or blue-white), those tinged with yellow or brown can also be used as gems. Shades of yellow, pea-green, light-blue, blue, pink and red, brown-red and black are also found. A variety of diamond called *bort* and the *carbonado* (black diamond) are used in industry and also for cutting other diamonds.

Diamond powder and tiny stones were found in meteorites which fell in Russia in 1886 and in the United States in 1891. Their discovery was of sensational interest, since it demonstrated the presence of the precious mineral on other planets in the universe.

Indian Diamonds India is probably the oldest known source of diamonds; it is believed that the gem was already in use in the 3rd millennium BC, but for a long time it was confused with other stones of similar appearance. It was not until the 1st millennium BC that the diamond's true value was realised. Apart from the Sanskrit poems and Pliny's writings, the presence of diamonds in India was confirmed by Marco Polo, who mentioned the kingdom of Mutfili as being a diamond trading region. Descriptions of actual deposits, however, are only recorded towards the middle of the 17th century by the Frenchman Jean Baptiste Tavernier who journeyed as far as Golconda in India and who wrote a report entitled *Voyages en Turquie, en Perse et aux Indes*.

The Indian diamond deposits, like those of other precious or semiprecious stones, were mostly of the secondary type, that is to say of exogenous origin. They were chiefly situated on the eastern side of the Deccan plain in three definable zones stretching from the river Pennar northwards as far as the Ganges. The mines, which go back to remotest antiquity, were practically exhausted in the 18th century, although they have been mined, and a very few famous crystals found, right up until today. The Indian diamond mines usually consisted of square pits sunk into the gravel layers. If quartz crystals were found in the first layer, this was a sure sign that there would be diamonds lower down between large rock boulders. The deep pits were often linked to galleries. Famous diamonds such as the Great Mogul, the Koh-i-Noor and the Hope were probably found in the Kollar mines on the left bank of the river Kistna. Another famous diamond, the Regent or Pitt diamond, was found in the Partial mines in the same region.

Frequently searchers treated their work casually; they would wait for the end of the monsoon rains before going off to the mountains or sifting river beds. Sometimes, however, the gems were extracted, with great effort, from diamondiferous rocks or gravel by grinding and repeated washing and sifting. In India, traditional methods were generally used in diamond mining. It has been calculated that the country has probably produced about ten million carats or $2\frac{1}{2}$ tons of diamonds.

South American Diamonds At the beginning of 1670 important diamond deposits were found in Brazil. Here, in a similar way to the finding of gold in Australia, the discovery was made by someone (apparently a missionary who had previously been in India) who remarked that the geological nature of the land was similar to the diamondiferous zones in India. Another tradition relates that gold prospectors were using rough diamonds as tallies in gambling games until one day a few such stones came into the hands of a Dutch consul from Lisbon, who recognised them for what they were. However, since Tejuco, now Diamantina, the first place where diamonds were found, is near auriferous deposits, it is probable that the real finders were the gold prospectors themselves.

When the news first reached Europe, it was received with incredulity and fear that the value of Indian diamonds would decrease. Rumours were started that the Brazilian stones were softer and of inferior quality, so, when Portuguese traders found difficulty in getting a good price for Brazilian gems, they shipped them to Goa and passed them off as Indian.

Soon, diamonds were being found over a vast area, from the region of São Paulo and the Paraná river to the west region of Goya and the Mato Grosso and to the north at Bahia. At the beginning, there was a great deal of confusion and disorganisation. Governments in trying to extract the greatest possible profit from the mines perpetrated a series of frauds and appropriations. Finally in 1891 the territories were restored to their owners.

For the most part, the Brazilian deposits were secondary alluvial deposits and, therefore, found in river beds. Large quantities of diamonds are found in gravels embedded in a clay cemented conglomerate known as *cascalho*, along with other minerals such as quartz, tourmaline, topaz and zircon. They have also been found in caves or grottoes whose surfaces were covered in *cascalho* which has a variable thickness of between four and thirty centimetres. From some of these grottoes between eight and ten thousand carats of diamonds have been extracted. One crystal found there of $726\frac{1}{2}$ carats was called after President Vargas.

Apart from the alluvial deposits in river beds and valleys, there are also some high plateau deposits (Diamantina is 1200 metres high). These are found embedded in another kind of coarse surface rock conglomerate cemented by red silicate clay known as *gurgulho*. In this type of deposit the concentration of diamonds, always found with other minerals, is less, but the stones are bigger and their crystal shapes more perfect Yellow, green, brown, red and black diamonds are found in Brazil. The Brazilian mines, many of which are still productive today, have proved richer than the Indian ones, but, because early records are extremely vague, the calculations on which this is based are very approximate. Nevertheless, compared to the much shorter period of time in which Brazilian deposits have been mined (1725-1910), the total production of Brazil is estimated to be about a third more than that of India. In 1946 alone a record amount of 325,000 carats was mined. Almost the whole of Brazil's produce is absorbed by North America.

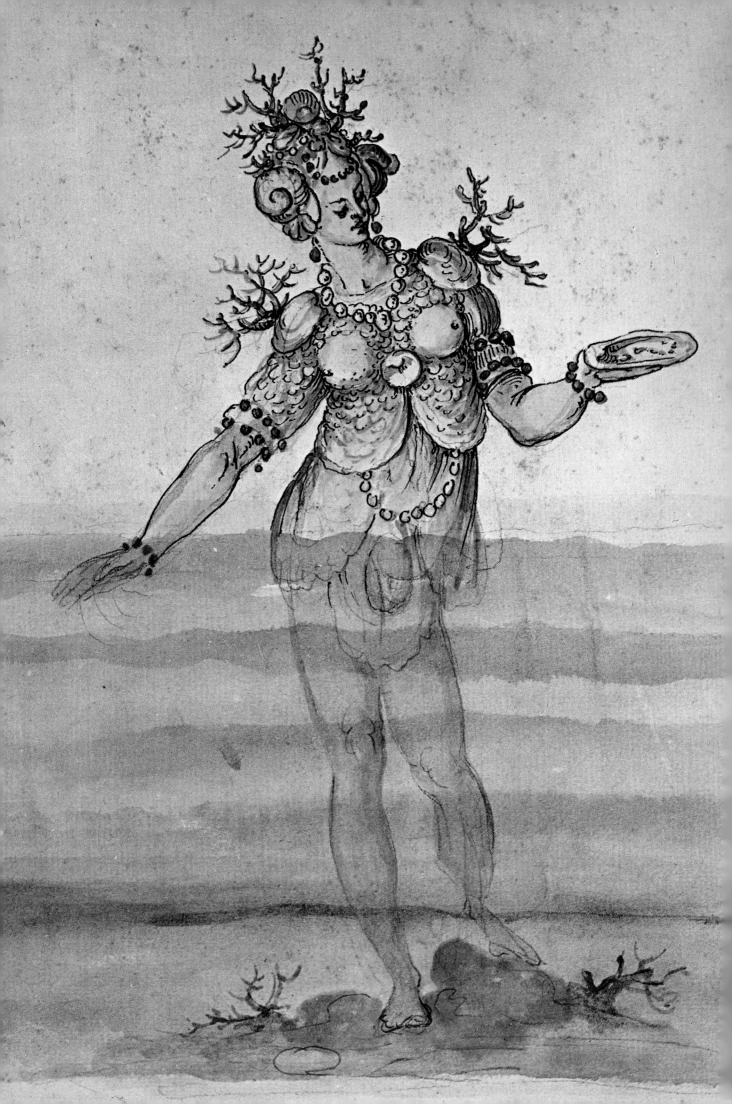

The Baroque period

Coral

In addition to diamonds, coral, a much less valuable gem, also became very popular in 17th-century jewelry. It already had a long and distinguished history, having been used by the ancient Egyptians, particularly for making scarabs, as well as by the Greeks in the Hellenic era and by the Etruscans, who also skilfully engraved it for decoration or for use in seals. It was exported in ancient times from fishing ports in the Mediterranean, the Red Sea, and India and China, where it was attributed with magic powers. Its fiery colour blended well with the colour schemes which were fashionable from the 17th century onwards, and it became widely used in Europe, not merely in cheaper jewelry.

Until the 18th century it was believed that coral was a form of marine vegetation. However, this theory was disproved by Peyssonel, a doctor from Marseilles, who discovered that coral was the skeleton remains of the minute coral polyp, which reproduces itself for eggs and secretes calcium carbonate. It lives in colonies which together assume very varied shapes.

Coral is mainly fished, at a maximum depth of two hundred metres, in Mediterranean regions, off the coasts of Sicily, Sardinia, Corsica and other smaller islands and along the coasts of Africa, Provence and Liguria down to Leghorn. The most beautiful red coral comes from the banks of Sciacca, south of Sicily. The Tunisian government has divided the coral sea coasts into ten sectors, only permitting the fishing to go on in one sector every year, so as to give the banks time to grow again.

Other ancient fishing sites are in the Red Sea and more recently in the seas off Japan. The fishing is carried on by means of traditional methods with a wooden dredging device made of two long, thick beams in the shape of a cross with a ballast at the centre; at the ends are fixed iron hooks called scrapers in the middle of a tangle of old nets. This dredger is lowered into the sea over the coral bank by means of a long rope and is then scraped backwards and forwards so that the hooks catch on the coral branches, toppling them into the nets. The dredger is then pulled back on board. In Japan a device based on the same principle is hauled up on a bamboo cane.

Bernardo Buontalenti, sketch of Anfitrite for the *Favola di Orione e Anfitrite*, the third intermezzo of *La Pellegrina*, performed for the first time in Florence in 1589 on the occasion of the marriage of Ferdinand I de' Medici and Christina of Lorraine. Biblioteca Nazionale Centrale, Florence.

223

Black coral is a product of the horny skeleton of certain species of polyps and only comes from the Red Sea. In jewelry the dark red, red, pink, pale pink (*pelle d'angelo*, 'skin of an angel') and white are used. There is also a rare variety of blue coral called *acori* which comes from the west coast of Africa near the Cameroons.

Necklace of gold, coral and small pearls, Italy, 19th century. Victoria and Albert Museum, London.

Coral *parure*, 1830s. Musée des Arts Décoratifs, Paris.

The Baroque period

The Far East

China, which has a very ancient artistic tradition, began to use precious metals relatively late. Gold, like silver, was used in the most ancient times in the form of inlay on bronze objects. Some rare references to personal ornaments date from the T'ang period (618-906), but it was only with the beginning of the Sung period (960-1279) that the Chinese showed any great interest in jewelry.

As far as style was concerned, in the early period goldwork in general and jewelry in particular was influenced by Persia and India. Only towards the end of the 11th century did the assimilated techniques and methods begin to manifest local characteristics, realised with delicate skill. From the late Sung period onwards jewelry forms tended to remain static or repeat themselves, with only slight variations, as the country's more developed social classes clung to ancient traditions in every field of art.

Characteristic of Chinese jewelry is highly skilful punched work, pierced work and filigree. The gems chiefly used were turquoise, jade, coral and pearls. The decorative themes mostly concern animals (dragons, birds, particularly the phoenix) and other symbols of good luck, such as clouds, flowers, branches and leaves and abstract decorative shapes.

Forms of Jewelry The most important type of jewel was traditionally worn on the head and could vary from a plain diadem to an elaborate tiara; in the most ancient examples of religious sculpture the decorations of these bear a close relationship with Indian jewelry of the time. However, the range of animals represented in Chinese ornaments is different, as is the texture of the works. Necklaces are very heavy, often embellished with two or three central motifs, mounted with large cabochon gems and pearls and richly ornamented with tracery and volutes. Less ancient necklaces are often lighter, being composed of rows of pearls and precious stones arranged in garlands, with rich embellishments at the points of contact and drop pearls hanging below. A secondary type of necklace was often worn across the stomach reaching as far as the thigh and winding round across the spine. It consisted of engraved and jeweled gold pieces, with a medallion decorated with relief and filigree and a huge gem in the centre, suspended

Portrait painted on silk of the wife of a high dignitary, Chinese, 1st Ming dynasty, early 15th century. Private collection, Milan.

227

from the crossing point. Some statues of Bodhisattva wear armbands and bracelets bordered with stones and pearls from which richly worked medallions hang.

A gold breastplate, which is thought to have belonged to a 15th-century emperor, is copied from a type which was certainly much older and shows ancient Iranian influences. On a rectangular gold sheet bordered with a double row of bezels set with various uncut precious and semi-precious stones is a scene depicting two dragons engaged in a lively struggle on a background of pierced-work clouds scattered with gems. The *repoussé* work reveals a surprising naturalism and the pierced work looks like an elaborate cobweb. Some solid bracelets and torques also reveal Iranian derivations. Tiaras, diadems and small decorated combs were widely used by ladies of high rank, both in and outside the court circle. Their size and richness of decoration depended upon the wearer's social status, but all designs were very varied and generally dominated by a lavish use of colour, with turquoises, jades, corals, pearls, gold and silver. Headdresses were long, with four elaborate pendants hanging from the highest and most prominent point and falling two on each side of the head. The pendants usually consisted of strings of pearls interspersed with decorated gold plates and finished off with a coloured stone. If they lacked more important ornaments, the women wore magnificent pins, the heads of which were very finely worked with gold floral motifs and set with precious stones. The appearance and aesthetic conception of these pieces bear a striking resemblance to modern jewelry. If earrings were worn with a rich headdress, they would either match it or be of a bizarre design, often a stylised bird form or an original inventive abstract pattern.

Jade A tradition found only in Chinese jewelry was the use of the breast feathers of a rare sea bird (Fei Ts'ui) a type of martin. The feathers would be mounted in a gold or silver support, with finely carved and pierced jade, pearls and filigree. The feathers are an iridescent blue and look in colour like enamel. The name of the bird came to be used to designate the most valuable jade, which in Europe is called gem jade or emerald jade.

228

Neck ornament inlaid with coral and inscribed, Tibetan. British Museum, London.

Hair ornament in the shape of a phoenix, Chinese, Sung dynasty, 960-1279. Private collection, Sweden.

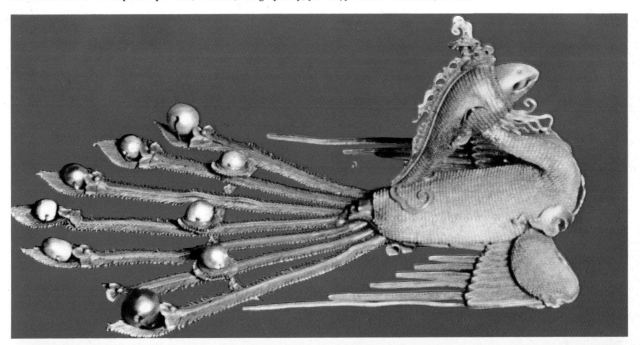

Gold plaque with the imperial dragon depicted in *repoussé* and cabochon precious and semiprecious stones. Possibly from the tomb of Emperor Hsuan Je, 1426-35. British Museum, London.

Pin made of pearls, jade and birds' feathers, Chinese. Private collection, Milan.

Gold earrings, T'ang dynasty, Chinese. British Museum, London.

above Gold earrings, T'ang dynasty, Chinese. British Museum, London.

Jade or jadeite (aluminium-sodium silicate), like nephrite (calcium-magnesium silicate) which, although it is a slightly different mineral, is always included with jade, is found in boulders or pebbles in alluvial deposits on hillsides and in water courses or in nests and veins through serpentine or stratified rocks. The most important jade deposits are in the Mogaung region of Burma, while others are in Turkestan, China, Tibet, Mexico, Venezuela, Alaska and New Zealand. The most valuable nephrite is found in alluvial deposits in China, with other deposits in Siberia, the Urals, New Zealand, New Caledonia, Brazil, Venezuela, Peru and Alaska.

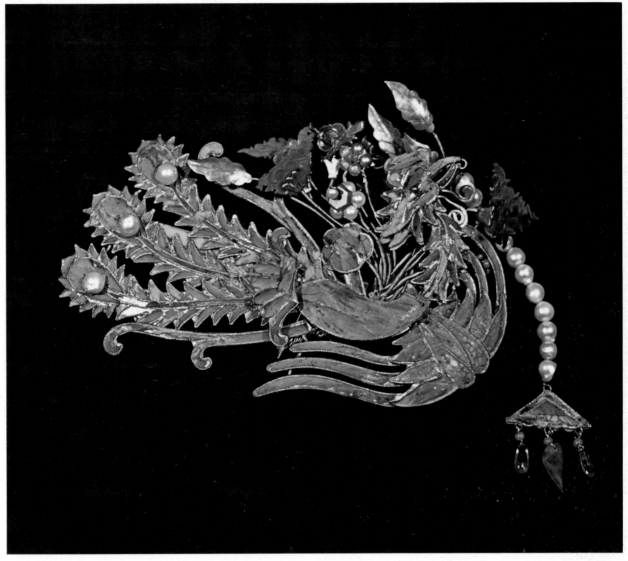

Bird-shaped jewel made of pearls, jade and feathers, Chinese, 18th century. Private collection, Milan.

There are also some scattered deposits in Italy in the Ligurian Apennines, Basilicata, Calabria and Sicily.

Both jade and nephrite come in several colours: grey, green-grey, olive-green, pink and, the rarest, emerald or imperial green. The production is not very important and is almost totally confined to China and Japan.

It is made into plain or carved beads for necklaces and in the Far East also into ornaments cut in fine sheets, moulded, pierced and engraved. Rich mandarins used to wear long necklaces of jade and pearls, finger covers in gold and mother-of-pearl rings.

Japan The Japanese civilisation developed much later than the Chinese and followed much the same pattern. The few slight variations are of a local character usually concerning ornamental details peculiar to the elegant Japanese decorative repertoire. Here, too, most of the evidence is from sculpture, above all in the numerous coloured wooden idols preserved in the temple of Nara and in various secular portraits of the Kamakura period (1185-1337) and later.

VI

The 18th century

The period of French influence

The 18th century was a period of great evolution and development in jewelry. Decorative forms changed radically, and tastes were completely transformed. The symmetrical and architecturally derived Baroque forms gave way first to the artificial and asymmetrical rocaille style derived from Rococo, with its voluptuous elegant lines, and finally to the florid but refined forms of the Classical revival.

France of Louis XV In France the great expansion in the decorative arts begun by Louis XIV continued, and in furnishings and costumes Europe, from Spain to Russia, became a French province. The quality of the products is far superior to that of previous centuries. In order to obtain the required standards of refinement, furniture makers would even send their pieces, or parts of them, to China to be decorated with the authentic lacquer.

The five official favourites who were always by the side of Louis XV were very important in the development of jewelry. Similarly many other ambitious aristocrats encouraged, by their demand for precious ornaments, the opening of numerous new jewelry shops in the French capital. Jewelry also became increasingly popular amongst the prosperous bougeoisie; the demand became so great that by 1767 there were in Paris at least 314 jewellers, working exclusively with imitation gems, particularly diamonds. Doubtless the workmanship and design of pieces made with these stones differed little from those in which real gems were used; in an age when labour was cheap and, therefore, added little to the price of the article, the lower cost of the material was of a great advantage to the buyer.

Towards the end of the 17th century the Venetian lapidary, Vincenzo Peruzzi, discovered the brilliant form of diamond cutting. The shape and position of the fifty-six facets in Peruzzi's cut caused the light which entered the stone to be reflected back through the same facets which received it. Thus far greater brilliance was obtained than in the Mazarin cut of thirty-two facets used hitherto. The already increasing predominance of gems in jewelry now knew no bounds, while the goldwork declined to merely being used inconspiciously in settings and frames.

Raphael Mengs, portrait of Infanta Maria Ludovica. Kunsthistorisches Museum, Vienna.

Earrings predominantly made of cut diamonds, 18th century. Museo Poldi-Pezzoli, Milan.

In addition to imitation stones, there was imitation gold; the type evolved by the Englishman, Christopher Pinchbeck, consisting of an alloy of copper and zinc, was the best. It had great success and was widely used in the making of shoe buckles, buttons and particularly watch cases.

Topazes, amethysts, white and blue sapphires, opals, peridots were used in the same ornamental motifs as diamonds; these stones and rubies and emeralds, in smaller quantities, were among the favourites. The constant changes in fashion were a disaster as far as the survival of pieces is concerned, and for this reason the richest documentation of 18th-century jewelry is to be found in designs and engravings. However, jewels are rarely shown in contemporary portraits; neither Queen Marie Leczinska nor Madame de Pompadour in the portraits of them by Jean Marc Nattier and Maurice Quentin de Latour wear any jewelry.

Decorative motifs continued to be inspired by floral forms, often embellished with leaves

234

Silver necklace and earrings with imitation brilliants, 18th century. Victoria and Albert Museum, London.

Johann Storff, bow-shaped hat pin of brilliants with rose-cut brilliants suspended from it, commissioned by Joseph Maximilian III, 1765. Schatzkammer der Residenz, Munich.

Gold and silver necklace set with rubies and diamonds, Sicilian, 18th century. Victoria and Albert Museum, London.

and branches, the occasional scroll work and ribbons arranged in one or more tassels or in decorative bows; sometimes all of them would be grouped together on one piece. Until the advent of Neo-Classicism 18th-century jewelry was composed almost exclusively of precious stones of various sizes, shapes and colours.

Necklaces Necklaces in the first half of the century were of the collar type, often consisting of a velvet ribbon with one or two pendants suspended from it in succession or with one pendant in the centre and one on each side. A very good example of this style is a piece in the Museo Poldi-Pezzoli in Milan; it consists of a band with a ribbon entwined through it interspersed with little flowers all made of topaz; the elaborate pendant in the centre front is in the form of a flower, surrounded by an interwoven ribbon from which hang petal-shaped pieces.

Silver brooch set with brilliants, Spain, 18th century. Victoria and Albert Museum, London.

Necklace and earrings of emeralds and brilliants, Russian, late 18th century. Victoria and Albert Museum, London.

The flowers and ribbons are all made of topazes surrounded by little diamonds, while the leaflets are in amethyst. Like nearly all the settings of the time, it is set in silver, and each stone is held in place by a convex element which is designed to enhance the reflection of light from the stones.

A style of necklace which was very fashionable was the *rivière* – a name still used today – which was usually composed of a row of large single stones, generally diamonds, often bordered by rubies or emeralds. A famous and enormously costly example of a *rivière* necklace was the one which involved the unfortunate Queen Marie Antoinette in a scandal of such dimensions as to shake the very foundations of the French monarchy. The necklace is only known through an engraving and consisted of a collar of seventeen huge diamonds from which were suspended three festoons and four pen-

dants entirely of diamonds; it was completed with another double *rivière* with four tassels also in diamonds.

The Du Barry Jewels Louis XV had ordered the piece from his jeweler as a gift for his mistress, Madame du Barry; when he died in 1774, before the jewel was finished, the jewelers offered it to Louis XVI, who could not afford it. At this point there enter the story two adventurers, Jeanne de Saint-Rémy and her husband La Motte, who persuaded Cardinal Rohan to be the unwitting accomplice in a plot. Saint-Rémy visited the cardinal to ask for money for the queen's works of charity. Having ingratiated herself with the cardinal, Saint-Rémy showed him false letters leading him to believe that he could regain the queen's favour, which he very much wanted to do, by helping her to buy the famous necklace without the king knowing. He

237

  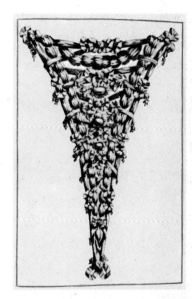

consented to negotiate the purchase of the necklace, which he then gave to Saint-Rémy who, however, sent it to England where it was broken up and sold. The complicated events which followed the ultimate discovery of the fraud involved the arrest of many accomplices. The cardinal, however, was exiled to his abbey, and Saint-Rémy was imprisoned, although she escaped soon afterwards and lived to blackmail the king.

18th-Century Forms A portrait, which perhaps gives the most complete idea of the precious ornaments which might have been worn by an 18th-century noblewoman, is of Matilde Querini painted by Pietro Longhi (Musée Nationale des Beaux Arts, Algiers). She wears a rich *parure* of diamonds consisting of an *aigrette*, together with at least seven other jewels scattered in her hair, as well as earrings made of three round gems set in a triangular shape with briolette pendants, and a diamond collar necklace made of curved elements matching those on the bracelet. In addition to rings, she has a long pearl necklace pinned to the left side of her décolleté by an *aigrette* brooch.

A jewel which had already appeared by the end of the preceding century and which developed greatly in proportions and richness in the 18th century was the *Sévigné* brooch, which probably originated in Spain. It was a bodice ornament in the shape of a bow or fan which could be lavishly embellished with openwork

239

Pietro Longhi, portrait of Matilde Querini. Musée Nationale des Beaux Arts, Algiers.

Gold, diamond and enamel bouquet. Victoria and Albert Museum, London.

floral motifs covered in faceted precious stones. As the century advanced, it became enlarged into a type of stomacher worn down to the waist. It was very popular in France and England, but less so in Italy. Queen Marie Leczinska wears a beautiful *Sévigné* on her bosom in Toque's official portrait of her in the Louvre; it is a triangular shape, with complicated ornamental motifs along its upper part and scrolls and floral motifs lower down; it extends from just under the decolleté, gradually narrowing towards the bottom which is finished off with three large pear-shaped pearls.

Bodice ornaments were very varied; among the most elegant were sets of three bows, with large gems at the knots, which were pinned one under the other in diminishing size. Later, in the second half of the century, brooches in the shape of bunches of flowers made of diamonds or stones of various colours appeared. At first their designs were somewhat stylised, but then they began to be more naturalistic. The little leaves and branches were often enamelled, while the corollas and petals scintillated with diamonds or other coloured stones. Brooches in

the shape of one or more bows from which might hang pendants of various shapes and designs were the mode in the first half of the century.

Jewelry, especially brooches, submitted for a short period to the capricious asymmetry of Rococo, using shells, scroll, volutes from the Rococo repertory. Some Rococo jewelry designs attributed to Girolamo Venturi are conserved in the Cooper Union Museum for the Decorative Arts, New York. Brooches of various designs and importance were used to fasten the tucks in the elaborate sleeves.

Many necklaces of this period are also very colourful: emeralds, rubies, diamonds and topazes are matched together in colourful harmony giving the best exposition to the floral elements which make up the design of the jewel.

The insignia of the golden fleece, worn by sovereigns, began the vogue in the 18th century for jewels of spectacular magnificence. The most rare and beautiful gems in royal collections were mounted in splendid ornamental compositions which became sumptuous symbols of distinction.

Among the simplest of earrings were those

using one or three drop pearls, in which the central one would be the longest. The *girandole* earring consisted of three pear-shaped drops suspended from a large stone, nearly always a diamond and usually circular, set at the top. A rich example of this type of earring is worn by Queen Maria Amalia Christina in a portrait painted by Raphael Mengs in the Louvre, Paris.

Bracelets with diamonds set in lined ornamental elements in openwork were very popular; some have a medallion finely painted in enamel at the clasp. Another ornament characteristic of this century was the chatelaine. This was an ornamental chain which was fastened to the belt or pocket sometimes composed of elaborate linked and moulded gold elements in various shapes and sizes, with *repoussé* scenes depicting biblical or allegorical subjects or themes from Classical history in elaborate Rococo frames. Chains of various lengths hung from projecting points, terminating in spring hooks, which were used by men to hang their watches, keys and other accessories

Earring of silver and brilliants, Spanish, 17th century. Victoria and Albert Museum, London.

A golden fleece of oriental garnets, brilliants, rubies and gold, German, 1760-70. Schatzkammer der Residenz, Munich.

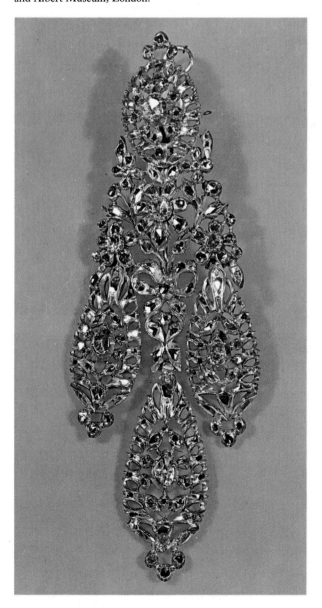

Chatelaine in *repoussé* gold, French, 18th century. Museo Poldi-Pezzoli, Milan.

Chatelaine, early 19th century. Musée des Arts Décoratifs, Paris.

on, while ladies would hang such objects as keys, little prayer books, sewing cases, scissors or little jewels. Already in use by the end of the preceding century, they became in this period, together with the watch case, the only things in which gems were rarely used, and the most refined expression of the goldsmith's art.

Ornaments such as the chatelaine were con-sidered to be day jewelry, along with imitation jewelry or rock crystals, imitation stones or semiprecious stones such as garnet, agate, cornelian or amber. Such jewels, which, as has been noted, were just as finely executed as real ones, might be worn by wealthy people too, in order to save their expensive jewels for the lavish evening receptions.

Chatelaine, late 18th century. Private collection, Rome.

more valuable articles. Other forms of imitation jewelry were marcasite and cut steel. These were so successful that by the 19th century there were firms in England specialising exclusively in the manufacture of cut-steel jewelry.

In Louis XV's time the *aigrette*, a spray of gems, enjoyed great popularity and was worn until the advent of Neo-Classicism. Its jeweled stems were often made in such a way that they shook when the head moved, thus showing off to greater advantage the brilliance of the diamonds.

The same stylistic motifs were used on rings. The hoops were often finely wrought in leafy or scroll designs, and the bezel would be in the form of the petals of a flower. Oval gems were preferred for settings. In the second half of the century and particularly in the Neo-Classical period the marquise ring enjoyed a great vogue. This is characterised by an oblong bezel set with

In the field of imitation gems, the 18th century saw the development of a huge industry, above all in England and France, countries where remarkable results were achieved. Apart from the lead glass or strass pastes, which were faceted and mounted just like real stones, another imitation of the diamond was made from fused beryl or quartz, but this was only used in

243

Hercules, design for a gem engraving. Civica Raccolta di Stampe Bertarelli, Milan.

Ring with a cameo framed in diamonds, c. 1760. Victoria and Albert Museum, London.

one large coloured stone, most often a sapphire, encircled by a double or even a triple row of little diamonds; later the central piece was often a cameo framed in plain gold or a stone engraved in the antique manner. Onyx, chalcedony or rock crystal were also used, and the types and combinations of the stones were innumerable. Many rings had bezels decorated with figures, sometimes in silhouette, finely painted in enamel.

Classical Influences The great events of the last thirty years of the 18th century were the amazing archaeological discoveries at Pompeii and Herculaneum, which drew scholars, architects, artists and engravers, particularly from France and England, to Rome and Naples to study the excavations. The man whose studies and writings had the greatest effect on the art and tastes of this period was the Prussian Johann Joachim Winckelmann. His views on harmony based on Classical Greek ideals found favour and provided inspiration in all branches of the arts. The study and appreciation of the architectural, plastic and decorative works, which were revealed and which were publicised through prints, had a decisive influence on the tastes and form of European decorative arts and ushered in the period of Neo-Classicism.

Florid ornamental lines were gradually abandoned for greater simplicity and more disciplined composition. Unlike the Renaissance era when Classical forms had been reinterpreted in terms relevant to the contemporary arts, Neo-Classicism took ornamental motifs almost directly from the Greco-Roman models. Thus, for instance, cameos depicting mythological figures and scenes came back into vogue.

An important contribution to the new jewelry styles was made by the English pottery manufacturer Josiah Wedgwood. In his famous factory he perfected a technique of producing cameos with special, very hard, fine pastes called black basalt and jasper. He worked in collaboration with sculptors such as John Flax-

left Silver-gilt ring with a porcelain Wedgwood medallion, English, 18th century. Musée des Arts Décoratifs, Paris. *right* Gold ring, French, 18th century. Musée des Arts Décoratifs, Paris.

man on jewelry which was mounted and sometimes decorated with cut steel. The subjects were Classical scenes taken from Greco-Roman models. An exaggerated refinement, a charming fluidity of line and a note of romantic sentiment characterised Wedgwood cameos, giving them a certain vitality which was very far from the severe Classical spirit. These oval, round or octagonal plaques, framed in gold, were used as medallions, brooches and as parts of diadems, belts or bracelets. The colours were usually white on a light-blue, light-green, black, lavender or buff background.

This period also saw the revival of the use of enamels on decorated plaques. Again the subjects most frequently depicted were pagan gods, Roman emperors or signs of the zodiac in oval metal frames embellished with gems. Brightly coloured rustic or domestic scenes were also popular, as were sober enamel pictures in the grey monochrome grisaille technique. The quality of the workmanship was very high,

particularly in French enamels, and the enamel painters justly enjoyed wide fame.

Pearls and precious stones, though still frequent in important jewelry, were less popular. In keeping with the new styles, they were used more sparingly, with stricter symmetry and greater disipline. Although only a short space of time had elapsed since the sumptuous jewels of the Louis XV epoch, the change in taste had been so radical that the old conceptions of form were completely rejected, resulting, as has been mentioned, in the destruction of innumerable pieces in order to recover the precious materials.

The French Revolution brought an abrupt end to the manufacture of and taste for sumptuous jewelry in the country which for over a century had dictated the fashion in elegance and luxury. From this time jewelry styles in Europe began to become more international; fashions in taste and quality which had hitherto mainly followed the French example were now open to other influences.

245

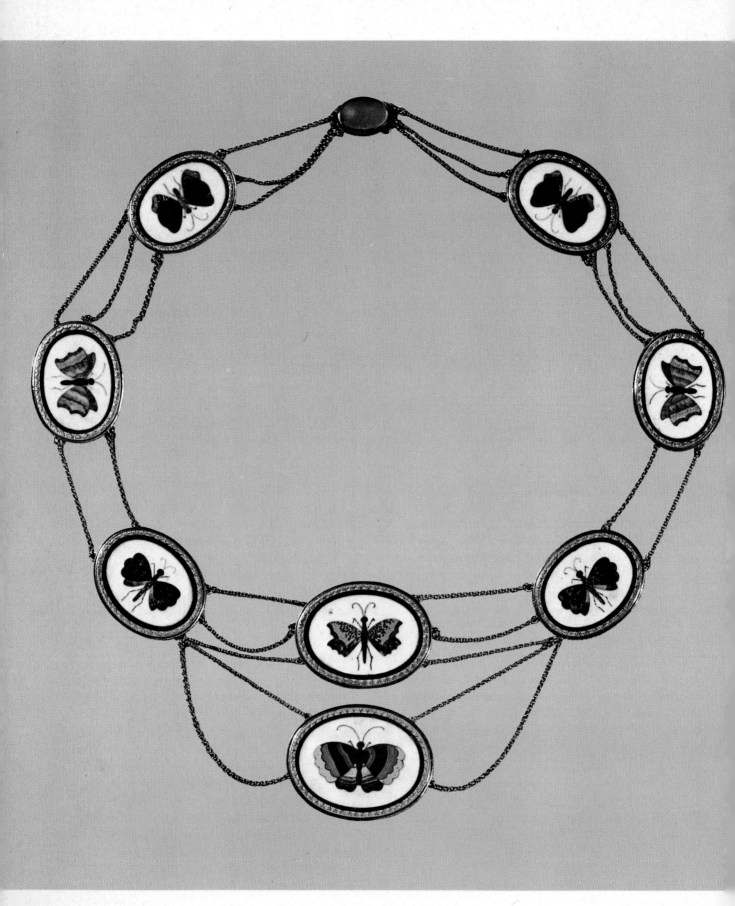

VII

The 19th century
The industrial revolution

The new phase which had begun just before the end of the 18th century witnessed an ever-increasing demand for jewelry. Hitherto, precious ornaments had been directly related to the social rank of the wearer, but this relationship was completely and for ever destroyed by the industrial revolution. The social evolution worked against the aristocracy, and they were forced finally into adopting the tastes of the triumphant bourgeoisie. The first symptoms of this phenomenon had already manifested themselves with the manufacture of imitation precious stones, pinchbeck gold and the use of cut steel and ceramics. This now expanded widely, and the results are often of little artistic interest. The era of the machine had arrived, and jewelry, too, succumbed to mass production methods. The industrial revolution had its first stirrings in England, where in the field of jewelry Birmingham became the manufacturing centre for pierced-work iron medallions depicting ornamental scenes and figures for mounting in gold for necklaces, bracelets and brooches. However, besides mass production, there still survived in the 19th century craftsmanship of quality.

In France the revolution was followed by a period of austerity imposed by the political climate in reaction against the excesses of the court circle. Simplicity was the keynote of fashion in clothes, and jewelry designs tended to be plain and to consist of semiprecious or even ordinary stones in decorated gold or silver mounts. However, with Napoleon's re-establishment of the court, the *citoyen* style gave way once more to the old extravagances.

Napoleon lost no time in repossessing himself of what remained of the crown jewels, carried off during the troubled days of the revolution, and in having new and sumptuous jewels made for his empress, Josephine, to wear on official and semiofficial ceremonial occasions. Her example was widely followed in the court circle.

Paris soon acquired again her old and glorious position as the leader of European fashion, both as regards clothes and precious ornaments. In the field of jewelry the revival of French supremacy concerned above all the tradition of refined workmanship. The forms produced by the master jewelers no longer achieved the high

Necklace, 19th century. Victoria and Albert Museum, London.

standards which had helped to create their fame in the past; and the quick pace of the variations in fashion gradually turned public taste towards other centres of production.

Changing Fashions The precious ornaments produced for the well-to-do bourgeois upper classes were characterised by a stylistic eclecticism. Their inspiration derived above all from fashionable literary sources and from archaeological discoveries, while political and artistic events and the industrial revolution also contributed to the sudden and radial changes in jewelry forms and materials.

In the many fashions of varying duration which succeeded each other during this period jewelry styles all drew on past eras for inspiration, according to what suited the current political mood. There were revivals of Gothic, Renaissance, Greek, Etruscan and Roman, of Rococo, Naturalistic, Moorish and Indian styles and even imitations of the jewels found during the excavations of Troy. None of these forms escaped the embellishments of Romanticism. In England, commemorative and mourning jewelry, depicting subjects full of pre-Romantic sentimentalism and melancholy,

which had a vogue at the end of the 18th century, returned to fashion during Queen Victoria's widowhood. However, these revivals rarely contained anything of artistic interest and are often mere pastiches which have no meaning or depth. They are responsible for the indiscriminate discrediting not only of jewelry, but of all 19th-century decorative art. From the technical point of view, however, the average level of craftsmanship was high despite the increasing use of the machine, which tended to produce stereotyped and lifeless forms.

Fashionable settings for stones were the collet and the claw setting. Later the pavé, which had already been in use in the previous century, became very popular; small turned over metal beads made it possible to hold in place many tiny diamonds or other stones (such as turquoises) very close together. The idea was that the stones should cover as large a part of the surface as possible with very little metal showing between them. In the illusion setting the

Unknown French artist, portrait of the Maréchale Lefèvre wearing a bracelet, a necklace of three rows of pearls linked with gems, a diadem and earrings, 19th century. Versailles.

Jacques Louis David, detail from *The Coronation of Napoleon* showing princesses wearing necklaces, Greek-style garland diadems, earrings and jewelled belts. Louvre, Paris.

edges of the metal rim surrounding the stone, usually a small diamond, are cut in such a way as to appear to be part of the gem, and thus enhance its size. From 1880 onwards the solitaire, a large diamond set in a ring without any other stones around it, became popular and was worn by men too. The cuts most widely used during this century were the rose and the brilliant, except, of course, where imitation antique gems were used.

In the second half of the century elaborate necklaces were sometimes made so that they could be dismantled at various points and turned into a *parure* consisting of a shorter necklace, one or two brooches and a bracelet.

Preferences as regards precious and semiprecious stones varied throughout the century, as a greater number of gems became available. Diamonds, emeralds and rubies remained the favourite stones for important or court jewelry; less valuable gems, however, were widespread in more ordinary pieces. Small diamonds often

served to frame large coloured stones, usually sapphires, amethysts and topazes. The opal became widely used as a result of the discovery of vast deposits in Australia, and jet (often called black amber) and coral were also popular at different periods.

The Age of Napoleon After the interlude of the *citoyen* style, which was a mixture of mild Classicism with patriotic emblems and motifs in semiprecious ornaments of little intrinsic value, the rhetorical conventionalism of the Empire style came in with the Napoloenic era. This was a stiff and heavy interpretation of Classical motifs in which eagles, rams' heads, Greek key patterns and laurel wreaths, together with other motifs of the Greco-Roman period, constituted the principal elements.

The painting by David of Napoleon's consecration as emperor admirably records the pomp and magnificence of the ceremony. Among the numerous onlookers, one group of lavishly jeweled noblewomen stands out. They 249

François Gérard, detail of a portrait of the empress Josephine wearing a diadem, necklace and earrings of precious stones and drop pearls, c. 1803. Musée de l'Armée, Paris.

Robert Léfebvre, detail of a portrait of Pauline Borghese wearing a classical style diadem. Versailles.

all wear jewelry reminiscent of Greek ornaments of the 4th century BC. Two of their coronets are in the form of laurel wreaths and three are bands decorated with Classical garland and key motifs; all are studded with diamonds and other precious stones and bordered with pearls, and each has one important decorative element in the centre. Their earrings are simpler, mostly the pendant type with one or more drop-shaped gems. Their necklaces, too, are inspired by Classical models; the gems or cameos of various shapes framed in gold are linked by little chains or by two or more rows of pearls each with a gem in the centre. The high waists of the dresses are encircled by belts made of linked elements (gems or cameos framed with stones), with a large cameo or some other diamond-framed motif at the centre. The motifs on the belts are repeated along the edge of the short sleeves. On the long white gloves which were customary, bracelets of pearls or

jewels would be worn, with a large cameo at the clasp which would match the belts and necklaces. Numerous precious stones would also be sewn onto the dresses.

This and other pictorial evidence, such as the portrait of the Maréchale Lefèbvre (*Madame Sans Gêne*, painter unknown) at Versailles and that of Queen Caroline of Naples by Gérard at Malmaison, show how the taste for luxury had revived and was reflected, with slightly less abundance, in the wealthy bourgeois circles.

Together with the large number of precious stones and pearls, one finds in this period a certain basic stylistic trend through which jewellers, goldsmiths and enamellers found the means of showing off their skill. Amongst the famous jewelers who worked for Napoleon was Etienne Nitot who, amongst other things, created the tiara of gold and precious stones which the emperor gave to Pope Pius VII. For gala occasions *parures* returned to fashion, and

left François Gérard, portrait of Queen Caroline of Naples wearing a necklace, earrings, and diadem of gold, pearls and turquoises. Malmaison.

right and left Two pairs of gold earrings in the Neo-Greek style, *c.* 1878-1900. *centre* Eugène Fontenay, gold earrings with busts of children in lapis lazuli. Musée des Arts Décoratifs, Paris.

shell and Wedgwood cameos, imported by the Paris jewelers and mounted in various articles such as chains, bracelets and chatelaines, were widely used. In addition to the ear of wheat motif, flowers, particularly jasmin branches, were widely used for diamond jewelry.

Revivals of the Past During the Restoration period, when Louis XVIII and Charles X reigned, jewelry styles were dominated by imitations of Roman jewelry. Earrings and small Spanish-style combs were decorated with Pompeian motifs, miniature mosaics (especially favoured by Roman jewelers) and embellished with pearls, ivory, tortoise shell and, above all, coral. From now practically until the end of the century, and not just in France, the taste for reviving past styles prevailed.

Paris continued to dictate fashion, but England, too, interpreted the literary and archaeological events in fashions. New vogues were set off by the successful novels of Sir Walter Scott or poems by Lord Byron. Thus the 'cathedral' or Gothic style influenced jewelry, with its crenellations, gargoyles, vertical lines and allegorical figures modelled in high relief in silver on buckles or brooches, embellished with coloured cabochon stones. The uniformity of the finish and a certain coldness in the forms of

252

Gold earrings with cornelian cameos framed in filigree, early 19th century. Musée des Art Décoratifs, Paris.

Bracelet, *c.* 1830. Private collection, Rome.

these jewels are evidence of the futility of taking artistic elements of one epoch from the environment in which they had evolved and transposing them into objects inspired by a superficial romantic admiration. Little models of ornamental sculpture taken from ancient architectural monuments were repeated with pedantic correctness.

The only name worth mentioning with re-gard to valid work in this style is that of Froment-Meurice, who lived in Paris. His jewelry, created in the medieval style, is the work of a man of culture and it has a certain significance. A fine silver bracelet by him in the Musée des Arts Décoratifs, Paris, is made of linked elements, each consisting of a pair of scrolls entwined in such a way as to look like decorative grilles. In the centre is a sort of niche containing

Solid silver pin in the style of Wagner and Rudolphi, *c.* 1840. Musée des Arts Décoratifs, Paris.

Enamelled silver pin in the style of Wagner and Rudolphi, 1838. Musée des Arts Décoratifs, Paris.

Gold and amethyst bracelet and brooch, 19th century. Private collection, Milan.

a figure modelled in high relief.

Although one can establish approximately when the various styles of the past were fashionable in the jewels of the 19th century, it is, however, in certain cases almost impossible to say when and where a jewel was made. Classical styles, for example, returned to fashion at various points throughout the century, and the last craftsmen worthy of note were the Roman Augusto Castellani and Carlo Giuliano, a Neapolitan who worked in London.

The Louis Philippe era in France, lasting from about 1830 to around the middle of the century, saw a return to the Renaissance styles with jeweled hair nets, chains (*chaîne de forçat*) and jewels with enamelled panels of markedly romantic subjects. In the same period the jeweler Frédéric Philippi created pendants and pins representing centaurs, using baroque pearls and vividly coloured enamel.

The middle of the century saw a return to naturalism in France, with ornaments again in the shape of flowers, bouquets, stems and branches, while in England the publication of Layard's *Nineveh and its Remains* in 1848 introduced Assyrian motifs into jewelry. Between 1850-60 jewelry inspired by Moorish sources was all the rage both in France and England. During the Second Empire brilliant-cut diamonds and other precious stones came back into

fashion: the emperor wanted to revive the pomp of Napoleon I's court, but in form, jewelry adhered principally to Louis XVI styles. At the same time Carl Fabergé was building up a great reputation in St Petersburg. At his factory the most refined jewels in all styles, including the archaeological, were produced. Full of clever ideas from the formal point of view, they were executed with unsurpassed technical mastery.

In Victorian England much the same developments were in evidence. The jewelry manufactured in Birmingham and London was of a very high quality, particularly in the finish and detail, and, since artistic creativity in jewelry was at a low ebb throughout Europe at this point, the English products were considerably admired everywhere, and above all in Germany.

Paris and Rome showed greater inventiveness in their interpretations of the past, the former excelling in imitation of the 18th century, and the latter in archaeological styles. This return to the past in the period between the restoration of the monarchy and the ascension of Napoleon III caused the popularity of diamond jewelry to decline save for the brief interlude of naturalistic fashion around the middle of the century.

Machine-made Jewelry However, gold once again became fashionable, all the skills of the goldsmith benefited greatly from the introduc-

254

right Parure of gold and precious stones, English, mid 19th century. Private collection, Rome.

tion of mechanical equipment which, perfected over the years, made possible greater complexity in composition. Identical gold pieces for use in various ornaments would be mass produced. A Louis Philippe *parure* consisting of a necklace, two bracelets, earrings and a belt-buckle in the Musée des Arts Décoratifs, Paris, consists almost entirely of machine-produced elements linked together. However, stamping machines did not play the main part in the manufacture of jewelry of this period and, in fact, this *parure* is an exceptional case. It is an example of a kind of mechanical virtuosity, for the handmade elements are scarcely distinguishable from the rest.

Many jewels, especially important ones, were decorated with traditional techniques, and others such as gold used in brooches, elements for bracelets, necklaces and earrings were stamped with a scroll design and then embellished by hand with filigree bezels for precious and semiprecious stones and pearls. While in Louis Philippe's France 18th-century styles were the vogue, in England, in addition to the Gothic revival which was more popular there than elsewhere, jewelry inspired by Holbein's designs and paintings came into fashion.

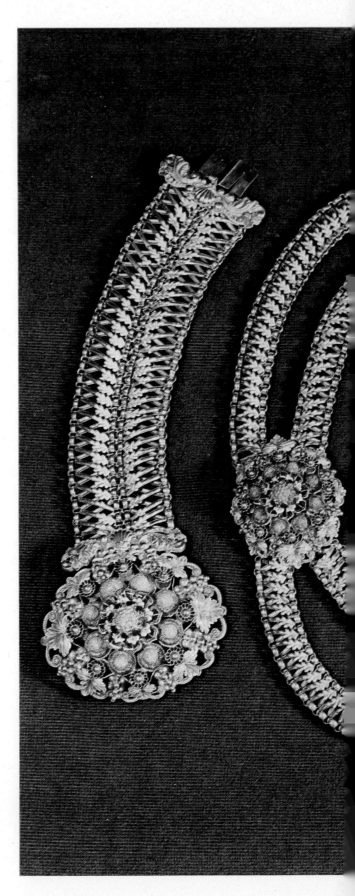

256

Gold filigree and pearl earring, Portuguese, 1800-50. Private collection, Rome.

257

Parure of gold and enamel, parts of which are machine made, consisting of a necklace, two bracelets, earrings and a belt buckle, French, 1830-40. Musée des Arts Décoratifs, Paris.

Necklace of gold mesh, pin topazes and emeralds, English, 1800-50. Private collection, Rome.

The Renewed Popularity of Diamonds

As has been mentioned, the naturalistic style brought diamonds back into the limelight for a certain period, but few very large crystals were used; the flowering branches which generally formed the subject of these pieces were nearly always covered with tiny diamonds and other coloured stones pavé set. This technique was also used for mounting half pearls. Small diamonds were used for framing other larger gems, and the rose cut was used as much as the brilliant. The pear-shaped cut, or briolette, was also often used for earrings and pendants on pins. For collet or claw settings highly polished silver was preferred even if the rest of the object was of gold, and coloured stones were often set in delicately wrought filigree mounts.

At the Great Exhibition in London in 1851 a diamond bouquet was shown which contained nearly six thousand stones, the largest of which weighed ten carats and the smallest one thousandth of a carat. The whole design, especially the outlines, the veining of the leaves and the petals of the flowers were a result of the great skill of the goldsmith, who arranged with meticulous care the thousands of little bezels in which the numerous gems were mounted.

Old Forms Again Some 18th-century forms such as the *Sévigné* were revived, and the *parure* was more popular than ever before. The great respect in which the art of Leonardo da Vinci was widely held caused a revival of the 15th-century ornament worn on the forehead called a *ferronière* after Da Vinci's portrait, *La Belle Ferronière*. A young lady in a portrait by Corot in the Louvre wears a jewel of this type.

The technique of enamelling was used both for embellishing the decorative parts of a jewel and for painting on medallions portraits of kings, great men or allegorical figures, often copied from pictures by famous artists. The medallions were always richly framed with pearls, gems, filigree or coral.

In England at the time of Mariette's excava-

right Vincente Lopez, portrait of Maria Christina de Bourbon wearing a Neo-Classical-style necklace and bracelets. Prado, Madrid.

tions in Egypt, there was a brief vogue for jewelry imitating Egyptian forms encouraged by the studies and all the publicity. Similarly, for a short period around the 1840s, Moorish styles were fashionable in England and France, following the interest shown in oriental painters and their work and echoed in the publication of Lord Byron's *Lara, a Tale* and *The Corsair*.

The return to fashion of the crinoline and heavy fabrics such as velvet around the middle of the century meant a demand for ornaments richer in appearance if not in substance. The shell cameo, so abused in the Napoleonic period, reappeared, as did coloured stones such as amethysts, emeralds and sapphires for more important pieces, and agate, jasper, cornelians, garnets and haematites for more popular works. **The Castellani** Meanwhile in Rome Pio Fortunato Castellani (1793-1865), in collaboration with Michelangelo Caetani, applied themselves, with great success, to the study and imitation of Etruscan, Greek and Roman jewelry. Castellani retired from his workshop in 1851, ceding the rights of direction to his

sons Augusto and Alessandro. Augusto Castellani, continuing his father's work, considerably improved his technical virtuosity. He inherited his father's passion and enthusiasm and, fascinated by the delicacy of workmanship in Etruscan jewelry, made a thorough research into ancient techniques and collected antique and peasant jewelry. The rediscovery of granulation was one of the results of his long studies,

Théodore Chassériau, *La Toilette d'Ester* showing Neo-Classical-style necklace and bracelets. Louvre, Paris.

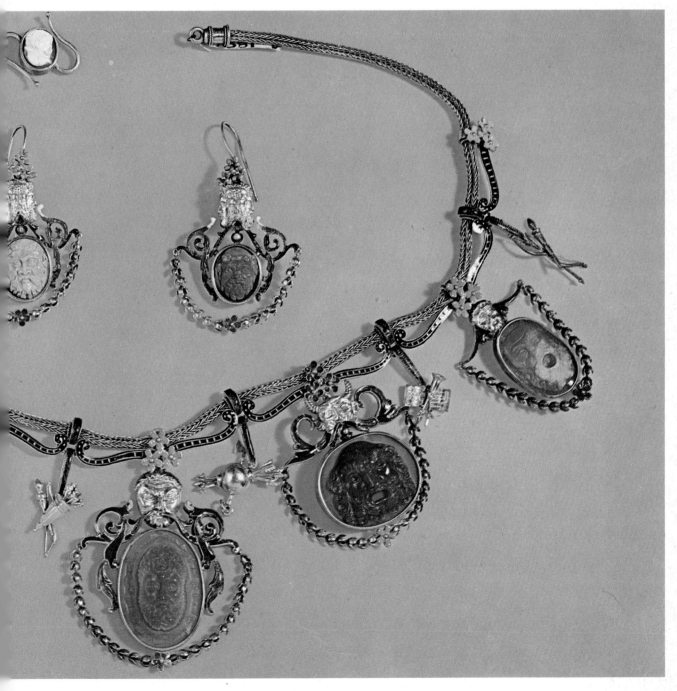

261

Necklace and earrings of gold, enamel and cameos. English, 1867. Victoria and Albert Museum, London.

but, although he achieved far more than anyone in the use of this technique, he never managed to equal the perfection of the ancient examples. At the Paris Exhibition of 1867 he exhibited an Etruscan-style coronet which was greatly admired, especially for the delicate 'reticulated' gold. The jewel was bought by the earl of Dudley for one thousand guineas which, since the intrinsic value of the material was estimated at not more than £100, indicates how greatly the Italian goldsmith's worth was esteemed.

Castellani's collection of Greek and Etruscan jewelry is today in the Museo Nazionale di Villa Giulia in Rome, while that of Italian peasant gold and silver has been acquired by the British Museum, London. His products, marketed under the name Italian Archaeological Jewelry, might include miniature Roman-style mosaics and also Byzantine-style enamel decoration. Another aspect of Castellani's artistic activity was his interest in traditional Italian peasant jewelry. He made silver hair pins in the form of daggers, arrows, anchors and javelins, bracelets as heavy as handcuffs and lockets as big as hand mirrors, which were popularly received and influenced jewelry production in the European capitals. Among the essays published by Augusto Castellani are *L'Arte nell'Industria* (Rome, 1878), *Della oreficeria italiana* (Florence, 1862), *Sulla necessità di abolire il bollo coercitivo* and *Delle gemme* (Florence, 1870).

England At the same time the Neapolitan jeweler, Carlo Giuliano, was working in London. His jewels, also in imitation of Classical styles or consisting of varied stylistic elements, were executed with a highly refined use of gold as well as enamels, pearls and precious stones. The work of Castellani and Giuliano and their followers rarely included valuable gems; the interest in the antique and the Classical meant that they used polished rather than faceted stones, chosen from the limited range of cornelian, onyx, cat's eye, lapis lazuli, chrysoprase and numerous pearls.

Mourning jewelry, making extensive use of jet, was widely worn in England from 1861, the year in which the Prince Consort died. This substance, which cannot really be called precious, is mineralised vegetable matter similar to lignite and anthracite, of a velvet-like black and easy

to work. One of the best and oldest sources of jet is the Yorkshire coast around Whitby. In addition to its use in mourning jewelry, it was used in styles imitating those of Pompeii. In a *parure* in the Museo Poldi-Pezzoli, Milan, the necklace consists of a very fine gold band made from a network of the finest interwoven filigree, attached to which are three jet rams' heads carved in high relief, two in the centre and one on the clasp. Another twenty-one jet medallions carved with gods' heads and little amphorae, hang alternately from the lower edge of the band. The brooch and earrings have similarly decorated pendants on a gold framework of scrolls. These jewels are embellished with great delicacy. On the earrings and the matching ring there are tiny frogs modelled in solid gold between each piece of carved jet.

Of the same period is another *parure* in the Egyptian style in the Musée des Arts Décoratifs, Paris. It comprises a necklace, a Spanish-style comb, two pins, earrings and a brooch. Egyptian influence is apparent in the agate and onyx scarabs which constitute the chief motif of each piece, but other elements such as the series of gold pendants on the necklace, the earrings and the brooch are derived from Assyrian models.

France Under Napoleon III With Napoleon III's accession to the throne and his marriage to Eugénie de Montijo in 1853, the court of

Egyptian style *parure* with agate, onyx, lava and jade scarabs, Italy, *c.* 1860. Musée des Arts Décoratifs, Paris.

Necklace, brooch and earrings in gold mesh and carved jet, 19th century. Museo Poldi-Pezzoli, Milan.

France once again held great balls and displayed an elegance and luxury the like of which had not been seen for many years. With it came a renewed vogue for sumptuous and valuable jewels. The empress had a predilection for pearls and diamonds and, as a result, they enjoyed a greater popularity in the second half of the century than ever before. Many of the most important crown jewels were dismantled and remade in styles more to the empress's liking. Among them was a spectacular brooch, now in the Louvre, entirely made of exceptionally large diamonds, which were especially cut in shapes to fit the design. Diamonds and coloured stones, in particular, large oval, octagonal, round or briolette sapphires and topazes framed in rosettes or pearls, were made into magnificent *parures* of necklaces, bracelets, earrings and pins in which the sparkling of the gems was predominant over the metal. Large pins in designs imitating natural flowers returned to fashion at this period.

Paris jewelers had once more recovered their supremacy, and their products, encouraged by the court, again dictated the fashion in Europe. The rise in the standards of living in the 19th century, especially in the countries where the industrial revolution was most advanced, created a demand for the manufacture of jewelry at prices which were more acceptable to the newly prosperous middle classes. Factors which determined this diffusion were the invention of electrogilding, the increased production of imitation stones and the use of machines which made possible the stamping of hundreds of different elements for jewelry.

New Materials Electroplating is a process which makes possible the covering of a metal object (silver, copper or bronze) with a thin uniform layer of another metal (gold and silver) for decorative or protective purposes. In 1802 the Italian chemist Luigi Valentino Brugnatelli succeeded in covering some silver medallions with a thin plating of gold through a cathode process in an electrolytic bath consisting of a solution containing ions of gold. The plating is obtained by passing an electric current through a solution containing the metallic salts to be deposited, an anode of pure metal to be transferred and the object to be plated. The fineness

A diamond brooch of Empress Eugénie. Louvre, Paris.

Diana bracelet of red engraved gold and enamel. Design by Alphonse Fouquet, sculpture by Carrier Belleuse, enamel by Granhomme Musée des Arts Décoratifs, Paris.

of the platings can be controlled by adjusting the intensity of the current; with gold it is possible to obtain layers of only a thousandth of a millimetre in thickness. The practical application of electroplating for the gilding and silvering objects became possible only from about 1840 onwards through the work of G. R. and H. Elkington and J. Wright in England, the firm of Christofle in Paris and W. Siemens in Germany.

Methods of imitating diamonds have already been mentioned. There was a great increase in the use of lead glass pastes with Ravenscroft's methods being used in England and those of Strass on the continent. Iron pyrites, called marcasite, mainly produced in France were used in ever greater amounts, as was cut steel which was a speciality of Birmingham. Faceted pieces of these two minerals were prepared by the manufacturers mounted on steel plates and supplied to jewelers ready for use. They were used above all for framing medallions, or in pavé settings. The crew or lever press was widely used for a great variety of elements for mounting or soldering and for all kinds of filigree.

Fouquet Towards the end of the century the distinguished Parisian goldsmith Alphonse Fouquet, in collaboration with the sculptor Belleuse, the engraver Honoré and the enameller Grandhomme, produced a series of heavy jewels in the Italian Renaissance style (Musée des Arts Décoratifs, Paris). There are enamelled medallions of various shapes and busts of beautiful

Design by Alphonse Fouquet (1878), enamel by Beranger. Musée des Arts Décoratifs, Paris.

265

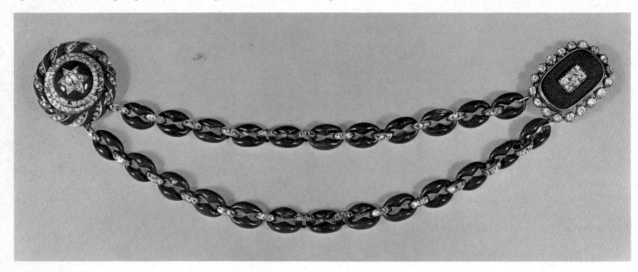

Bracelet, English, 1860-70. Victoria and Albert Museum, London.

16th-century Italian women taken from the pictures of famous masters. The sculptural versions were derived from architectural forms, with cherubs, caryatids, gargoyles, sphinxes and other fantastic images modelled in full relief.

Fouquet's very personal style and the very different one of Castellani and of other gold-smiths and jewelers did not affect the continued production of jewelry of high intrinsic value in which diamonds were the chief and undisputed centre of the designs. The period of the *belle époque* in Paris was at its height; balls, theatres and society parties provided many occasions for the nobility to don their fabulous tiaras, *rivières* and *parures*. The spread of the use of diamonds at this time was made possible by the ever-increasing number of stones coming into the market from the newly discovered rich South African deposits.

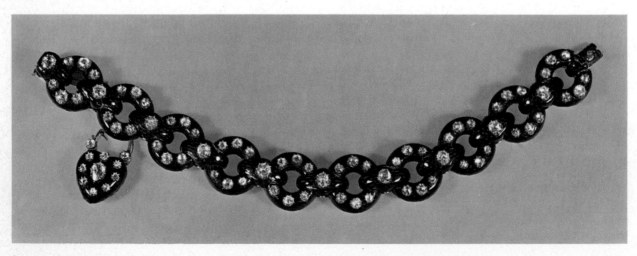

Bracelet of brilliants and enamel with a heart-shaped pendant, English, 1860-70. Victoria and Albert Museum, London.

The 19th century
Diamonds

South Africa The South African diamond mines are the most recent to have been discovered of those so far mentioned. Their development, therefore, is the best documented, richest in names, dates, places and anecdotes which recall, in their fascinating details, the adventures typical of the pioneering life of the last century. Their history shows how the small beginnings of individual men of initiative grew in a relatively short space of time to major proportions until the individuals and small groups became powerful industrial and financial companies whose interests are bound up with those of nations.

The First Discoveries The first diamondiferous region to be discovered in South Africa was about a thousand kilometres from Cape Town on the grassy steppe of the Karro thirteen hundred to sixteen hundred metres above sea level, through which flow the three rivers Orange, Vaal and Caledon. This area, which was a patriarchal republic called the Orange Free State, was inhabited by Boers who lived mostly on farming and cattle rearing. Overthrown after a treaty of alliance with the Transvaal during the Boer War, it was annexed by England in 1900. Ten years later it became part of the Union of South Africa and is today one of its four states.

The children's game of five-stones – coloured stones thrown up and caught on the back of the hand – is the first small link in the chain of events which led in 1867 to the discovery of diamonds in this area. Near Hopetown on the river Orange the son of a Boer, Erasmus Jacobs, found while playing near the river a large bright pebble whose irregularity caught his attention. He put it in his pocket together with others he had there, planning to use it in his games. However, one day a neighbour, Shalk von Niekerk, noticed the stone; he wanted to buy it, but was given it free by the boy's mother. He had a vague idea that the stone might be a diamond, but, although he offered it to several traders, they did not share his opinion. Finally, after many fruitless attempts to sell, the lion hunter and trader Jack O'Reilly bought it for very little. He was convinced that this piece of mineral, with which he had managed to write his name on a window pane, must be a diamond,

The Grand Condé diamond set in the centre of a diamond necklace. Musée Condé, Chantilly.

and on the advice of the civil commissioner of Colesberg he sent it to W. Guybon Atherstone, a minerologist at Grahamstown, who pronounced it a genuine diamond weighing twenty-one carats.

As was to be expected the area around the Jacob's farm was combed for more stones after the news, but no more diamonds were found. Experts in London did not attach much importance to the original find which was presumed to be a freak.

The case was not, therefore, recorded, but rumours began to spread. In 1869 the same Van Niekerk encountered a native African who had found a stone much bigger than the first one on the bank of the same river and, according to the story, traded five hundred sheep, ten oxen and a horse for it. It weighed 83·5 carats and was later named the Star of Africa. Prospectors, miners, merchants and adventurers poured into South Africa in search of fortunes. By the end of that year more than ten thousand people swarmed over the huge previously deserted area along the banks of the rivers Orange and Vaal.

In Griqualand West in a locality called Dorstfontein a Boer called Adrian J. van Wijk bought a farm from a certain Du Toit. One day he noticed that the plaster binding the stones in the wall contained little diamonds. The mortar had been made with mud from a pool near the farm. One of the four most famous mines in South Africa, Dutoitspan, was to rise on that site.

On each side of Du Toit's property were two farms relatively nearby. One of them called Bulfontein was owned by a certain Du Plooy, who as soon as he heard of his neighbour's fortune, had no difficulty in getting £2000 for his own land. Here arose the second famous mine of the four mentioned, the Bulfontein diamond mine. The other farm, called Vooruitzigt, belonged to the De Beer brothers who had paid £50 for their sixteen thousand acres. Being shrewder than their two neighbours, they aimed to make some real profit out of it. Their efforts were, however, unsuccessful, and they decided to sell for £6000. Later De Beer's farm was to prove the richest diamond mine of all time, the third of the most famous mines.

On a hill about two miles from the De Beer's property were camped some miners who became known as the Red Cap Company on account of the red berets they wore. One Saturday evening in July 1871, while some of them sat at a game of cards in their tent, they were joined by one of their companions who had just discovered a fistful of little diamonds. The next day the area for miles around was full of prospectors. The reddish sandy earth on which grew thick grass was about three feet deep and covered a thicker layer of limestone; under this was found a stratum of the characteristic diamond-carrying yellow clay, known as yellow ground. At first, the locality was called the Red Cap Company, then New Rush and finally Kimberley.

Early Diamond Mines In the area diamonds were found both in secondary, alluvial deposits and in primary deposits, that is in the mineral strata in which they were originally formed. Crystals of the secondary type are often found near water courses, as are primary ones if they have become dislodged, although at one time it was believed that these were only found in the deep strata of yellow clay. The size and thickness of yellow ground strata are variable (from ten to eight hundred metres in diameter and ten to twenty-five metres in depth) and are surrounded by rock walls of various geological types.

Digging was carried on in enclosures of yellow ground, called claims, for which the miners had to obtain a digging licence. These small areas were often subdivided by private agreements between the miners themselves or ceded according to their fruitfulness at greatly inflated prices. Gradually as the ground was dug away an enormous ever-deepening hole was formed, and the diamondiferous material had to be transported to the surface for the washing and sifting for crystals. At Kimberley the hole, or more properly the pipe, became so deep that electric cables had to be installed to transport the materials to the surface. Each prospector had his own, and soon the Big Hole resembled a huge spider's web.

Yellow ground is in fact the decayed upper surfaces of kimberlite, the volcanic rock in which diamonds and also other gems are found. The pipes of kimberlite, called blue ground because of its bluish colour, come from the depths of the earth's crust from sources that have never been traced. South African mines are usually about eight hundred to nine hundred metres deep, but in Kimberley, which is still mined today, depths of over twelve hundred metres have been reached. The distribution of the gems in blue ground is variable. When the diamond-bearing pipes are very deep, as at Kimberley, a vertical shaft is sunk parallel to them, and from this horizontal tunnels are drilled into the kimberlite.

Already by the end of the last century mining operations had become better organised due to centralisation under large enterprises. Gradually all the individual claims on one mine would be bought up until it was owned by a sole proprietor which brought greater benefit to the shareholders and more efficient recovery.

Cecil Rhodes and Barney Barnato At this point one must introduce the extraordinary adventures of two Englishmen who played a very important role in the development of the mining, political and financial activities of the country. The first arrived in South Africa with a Greek dictionary and £2000 borrowed from an aunt; the second with £100 and forty packets of cigarettes. One lived to the age of forty-nine and the other to forty-four, and they were to come into contact only through the conflict of their powerful financial interests.

Cecil Rhodes was born at Bishops Stortford, Hertfordshire, in 1853, one of ten children of a rural vicar. He was intended for the church, but his studies were interrupted by the breakdown of his health, and he was sent to stay with his elder brother Herbert, who was a cotton planter in Natal in South Africa. Herbert, attracted by the news of the diamond discoveries, collected together some money and set off to Colesberg Kopje where the Red Caps had discovered the mine. Cecil joined him soon afterwards, acquired a claim in the De Beer's mine and succeeded in making about £100 a week out of it. His first ingenious idea was to acquire a pump and offer it for hire to the miners for pumping out the Big Hole. By the age of twenty-one, when he returned to England to continue his studies at Oxford, his health was quite restored by the South African climate, and he was rich

Negro slaves digging and transporting diamonds, from an engraving, 1800. Civica Raccolta Bertarelli, Milan.

enough to repay the loan from his aunt and finance his own studies.

At about the same period another man, of a lower social class than Rhodes, left Southampton for Cape Town. Born at Aldgate, London, in 1852, the son of a Jewish second-hand clothes dealer in Petticoat Lane, he changed his name from Isaacs to Barnato. He, too, went off to South Africa to join an elder brother called Henry, and when he arrived at Kimberley, after walking all the way from Cape Town behind a Boer's waggon, he had only £30 and a few packets of cigarettes left. He joined up with a diamond dealer and bought himself a pony at an auction. Barnato knew that the animal had been accustomed to wait outside the doors of the miners with stones to sell, whom his previous master, one of the shrewdest diamond buyers, used to visit every evening. He let the pony direct him to the addresses so important to a buyer, enabling him to obtain personally the best material for his trading. This was the beginning of a colossal fortune.

Breaking with his partner, Barney Barnato

formed a company in association with his brother Henry and began to buy up claims at the lowest point of the Big Hole at Kimberley. By that time the yellow ground was almost exhausted, and the miners, not realising that the yellow soil was simply weathered blue ground and that it was in the latter that the greatest riches lay, moved on elsewhere, thinking the claims were exhausted. The Barnato brothers, after consulting geologists and acting on their advice, bought up claim after claim on supposedly exhausted land, so that before long they controlled a large part of the Kimberley mine. Thus when the blue ground was thoroughly investigated and found to be even richer than yellow ground their fortunes were made.

During the period when the Barnato brothers were forming their company, Rhodes, having finished his studies, had returned to South Africa, and at the time when the Barnato's activities were in full swing, he had gained control of the De Beer's mine. Not content with that, he entered into negotiations with the Barnatos for their share of the Kimberley mine. Rhodes' ambitions for South Africa stretched far beyond mere financial ones. His dream was to extend the area of British settlement in South Africa and to bring the whole colony under the rule of the British empire. He saw the riches obtained from diamond mining as the means which would give him the power to achieve this end. He later played an active role in politics, becoming first finance minister at the age of thirty-seven and then prime minister of Cape Colony. In his dealings with the Barnatos, he used all possible cunning to gain control of all the Kimberley shares against their strong opposition, yet remaining on good formal terms with them. He finally achieved his ends, making Barnato a lifetime governor of the newly formed company, De Beers Consolidated Mines.

The story of these two exceptional pioneers, together with those of numerous other adventurers and prospectors for diamonds, shows how this activity made a notable contribution to the rapid development of this vast area. **Other African Mines** In addition to the four deposits described above, discovered in the short space of six months and all situated in the area around Kimberley, many others came to

light around the same time. They were mostly of lesser importance, with the exception of Jagersfontein (discovered in 1870) about a hundred kilometres from Kimberley on a farm belonging to a widow called Visser. Her overseer one day found some garnets in the bed of a stream which skirted the farm. This encouraged him to dig still further and he found a diamond of fifty-two carats.

The widow leased concessions on the brook to prospectors for £2 a month and before long there were about four hundred people there. Finally, the woman decided to sell the property for £2000, thinking she had made a good bargain out of the transaction. The mine, still fruitful today, has revealed splendid diamonds worth millions of pounds. The Excelsior diamond, which weighs 970 carats, was found there.

Another mine of some importance was that of Welleston, discovered near Kimberley in 1890. In 1902 the pioneer Thomas Cullinan discovered a very important mine in the Transvaal about forty kilometres from Pretoria. It was later called the Premier in honour of the prime minister Cecil Rhodes. When Cullinan went to see the owner of the land, a Mr Prinsloo, to make an offer for it, he was met with a loaded rifle. Cullinan had to wait until Prinsloo died, when he was able to negotiate with the dead man's sister, who was somewhat more reasonable. The mine has proved fruitful right until today and will probably continue to be so. From it came the largest diamond ever found, the Cullinan. The mine today belongs to De Beers.

Diamond Mines in America In North America, besides sporadic diamond finds in the Californian gold fields, primary deposits have been found in rock structures similar to the South African diamond pipes, but they are mostly of industrial rather than gem standard. In a mine in the state of Arkansas called the Diamond Crater tourists are permitted to search for diamonds during the day on the payment of one and a half dollars and may keep any stones they find, which is an average of only about two stones a day. The deposit does not merit any large scale operations but the soil is turned over once a month.

In 1870 news of the discovery of diamonds spread from San Francisco. Self-styled pros-

Diamonds from the Premier mine, Pretoria.

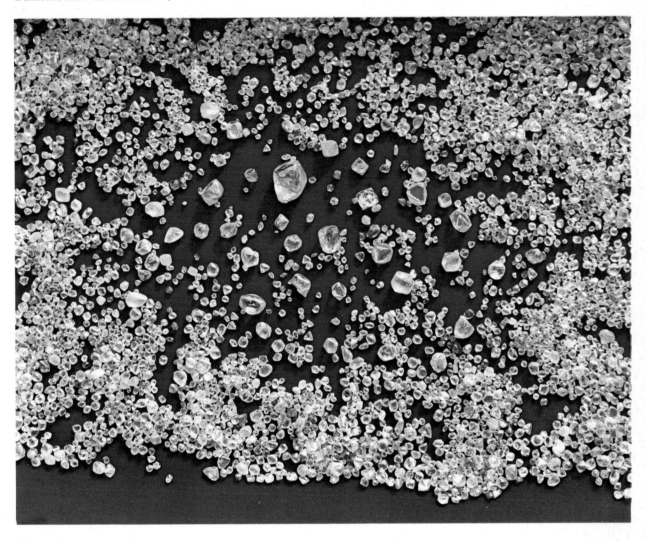

pectors put about rumours of the find of a fabulous deposit and, as proof of the truth of their assertions, placed in a bank a deposit of about eight thousand carats of rubies and diamonds, the largest of which was 108 carats. A second deposit followed the first, almost as large and equally widely publicised. Naturally information of the location of the site was sold at a high price to many people, and in the first week they found a thousand carats of diamonds and six thousand carats of rubies. Then an expedition from the Washington Geological Survey exposed the whole thing as a fraud: the diamonds were rock crystals and the rubies were garnets. The authors of the trick had scattered a few on the ground to be found by the gullible. They had made altogether the enormous sum of 900,000 dollars, far more than they had spent on the crystals and garnets.

The Modern Diamond Market The most important diamond mining companies all over the world sell their rough stones through the Diamond Corporation of London. The crystals are washed in acid, weighed and divided into those suitable for jewelry and those for industrial purposes and then despatched to London. There the gem stones are carefully classified by experienced specialists with keen eyesight by daylight in the brightest conditions surrounded by whitewashed walls. The boundary between a diamond for industrial use or for cutting is often decided by the volume of demand for one or the other. The best crystals, judged by the material, are the exceptionally fine, flawless ones. Then come the piqué, followed by medium quality, spotted and poor quality. Lastly there are the macles, which are misshapen and are really twin crystals. Melee is a 273

Different ways of cutting diamonds, from Diderot, *Recueil des planches sur les Sciences et des Arts*, 1780. Civica Raccolta Bertarelli, Milan.

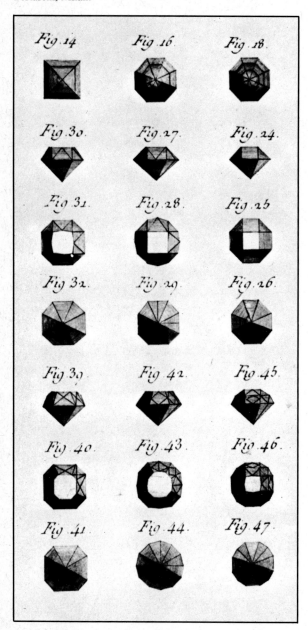

diamond sorter puts them into little heaps of equal value on his table. Having finished this difficult task, he places a certain number of stones of equal value into little white cones of paper. These cones are wrapped together in parcels. When the sellers are coming to some agreement with the buyers, they are permitted to examine the stones in the parcels and choose what they want. Twelve sales a year usually take place in London. In Johannesburg, too, several sessions are held during the year. Buyers usually carry with them a stone against which to judge and compare the colour of those which they might buy. A buyer's examination may last several days.

Some experts become so experienced that they can even tell from which mine a stone has come; the colour, shape and markings are for them signs of identification. Exceptionally large stones are always sold separately from the parcels. After this the diamonds for use in jewelry go to the cutting centres. The most important centre used to be Amsterdam, but today it is Antwerp where there are about fifty workshops. More diamonds are cut there than in the whole of the rest of the world; almost all the stones of average weight, as well as the lesser quality ones, are sent to Belgium for cutting. Good quality large stones are generally cut in America, and small ones are sent to Israel, a rapidly expanding cutting centre. West Germany too is an important centre.

Diamond Cutting A diamond cutter must have a profound understanding of the crystals and their colour. A Brazilian diamond in its natural state may appear to be covered with brown or green, but when cut may turn out to be a beautiful blue-white, while, on the other hand, a well-shaped apparently white crystal may on cutting reveal a yellowish tinge. Often the cutter will polish a 'window' on each side of the rough stone (which is greyish in colour) in order to examine the inside.

As has been said, the diamond is the hardest of all known minerals, but this is not to confuse hardness with fragility. A brilliant-cut diamond would split if dropped on the ground, accidentally hitting the crystal at a point of cleavage. The part which is broken off will leave a smooth bright surface parallel to the facets of the octa-

term for an assortment of small mixed diamonds with anything from between ten and fifty to the carat. The tiniest ones are called sand. The experts really qualified to distinguish and classify diamonds for colour are few in number. It is sometimes difficult to identify the perfect colourless, flawless diamonds, which are the most highly prized. There are various shades of capes and browns, the former being shades of yellow and the second brown. The diamonds which are of a definite yellow hue are known as fancy diamonds and constitute a separate category.

274   In the process of classifying the stones the

Cutting and polishing diamonds, from Diderot, *Recueil des planches sur les Sciences et des Arts*, 1780. Civica Raccolta Bertarelli, Milan.

hedron. The trained eye of the cutter knows how to seek out these points and use them for cutting.

In antiquity gems in general and diamonds in particular were chosen for their size and regularity of form. Later they began to polish them and to cut them slightly. For many centuries it was considered most important not to sacrifice the size by cutting except when a more regular shape was desired. The ancient saying that 'a diamond can only be cut by another diamond' suggests that already in remote times they understood the art of cutting to some extent. Therefore, if it was not very often applied, it must have been due to questions of taste. The four large diamonds in the brooch on Charlemagne's cloak are uncut octahedrons called *pointes naives*. Similar settings are encountered in royal jewelry in later epochs also. The inventories of Duke Louis of Anjou mentioned shield and heart-shaped diamonds, and we know that in Nuremburg around 1368 there was a workshop for polishing diamonds. Further progress was made in the art of cutting the stone at the beginning of the 15th century in Paris.

It is said that the Bruges lapidary, Ludwig van Berquem, cut diamonds with diamond chips in 1475, but this was doubtless a perfection of a technique rather than an invention.

At that time cut diamonds, even very simple ones, were a great rarity. There is some evidence that around the middle of the 16th century the Venetian lapidary, Ortensio Borgi, worked in India and cut the Great Mogul diamond. We also know that they had discovered a means of pulverising diamonds.

In the same century, the simple rose cut was introduced. The next stage of development was not until 1640, the year in which Cardinal Mazarin commissioned the first brilliant cut (also called the Mazarin or single cut). Towards the end of the century, the Venetian Vicenzo Peruzzi discovered the triple brilliant cut, and this is still used today. Apart from the two tables, a single brilliant has sixteen facets, a double one has thirty-two and a triple one fifty-six.

The master lapidary's work consists of three stages: cleaving, bruting and polishing. The

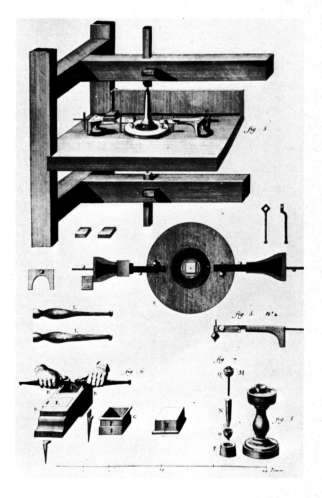

275

cleaving reduces the stone to suitable dimensions for further work. Once he has examined the stone for the natural cleavage planes, which will at the same time retain as much of its weight as possible, he mounts the stone on a solid base with special glue. Then a groove is made at the cleavage point by careful filing with progressively sharper diamonds until it is large enough to insert a fine steel wedge. A sharp blow correctly aimed at this wedge is enough to cleave the stone. The operation is repeated, changing the position of the stone according to the size desired.

This is followed by the bruting process, in which the diamond is held securely on a chuck lathe and ground and shaped by another rough diamond mounted on a long stick which is held under the operator's arm. Of course, all the diamond dust and chips rescued from the operation are gathered for further use.

Grinding or polishing the facets brings the stone to its final shape. The remaining facets are ground and any errors are corrected. This is done with a grinding machine consisting of a flat wheel called a scaif, which is smeared with a compound of olive oil and diamond dust. This spins horizontally as the diamond is held against it in a mechanical dop (an old Dutch word meaning hold), which looks rather like the arm of a gramophone needle. The master cutter carefully controls and adjusts the position of the stone according to the cuts desired.

The angles and shapes of diamonds and other gem stones are mathematically worked out so as to produce the maximum fire and brilliance from reflected light. Diamond cuts start from the octahedron shape, a geometric figure like two four-sided pyramids joined together at their bases; exceptions are the rose and table cuts. In addition to the single, double and full brilliant cuts, which have been mentioned, the other principal cuts are: round, American, classical, emerald (step or trap), marquise or navette (boat-shaped), square, pear, briolette, rose, table, half moon, triangular, star or Caire, French star, baguette. Less common are the arrow baguette, long hexagon, shield, key stone, kite, heart and old mine. The number of facets may vary from sixteen on a single brilliant to 156 on a star cut.

Great Mogul Information about this stone comes mostly from the descriptions by the traveller and merchant, Jean-Baptiste Tavernier (born in Paris, died in Moscow, 1605-89), in his *Voyages en Turquie, en Perse et aux Indes* (1679). It is thought to have been found between 1650-58 at the Golconda mines and originally weighed $787\frac{1}{2}$ carats. Tavernier also made drawings of it and claimed to have seen it in the treasure of Aurangzeb, belonging to the great mogul of Delhi. It was entrusted to the Venetian cutter Ortensio Borgis, who attempted to give it a rose cut in the shape of half an egg; however, it was so badly done that the stone was reduced to a mere 280 carats. The mogul was so furious that Borgis was deprived of all his possessions and was indeed lucky not to lose his head. All trace of the stone seems to have been lost after the first half of the 18th century.

Some authorities claim that the Koh-i-Noor is really the Great Mogul, and there is also a theory that the Koh-i-Noor and the Orloff are both fragments of it.

Koh-i-Noor The documented history of this stone (the name means Mountain of Light) appears to have begun in the 14th century when it was clumsily rose cut and weighed 186 carats. It belonged to the great moguls of India until 1739 when India was invaded by the Persians, led by Nadir Shah. He conquered Delhi, made the mogul his prisoner and seized the crown jewels. The story goes that he found that the Koh-i-Noor was missing and, hearing that the mogul always wore it hidden in the folds of his turban, he devised an elaborate plan whereby at a ceremony of friendship, the mogul was obliged to exchange turbans with him. Thus he obtained the diamond. The stone evidently brought Nadir Shah ill-fortune because he was assassinated during his return journey to Persia. The diamond, after many vicissitudes, came into the hands of the East India Company in 1849 as partial indemnity for the Sikh Wars in the Punjab. The company presented it to Queen Victoria who, thinking the stone lacked brilliance, decided in 1852 to have it recut. She entrusted the task to the foremost cutter of the time, a Mr Voorsanger of the firm of Coster in Amsterdam. Little additional brilliance was achieved and the stone was reduced to 109 carats. Queen Victoria wore the diamond in the form of a brooch and, later it was set in the Queen's Crown made for Queen Mary in 1911 and worn by Queen Elizabeth the Queen Mother at the coronation in 1952.

Orloff This diamond was first heard of as one of the eyes of a temple statue of Brahma at Mysore in India. It was stolen by a French soldier who gained admittance to the temple one night by disguising himself as a religious fanatic. He fled to Madras where he sold the stone to an English captain for £3500. The captain resold it in England for 300,000 francs,

and after several more changes of hands it was bought by Prince Gregory Orloff for £90,000 through the Russian crown jeweler Lazarov. Orloff presented it to Empress Catherine the Great in an attempt to regain her favour. Though she still spurned Orloff, she kept the diamond, having it mounted in the imperial sceptre, where it still survives today in the treasury of the USSR.

Some experts suggest that the Orloff may, in fact, be part or the whole of the vanished Great Mogul described by Tavernier, as it is similar in shape to descriptions of the Great Mogul. Its weight is between 194 and 199·6 carats.

Florentine There are many legends about this important gem which weighs 137·27 carats. One is that it belonged to Charles the Bold, who lost it in battle. Another version is that it belonged in antiquity to an Indian king conquered by the Portuguese in the 16th century. The rough stone was acquired in 1601 by Ferdinand, duke of Tuscany, for 35,500 scudi. It was entrusted to a Venetian lapidary living in Florence, Pompeo Studentoli, who gave it a double rose cut in a drop shape. The gem passed to the Hapsburg crown jewels through Francis of Lorraine, where it remained until the Germans invaded Austria and took it. It was restored after the war by the Americans.

Regent or Pitt This stone was found in the Partial mines in India in 1701. The 410-carat rough stone was acquired by Sir Thomas Pitt, governor of Madras, for £35,000 and sent to London where it was cut into a brilliant. Although 60% of the weight was lost, the resulting gem is so beautiful that it is one of the loveliest in existence. It was then bought by the duke of Orleans, regent of France, for about £175,000. During the revolutionary activities in France, it disappeared in the famous robbery of the crown jewels in 1792, but was later recovered when the thieves were caught. It was withheld when the crown jewels were put up for auction in 1886 and is today on exhibition in the Louvre. During the Nazi occupation of Paris in the Second World War it was hidden for safety in a pile of plaster behind the stone panel of a chimneypiece in the château at Chambord.

Shah of Persia This diamond is strangely shaped like an elongated irregular prism, only partially cut and with an incision of about half a millimetre towards one end. It is possible that it is the one which, according to Tavernier, decorated the canopy over the great mogul's throne. The Russian scholar, Fersman, has discovered that the inscriptions engraved on three of its facets dated 1591, 1641 and 1824, refer to three successive owners: two shahs and one sultan. The diamond weighs 88·7 carats and is a first-class example. Today it is in the great diamond collection in the Moscow Kremlin.

Sancy The story of this fifty-four-carat diamond is long and complicated. It has hardly been used as a jewel at all, but has often provided credit for raising troops, and during its long history it has, among other things, aided the acquisition of a kingdom and caused the sacrifice of a man's life.

The gem was found in India where it was cut in the traditional manner; then began its long journey along the caravan routes to the West. It finally reached Constantinople where it was bought in 1570 by Sancy, French ambassador to Turkey. Sancy returned to France where Catherine de' Medici was ruling in the name of her weak son Henry III. Sancy lent the diamond to the king, in return for which he was appointed colonel-in-chief of a regiment of twelve thousand Swiss soldiers. Henry III was assassinated, nominating Henry of Navarre as his successor before he died. Sancy was now made superintendent of finance and used his position to redeem his diamond. As the financial situation in France was at that time critical, Sancy decided to send the stone abroad. He entrusted it in great secrecy to a faithful servant, but despite all the precautions the news leaked out; the man was attacked during his journey, and in order not to surrender the precious stone he swallowed it, and was killed by his frustrated attackers. As soon as Sancy heard of this, he set off for the place where his faithful servant was buried, and, suspecting what he might have done to save the diamond, had the body cut open and thus recovered the stone.

Henry IV of France later wanted to buy the diamond, but did not have the resources. Sancy found a way of sending the stone to London to his brother, the ambassador to England, and he sold it to Queen Elizabeth for sixty thousand scudi. It passed to Charles I who, finding himself in grave financial difficulties at one point, sent his consort Queen Henrietta Maria to Holland with some of the crown jewels, including Henry VIII's ruby necklace, the Mirror of Portugal diamond and the Sancy, in an attempt to pawn them. She managed to pledge them to the duke of Eperon who later, not finding the pledges redeemed, sold them all to Cardinal Mazarin. The cardinal was said to have loved precious gems even more than his God; he already had a collection of eighteen large diamonds. On his death, he left them all to Louis XIV in order, so it was claimed, that the king would pardon all his misdeeds. The Sun King's collection of a thousand or more gems contained some of the most beautiful in the western hemisphere, including the Blue Diamond sold to him by Tavernier. In this period the Sancy was used in its true function as a jewel; both Maria Leczinska and Marie Antoinette wore it mounted in different ways.

On 17th September 1792 the royal *garde meuble*, where the crown jewels were kept in eleven closets, was emptied by the revolutionaries. This was in fact a major loss in capital to the country, but the citizens were too busy sending aristocrats to the guillotine to take much notice of the news of the robbery. In the anxious search which ensued, the Regent diamond was found in an attic, the Great Hortensia in the roof of a house in les Halles, the Duke of Guise diamond in the house of a certain Tavenal, and the police, tipped off by a sixteen-year-old fortune teller, found another heap of jewels buried beneath a tree in Avenue Montaigne. Nothing further was heard of the Blue Diamond, the Mirror of Portugal or the Sancy. Later the Sancy reappeared in the hands of the marquise Iranda at Madrid, who pledged it to pay the hussars of La Selle at Rivoli and the Kellerman cavalry at Marengo. It then became the property of Queen Maria Louisa of Spain, and Goya portrayed her with the jewel.

In 1822, it was acquired by Prince Anatole Demidoff, who took it back to Russia, and by 1865 it was in the hands of a Bombay jeweler. Finally, in 1906, Lord William Waldorf Astor bought it in Paris as a present for his daughter-in-law, who had it mounted in a tiara.

Reconstructions of six famous diamonds. *left to right starting at the top* Orloff, Regent or Pitt, Cullinan, Florentine, Koh-i-Noor, Grand Mogul. Museo di Storia della Scienza, Milan.

Hope This is a very rare sapphire-blue, brilliant-cut diamond which is probably the one which Tavernier brought from India and sold to Louis XIV. It disappeared with the Regent and Sancy in the famous robbery of the French crown jewels during the Revolution and as such it was never seen again.

Then in 1830, a remarkable blue gem weighing $44\frac{1}{2}$ carats appeared on the London market and was bought by the London banker, Sir Thomas Hope. It is now accepted that this stone was cut from the original 112-carat Tavernier blue diamond, which was so well known that the thieves could not have disposed of it in its original shape. There is also a Brunswick blue diamond, identical in colour to the Hope and weighing $13\frac{3}{4}$ carats, which is probably the other part of the Tavernier diamond.

The diamond remained in the Hope family until their jewels were sold in 1867. It then changed hands several times until finally it came into the possession of Edward B. McLean of Chicago.

In 1949, it was bought by the famous New York jeweler Harry S. Winston, who had one of the largest diamond collections in the world. He exhibited it in Milan in 1956, and in 1958 he presented it to the Smithsonian Institute in Washington.

Pigott This diamond, which weighs somewhere between forty-seven and eighty-five carats, was brought to England in 1775 from India by Lord George Pigott, governor of Madras. It appears that the governor was willing to accept valuable gifts from the maharajah in return for protecting his territory from invasion.

The arrangement displeased the British government, and Pigott was recalled and thrown into prison. The stone was inherited by his brothers who sold it in 1801. It passed into the hands of Napoleon's mother, and later it arrived how is not known, in the possession of Ali Pasha, renowned as the tyrant of Yannina. On his deathbed this semi-independent despot, believing the time had come to make his peace with God, called to his side his faithful follower, a French mercenary, and giving him the diamond, ordered him to destroy it together with his wife. No more is known about the stone,

but it is known that the soldier's wife, Vasilkee, lived a long time afterwards in great comfort.

The Empress Eugénie This is a fifty-one-carat diamond which belonged to Catherine the Great of Russia, who presented it to her favourite Potemkin. Later it was sold to Napoleon III, who gave it to Empress Eugénie as a wedding present. It is now believed to be in the collection of the Gaikwar of Baroda.

Famous Diamonds of Brazilian Origin
Star of the South This $245\frac{1}{2}$-carat diamond was found by a Negress in 1853 at the Bagagem mine, Minas Gerais. After cutting in Amsterdam, it weighed 125 carats and was bought by the Gaikwar of Baroda.

English Dresden This $72\frac{1}{2}$-carat diamond, found at Bagagem and cut into an oval brilliant, was named after its first owner, the London merchant E. Dresden. It is now in the Gaikwar of Baroda's collection.

President Vargas This 726-carat stone was found in alluvial deposits of the Rio San Antonio in the Bagagem region in 1938. It was acquired by the American jeweler Harry Winston and cut into twenty-nine pieces of between ten and forty-eight carats each.

Diamonds from South Africa
Cullinan On 25th January 1905 a superintendent of the Premier Mining Company in the Transvaal saw something glittering in the distance while he was making a routine check. On closer inspection he dragged from the ground a diamond which weighed $1\frac{1}{3}$ pounds avoirdupois. It was the biggest ever found; one side of the stone was smooth and some experts believe that the stone was part of a still larger one which had been split by natural processes. It weighed 3106 carats and was named after the president of the Premier Mining Company. It was acquired by the Transvaal government, who presented it to King Edward VII on his birthday in appreciation of the colony's newly acquired autonomy. To foil any would-be international thieves, the stone was sent to London through the ordinary post.

The firm of I. J. Asscher and Company of Amsterdam was entrusted with the cutting of the stone. After months of study it was decided to cleave the crystal into two parts, and thus two crystals of 2029 and 1068 carats were obtained; they were ultimately cut into nine large stones of the first water. The largest of these is a pear-shaped brilliant with seventy-four facets weighing 530 carats. It is called Cullinan I and is the largest diamond in the world. It is set in the Royal Sceptre. The second is a rectangular brilliant with sixty-six facets weighing 317·4 carats, making it the second largest in the world. It is set in the band of the Imperial State Crown.

Cullinan III and IV, 94·5 carats and 63 carats respectively, are set in the Queen's Crown. There were also five other large diamonds used

The Briolette diamond. An unusual Indian diamond in an elongated drop shape. Harry Winston collection, New York.

in personal jewelry, and ninety-six small brilliants. All the jewels can be seen in the crown jewel collection at the Tower of London. The cutting took eight months and 67·75% of the original weight was lost.

Excelsior This blueish-white gem of the first water was found in 1893 in the Jagersfontein mine. Weighing 995 carats, it was the largest in the world before the discovery of the Cullinan. It was found by a Negro who received in reward £500, a horse with harness and some pistols. The firm of Asscher was entrusted with the cutting of the diamond, obtaining from it ten brilliants, weighing in all 358 carats; the largest weighed 69·68 carats and the smallest 9·82. Some other small stones were also obtained, bringing the total used in jewelry to 379·75 carats, with a loss of 62·44% of the natural weight. Opinions vary as to whether the gems were put on the open market or form part of the English crown jewels.

Jubilee or Reitz This diamond weighing 650·8 carats was found at Jagersfontein in 1895. It was at first named after F. W. Reitz, president of the Orange Free State, but was renamed the Jubilee in 1897 in honour of the sixtieth anniversary of Queen Victoria's accession. It was made into a large cushion-cut gem of 245·35 carats, which was exhibited in Paris in 1900, and a drop-shape one of 13·34 carats, both of the first water. The rest of the diamond probably produced some more small stones which would have been used in jewelry.

Victoria, Imperial or Great White This diamond of 469 carats appeared on the London market in 1884 and is the type of stone found at the Jagersfontein mine. It was cut in Amsterdam to an oval brilliant of 185 carats and sold to the Nizam of Hyderabad. There was also a round stone of twenty carats.

Star of South Africa or Dudley When found in 1869 at Zanfontein on the Orange River it weighed 83½ carats. Cut to an ovoid brilliant, it was reduced to 46½ carats. It was acquired by Countess Dudley.

VIII

1870
to the present day

In the second half of the 19th century industrialisation and new ways of manufacturing were beginning to affect ever-wider areas. The small cottage and craft industries, often carried on by one family in their shop, were being gradually absorbed into the new large organisations. Industry brought other momentous changes too: coaches were replaced by trains, sailing ships gave way to steam, electricity took the place of candlelight, and bicycles were used instead of gigs.

Luxury was more ostentatiously displayed than in the past: the old Roman and Florentine palaces were reproduced throughout Europe, as were the châteaux of the Loire, Louis XV furniture and anything else which would contribute to an appearance of richness and nobility.

The new mechanical methods of industrialisation were admirably adapted to supplying the requirements of society. Jewelry was affected too on all levels. Apart from mass-produced articles, a factor of great influence in the history of jewelry was a new type of high quality jewelry shop that came into existence.

Fabergé Among the first firms to respond to these new demands was that of Fabergé, the Russian jeweler. Peter Carl Fabergé was born in St Petersburg on 30th May 1846. After thorough studies in Russia, Dresden and Frankfurt, and educational journeys to London, Italy and Paris, he joined the family firm, which his father, Gustave, had started in 1842. His first colleague and teacher was the Finn, Peter Hiskias Pendin (died 1882), who had worked with his father, and for whom he always felt the deepest regard and gratitude. A close examination of Fabergé's work in all its complexity makes clear that his visit to Paris had left a marked imprint on his style, as did his many trips to Dresden where he frequently visited the Grüne Gewörbe Museum.

On his father's retirement Carl, aged only twenty-four, took over the running of the family business. He began by acquiring new, more spacious premises on the Bolshaya Morskaya Street and reorganised the factory along progressive, modern lines. Later his younger brother Agathon, a fine sculptor and painter, collaborated with him, and later still his two sons Eugene and Alexander joined him also.

René Lalique, pendant, *c.* 1900. The woman's face is white carved stone; the long flowing gold hair is tied by two blue fleurs de lys and supports a large baroque pearl. Musée des Art Décoratifs, Paris.

283

The peak of Fabergé's career came at the World Exhibition in Paris in 1900 when he displayed for the first time all the imperial Easter eggs he had made, plus a selection of other 'luxurious objects', and was proclaimed Master and awarded the Légion d'Honneur. In addition to the tsars Alexander III and Nicholas II and the tsarinas, his other important clients included members of English and Swedish royalty and the king of Siam, and he had business contacts in India and China.

In 1887 he opened a branch in Moscow; in 1890 at Odessa, in 1903 in London and in 1905 in Kiev. Around 1900 the firm employed more than five hundred workers. After the 1917 revolution, the firm ceased to exist, the London firm having already closed in 1915 because of the war and the Kiev one in 1910.

Before beginning a new piece, Fabergé would call together the heads of the departments in the factory to discuss all the details of the execution and how the work should be divided between the goldsmiths, enamellers, jewelers and engravers.

In addition to jewelry Fabergé's products included small items of furniture, all kinds of boxes, little animal sculptures in semiprecious materials decorated with gold and gems, various useful articles, frames, flowering branches in vases or baskets, clocks and mechanical pieces. His most famous works are the jeweled eggs which were presented by the tsars to the tsarinas at Easter. The first of these was made in 1884 and was followed by about fifty others, the last being made in 1917. Each has a different theme either taken from nature or imaginative; they are miracles of enamelling and fine gem setting.

Refinement is the distinctive characteristic of all Fabergé's work: one object alone might have four different shades of gold, exquisitely blended and contrasted with the colours of the enamels and the gems. The surfaces of the metals too would receive varying finishes (polished, matt, satin) according to the material used and its position in the particular piece.

Enamels were his particular speciality, above all the different finishes which could be obtained: opaque, semipolished or brilliant, or the colour effects which varied according to the angle of the light or vision. His work in this

sphere achieved results only comparable with beautiful 18th-century pieces. He often used enamels on jewelry; some of his brooches are made of little elaborately enamelled panels framed in gold Rococo tracery, with a diamond in the centre. Others are in the form of bows interwoven with diamonds with perhaps a large pearl in the centre.

Fabergé used a greater variety of precious and semiprecious stones than any other jeweler in history. He preferred to set sapphires, emeralds and rubies *en cabochon*, and diamonds were almost always rose cut. As far as stylistic derivations were concerned, Fabergé had a strong liking for the Louis XVI period and also the 'old Russian style', which is a mixture of Byzantine and Baroque, but there are also numerous works inspired by the Italian Renaissance, the Rococo and the Middle Ages.

As a demonstration of his great skill, Fabergé made a copy of a Sassanian bracelet of the Hellenistic period from the Scythian treasure discovered at Kerch in the Crimea. The two works, the copy and the original, were presented to Tsar Alexander III, who was unable to distinguish which was which. A *rivière* made of thirty-three large diamonds of superb quality, known only from a photograph, shows the gems supported solely by tiny claws, each setting linked to the other by fine gold chains. Other groups of jewels using diamonds or small coloured stones, usually rubies and emeralds, were made in the form of garlands of leaves, zigzags, bows and briolette-cut pendants, pins with pendants, necklaces and *Sévigné* ornaments. Illustrated catalogues were printed so that sales could be made by post.

Fabergé contributed to all the most interesting forms of decorative art which were known at that time. His imagination was also captured by the fascination of the Far East, and its motifs often figure in his jewelry. He was a passionate collector of Japanese carved *netsuké*, and this is reflected in the engraved stones, particularly those representing animals, which formed an important part of his artistic output. At the beginning of the 20th century he adapted the fashionable Art Nouveau ideas to his designs, reproducing its floral forms with exquisite elegance in many of his pieces. He always main-

tained the highest standards, and his eclecticism and versatility were always tempered by a rare combination of profound knowledge and understanding of form and balance. His extraordinarily wide knowledge of a vast range of precious and semiprecious materials, always most carefully selected, was matched only by the technical standard which he achieved.

Fabergé and his factory were swept away by the 1917 revolution. Fabergé himself escaped to Switzerland where he died on 24th September 1920 at the Hotel Bellevue, La Rosiaz near Lausanne. His son Agathon was commissioned by the Soviet government to restore the crown jewels, but in 1928 he too left the country.

Art Nouveau The 19th-century tendency of reviving styles of the past had by the end of the century brought weariness to decorative art forms. Every possible avenue of repetition and imitation had been explored, until all art de-

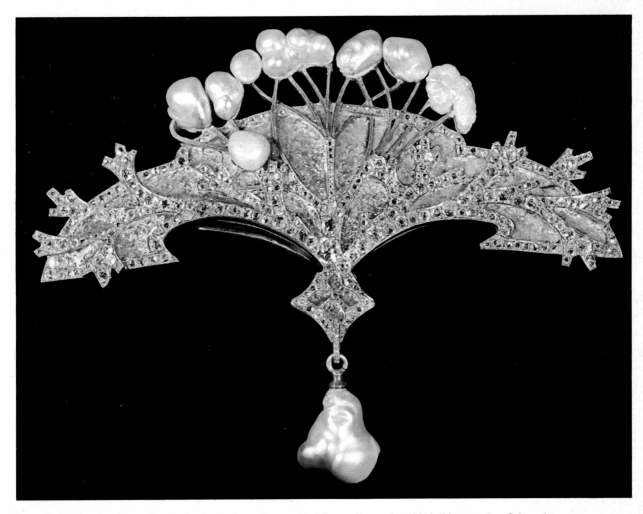

Peter Carl Fabergé, gold pendant in the shape of a snail suspended from a diamond studded ribbon, *c.* 1890. Schmuckmuseum, Pforzheim.

285

generated into a sort of unsatisfactory pastiche. It was perhaps one of the merits of the industrial revolution that its new efficiency caused the rejection of the old historic mannerisms in favour of a search for new original forms more appropriate to the society which was evolving.

The first of these movements concerned with the linking of industry to art began in England. Its leader was the painter-craftsman William Morris (1834-96), who considered the linking of functional and aesthetic considerations very important even in articles of every-day use. Another man interested in the same ideas was the Belgian architect and designer Henry van de Velde (1863-1957), who at that time had begun his career as a designer of tapestries, book decorations and furniture. He later designed the interior of the decorative art shop opened in 1896 by the Hamburg art merchant Siegfried Bing in Paris. It was called Art Nouveau, which was, of course, the French name for the new ideas in the decorative arts and architecture. But even earlier in London, where the young architect and decorator Arthur H. Mackmurdo (1851-1942) more than anyone else encouraged the new style, another art dealer, Arthur Liberty, displayed in 1875 the new-style artistic products in his shop.

In Germany the art magazine *Die Jugend* (which began publication in 1896) was the most enthusiastic propagator of the new trends, which became known in the German-speaking countries as the *Jugendstil*. In Italy, it was called the floral style or more snobbishly, the Liberty style. There were other names for this art movement: in France, the *style 1900, métro, coup de fouet*; in England, the Morris style, Yachting style or Glasgow style; and in German-speaking countries, *Sezession, Lilienstil* and *Wellenstil*. In France, Art Nouveau developed in Paris and also in Nancy, where Emile Gallé, known chiefly for his glass, had a large following.

Jewelry lent itself very well to Art Nouveau treatment. During the Second Empire the most important considerations in jewelry had been the purity of the stones and their composition. There was now a reaction against this and against imitations of ancient styles. Art Nouveau introduced many materials adapted to its symbolic or decorative ideas: bronze, glass,

René Lalique, a pendant brooch, representing a woman surrounded by lilies. It is made of carved ivory, gold, enamel, brilliants and a pink drop baroque pearl. Michel Périnet collection, Paris.

ivory and mother-of-pearl. The materials were not used merely for their intrinsic value but for their chromatic possibilities.

Symbolism, abstraction, vegetable and animal elements were the basis of expression of Art Nouveau, while the chief subjects were flowers (particularly lilies), thistles, women, geometric figures, butterflies, serpents and insects. Compositions were often asymmetrical, with wide use of enamels and few precious stones. The predominant influence in the figurative work was the romantic English painter

L. Gautriat, chain with a pendant in the shape of a peacock, *c.* 1900. It is made of gold, enamel, brilliants and moonstones, and has a drop pearl hanging from the bottom. Schmuckmuseum, Pforzheim.

William Blake; while in the abstract motifs and the designs of asymmetric and sculptural curves the influence of Celtic art and so-called auricula style of late 18th-century German goldsmiths is in evidence. Horticultural motifs as well as naturalistic ones were inspired by the movements of sea algae and by two-dimensional patterns in Japanese graphic art. There was a predominance of wavy lines which gave rise to the expressions *style fouet* and *style nouilles*.

Art Nouveau seems to be an anachronism in the world of the industrial revolution, which attempted to solve its aesthetic problems with rational ideas in keeping with the social evolution. Instead Art Nouveau ideas exploded in anti-structural and anti-static conceptions. From the Arts and Crafts movement it took only the innovatory urge and certain elements which lent themselves to its violent reaction from academicism. Its ideas centred on the instability of form and dynamism of line, accentuated by clear colours.

Lalique, Vever and Mucha René Lalique (1860-1945), the Parisian goldsmith and jeweler,

René Lalique, necklace with a large plaque decorated with leaves and hazel-nuts, 1900. It is made of gold, enamel, diamonds and precious stones. Musée des Arts Décoratifs, Paris.

had the most profound influence on his contemporaries in Europe, and his works exhibited at the Salon du Champ Mars in 1895 attracted much controversy. Art Nouveau greatly raised the artistic level of jewelry, which had been dominated for more than a century by designs which, for all their skill and nobility, never achieved a truly creative expression. Lalique personified the Art Nouveau artist-jeweler.

Often he used a specific theme in his creations. A corsage ornament by him (Gulbenkian collection, Lisbon) which was worn by Sarah Bernhardt consists of a long, flexible stylised lizard, with two enormous clawed feet, about to swallow a dragonfly in the form of a young woman whose nude body rises halfway out of the jaws of the horrible beast; in place of the woman's arms are long fine wings. Gold, enamels and chrysophrase are the materials out of which this large composition is made. Lalique achieved interesting colour effects with engraved and satined glass in his exquisite jewels. From glass and enamel he made the wasps on a hair ornament, which consists of a three-pronged branch, with a group of stylised flowers at the end of each branch from which insects are sucking the nectar (Musée des Arts Décoratifs, Paris). The serpent, with its complex contortions, was another of Lalique's principle themes.

Art Nouveau jewelry showed certain similarities in its taste in decoration and use of enamels to the Renaissance. It had its own symbolic repertoire. The pastel blues and greens of such stones as opals were associated with bad luck; frightening animals such as serpents, screech owls, vampires and bats were frequent; and the figures of enigmatic, dreamy women of an idealised type occur in Art Nouveau work. Every design of this era seems to have been conceived to render homage to women.

The jewelers Georges Fouquet (1850-1929) and Henri Vever (1854-1942) differed from Lalique in that they expressed themselves in more synthetic and geometric forms. A pendant by Vever (Musée des Arts Décoratifs, Paris) shows the bust of a woman with long flowing hair wearing a diamond helmet and holding lilies in her hand. The design has a vaguely triangular shape, and the base is bordered with

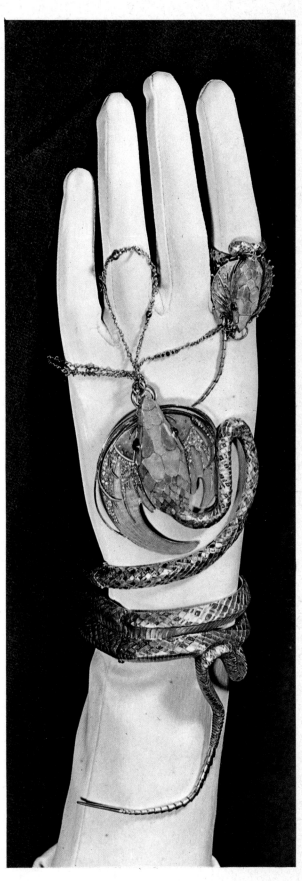

289

Georges Fouquet after a design by Alphonse Mucha, Sarah Bernhardt's bracelet and ring. The head of the snake is carved opal; the eyes are cabochon rubies; the coils are *champlevé* enamel. Michel Périnet collection, Paris.

an abstract design in various coloured enamels. This, together with another pendant called Sylvia, which shows a woman in the form of a butterfly seen from behind, are the two most representative and best-known pieces of Vever.

The Czechoslovakian painter and graphic designer Alphonse Mucha (1860-1939), who worked in Paris, produced various jewelry designs applying his lively talent for illustration to precious metals and gems.

Sezession The manifestations of Art Nouveau in France and Belgium (Philippe Wolfers 1858-1929), though only slightly different from each other in as much as they reflected the individual personalities of their creators, were quite different from the Sezession movement in German-speaking countries. In its chief centres at the beginning of the 20th century, Vienna and Pforzheim, the more abstract aspects of Art Nouveau were in the ascendancy; naturalistic motifs were abandoned for abstract and geometric ornamentation. Some of the decorative solutions and use of colour which characterise

the work of Klimt and Schiele were in the Sezessionist style. A single pendant by Kolo-man Moser (Oesterreichishes Museum für Angewandte Kunst, Vienna) consists of irregular cabochon turquoises, corals, lapis lazuli, agate, amethysts, mother-of-pearl, moonstone, sapphires, emeralds, opals and amber set in an octagonal design.

The new shapes which attachment to the Sezessionist style brought to jewelry, for example abstract lines, were most widespread in the Scandinavian countries. This tendency towards abstract forms, which foreshadow those of a later period, left their stylistic imprint on the decorative arts which were shown at the Paris Exhibition of 1925.

Tiffany In the United States Art Nouveau found in Louis Comfort Tiffany (1848-1933) one of its most individual interpreters. Tiffany was the greatest American decorator of his time. He started as a painter, but his lively interest in all branches of the decorative arts, from wrought iron to embroidery, and from stained glass to

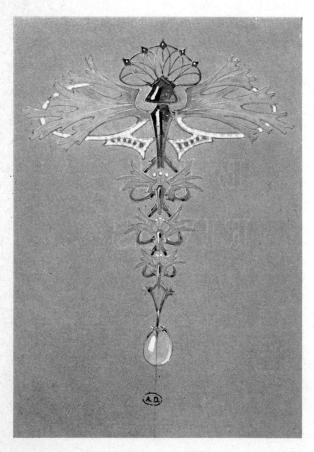 

Georges Fouquet *left* Preliminary drawing for *right* Gold and enamel pendant with a baroque pearl. Michel Périnet collection, Paris. Drawing, Musée des Arts Décoratifs, Paris.

Paul and Henri Vever, the Silvia Pendant, a young girl with dragonfly's wings, Paris, 1900. It is made of gold, enamel, agates, brilliants and rubies. Musée des Arts Décoratifs, Paris.

Paul and Henri Vever, gold and enamel necklace with a removable pendant which can be used as a brooch, *c.* 1900. The pendant is in the form of a young woman's head surrounded by gold branches with pearl flowers and a pendant amethyst. Michel Périnet collection, Paris.

René Lalique, brooch in the shape of a young woman's head surrounded by swallows, Paris, 1901. It is made of gold and enamel and has a baroque pearl. Schmuckmuseum, Pforzheim.

Eugène Feuillâtre, a young woman's head with dragonfly's wings. The head is opal; the wings are translucent enamel with silver scales; below the wings are three cabochon moonstones surrounded by diamonds. Michel Périnet collection, Paris.

mosaic furniture, resulted in all sorts of large-scale artistic undertakings. His most important contributions were the vases in his new oxidised iridescent glass, which he made in flowing shapes designed with great technical skill. In his jewelry Tiffany was at first fascinated by oriental and Byzantine ideas and colours, which he adapted to Art Nouveau forms; later he became interested in Lalique's French Symbolism, imbuing it with his own personal style; and finally a necklace in the Metropolitan Museum, New York, expresses with exquisite grace the Sezessionist style.

While this important new movement was trying to establish a closer collaboration between artists and craftsmen and between designers and industrialists, jewelry which satisfied bourgeois taste continued to be made throughout Europe. Imitations of past styles, using valuable stones as the main part of the design, were still as popular as ever.

The new trends once again gave prominence to gold and the goldsmiths' work. As in the fine arts, the revitalisation of jewelry was based on a reaction against the conservatism of the academies.

Pearls From the end of the 19th century until today pearls have enjoyed a greater popularity than ever in the past. Pearl production has been considerably increased by the introduction of cultivation. The history of cultured pearls goes back to the 13th century when a Chinese of an inquisitive nature attempted to insert metal fragments, pieces of mother-of-pearl or tiny Buddha images between the mantle and the shell of a mollusc, which was then replaced in the sea where it could be watched. After waiting patiently for two years, it was found that the little pieces of foreign matter which had been inserted had become encased in layers of mother-of-pearl. This practice became widespread and was carried on for centuries, but it was not until the beginning of this century that methods of producing perfectly spherical cultured pearls were discovered; up till then the pearls produced had always been attached to the shell. It was a Japanese, Kokichi Mikimoto (1858-1954), who, carrying on work started by predecessors, perfected the methods and became a legendary figure.

294

Koloman Moser. Oesterrichisches Museum für Angewandte Kunst, Vienna.

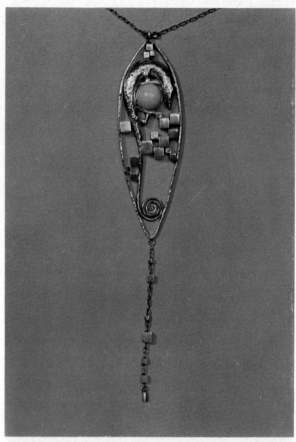

Henri van de Velde, gold pendant with a blue stone, about 1900. Bibliothéque Royale, Brussels.

It was easy for Mikimoto and his followers to organise sea beds in sheltered areas in order to ensure ideal conditions. There, from suitable molluscs the minute spheres of mother-of-pearl embedded in the secretive epithelium were made and were introduced between the valves of a live mollusc and returned to one of numer-

Sezession-style necklace of gold and precious stones, Vienna, 1920/25. Osterreichisches Museum für Angewandte Kunst, Vienna.

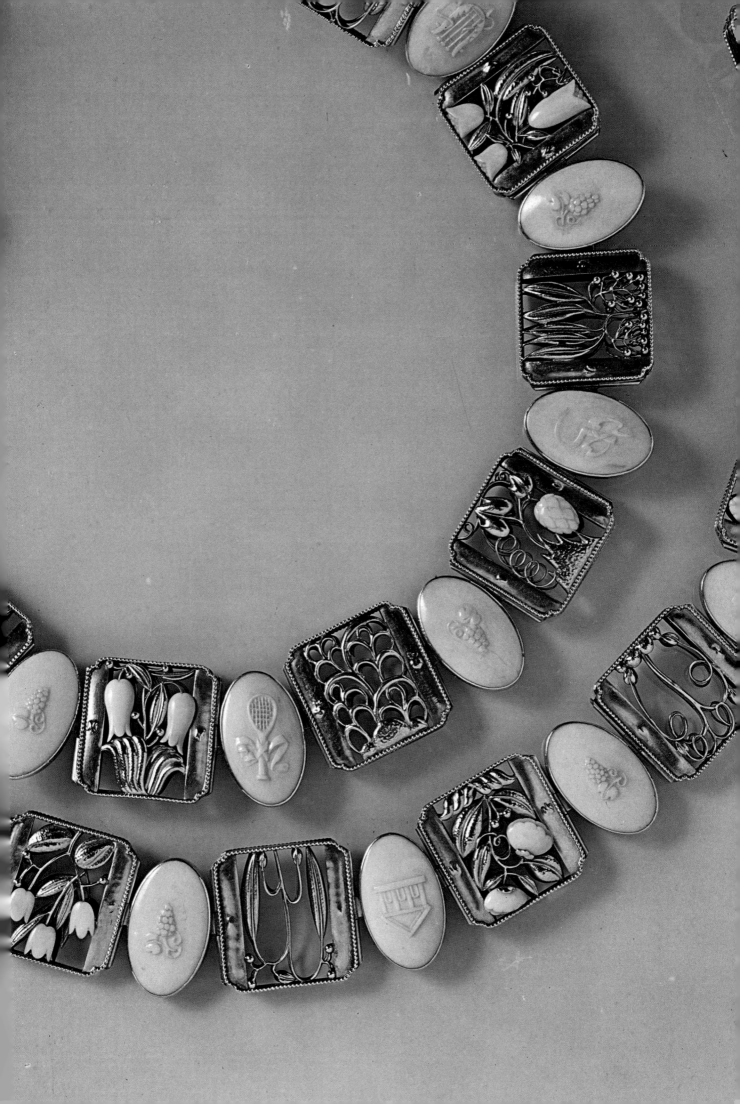

The Pearl of Asia, the largest known pearl, mounted with ordinary pearls and pink jade. Probably in a private collection in London.

A contemporary photograph of Queen Margherita of Savoy with a multi-stranded pearl necklace and a diadem, from *Les Modes*, November, 1904.

ous cages in the sea to begin its long work. The longer one waited, the larger the pearl would be. The value of cultured pearls depends on the thickness of the layers of pearly nacre. Except for its nucleus, the cultured pearl is composed in exactly the same way as the natural or oriental pearl.

Very different, however, are the manufacturing processes of imitation pearls. The wide use of and demand for pearls since the 16th century, even by less wealthy classes of people, had encouraged the manufacture of imitation pearls. The first to make them at that time was the Frenchman Jaquin, a rosary maker. He blew little hollow glass beads and coated them on the inside with a pearly paste called *essence orient*, made from the silvery scales of a little fish, and then filled them with wax. This type of imitation pearl became known as the parigine. Another type known as the Roman pearl is made by repeatedly dipping alabaster beads into a pearl solution made of the same fishscale

essence, and by polishing and spraying them with lacquer.

One of the most famous pearls is the Great Cross of the South. It consists in fact of nine pearls joined together: seven are in a straight line and the other two are joined on in such a way as to look like a cross. It was found in an oyster in 1866 on the west coast of Australia and is now part of the English crown jewels.

Stories, some fictional, of extraordinary pearls in antiquity have been passed down to us. Julius Caesar sent Brutus's mother a pearl worth six million sestertii and Caligula's wife, Lollia Paulina, had a jewel containing pearls worth forty million sestertii, which was part of plunder from the East. Among the fabulous jewels belonging to the Gaikwar of Baroda kept in the Nazar Bagh Palace in India was a rug made entirely of pearls bordered with precious stones.

The largest known pearl in the world is the Pearl of Asia which weighs 2400 grains. It is shaped like an aubergine and has been mounted

Countess de la Riboisière with a diadem and a high choker of pearls, from *Les Modes*, 1908.

Wedding veil attached to a widely spaced net of pearls, from *Vogue*, February, 1927.

with other large pearls and rose-coloured jade. It is apparently kept in a London bank. Another exceptional pearl, which is pear shaped and weighs 1800 grains, was part of the gem collection of the banker Philip Hope. It was fifty-one millimetres long. Another pearl, fished up off the Philippines in 1938, was about twenty-two centimetres long and ten across. It was shaped like a human brain and belonged to the American collector Wilborn D. Cobb.

Commercial Jewelers The Belle Epoque was a period of great economic expansion. The new wealthy aristocracy, who vied with the old nobility in their display of opulent luxury, favoured such artistic-commercial organisations in the field of jewelry as that typified by Fabergé. The activities of these firms moved in a different direction from that, for instance, of such artist jewelers as Lalique, Vever, Fouquet and others, who merit an important place in the history of art jewelry for their stylistic contribution.

While the products of these firms were always of the highest material and technical quality, from the aesthetic point of view they tended to reflect the taste of their bourgeois clientèle which was usually conservative. Thus though the large firms were ready to make stylistic concessions to avant-garde ideas, they only absorbed as much as they felt their bourgeois clients could accept.

Louis François Cartier, succeeding his teacher Piccard in 1846, produced jewelry inspired by the 18th century. The prosperity and luxury of the Second Empire period favoured the activity of the good jeweler of taste. Cartier, coming to the notice of the Empress Eugenie, who was particularly fond of jewelry inspired by the Louis XVI period, supplied her with this. However, he was very versatile and could work in any number of styles, including the Italian Renaissance and the Egyptian.

In 1874 his son Alfred joined him as collaborator and colleague, and the firm continued

297

to prosper even after the founding of the Third Republic, as Paris remained the centre of luxury.

In 1898 Alfred Cartier in partnership with his son Louis formed the company of A. Cartier et Fils, transferring their shop from the Boulevard des Italiens to its present address in Rue de la Paix. From that time one can distinguish the development of a certain kind of design peculiar to Cartier, which involved for the first time the widespread use of platinum. Delicate settings, designed so that only the precious stones, which were among the very finest gems available, were visible, were made possible by the strength of this metal. Cartier became the most famous jeweler at the beginning of this century, serving the prince of Wales, the future Edward VII, the Brazilian royal family, the king of Portugal, the prince of Saxe-Coburg Gotha and the grand dukes of Russia.

In America around 1850 Louis Comfort Tiffany produced vases and silver objects in New York. He was the first to make wide use of the sterling alloy which was later recognised by Federal Government Law. In 1866 he intro-duced the Tiffany setting which was a special fork for setting diamonds. Among his clients were President Lincoln and J. P. Morgan, and he made a silver mirror for Sarah Bernhardt's bicycle. The firm owns the Tiffany Diamond, the largest and purest canary yellow diamond in the world, found at Kimberley, South Africa, in 1878. It was cut in Paris with the unusual number of ninety facets and was exhibited un-mounted at two world exhibitions, Chicago in 1893 and New York in 1939. It has also been shown in other important exhibitions at Buffalo and at Chicago.

The noted designer, Jean Schlumberger, of Alsation origin, who had collaborated in designing costume jewelry for the famous couturier Schiaparelli in Paris, joined Tiffany's as a designer after the Second World War and recently became the firm's vice president. He was the first jewelry designer to be awarded the Fashion Critics' Award at a ceremony at the Metropolitan Museum, New York. The Tiffany Diamond has been set in a necklace designed by Schlumberger, which consists of a delicate

298

Cartier, necklace of gold, brilliants and pearls, mounted on a black velvet ribbon. Cartier collection, Paris.

tracery of knots with this exceptional diamond at the centre.

Van Cleef and Arpels In 1906 Julien, Louis and Charles Arpels and their brother-in-law, Alfred van Cleef, descendants of generations of jewelers, founded their firm of Van Cleef and Arpels in Paris in the Place Vendôme. Within a few decades their choice jewelry had become world famous, and, in addition to the elegant tourist shops at the international resorts of Deauville, Cannes and Monte Carlo, they have opened branches in London, Geneva, New York and Palm Beach. Always abreast of the times, the firm has opened two boutiques in Paris and New York where jewelry of a more 'accessible' kind is sold.

Unlike other great firms, Van Cleef and Arpels keep the names of their important clients a secret; the sole exception to this was when they made the crown for the empress of Iran's coronation in 1967, the first empress of Iran in the thousand-year history of the country. The firm's design for the crown was chosen by a special commission from fifty others submitted. The designer was not permitted to see beforehand any of the large number of jewels from the crown treasury which were to be used in the decoration of the crown; nor could the gems be taken out of Iran. Before the work could be finished Pierre Arpels had to make at least two dozen trips between Paris and Teheran. The visits he was allowed to make to see the collection of jewels in order to choose the ones he wanted for the crown must have been among the most exciting events in his life. Arpels first chose the stone which was to be the centrepiece, a magnificent 150-carat emerald; then he chose the rest: 1,469 diamonds, 36 rubies, 36 emeralds and 105 pearls, in all 1,646 pieces.

Among the most famous jewels in this wonderful Iranian collection are: the Darya-i-Nur diamond, which weighs 182 carats; the Nader-Shah *aigrette*, a magnificent example from Safawidi's treasure; the crown of the Kians; Nasser-ed-Din Shah's globe of the earth encrusted with more than 51,000 precious stones and the most modern piece, the emperor's crown.

Constantine Bulgari Boulgaris was the original name of the Roman jeweler Bulgari, whose ancestors were an ancient family of gold-

smiths from Kallaritis, a mountainous region near the old Greek frontier. Sotirio Bulgari (1857-1932) left his country as a youth, and after an unlucky sojourn in Naples went to work in Rome in 1881. He had a hard struggle at the beginning of his career as a goldsmith; however, through his skill and perseverance, he was finally able to open a shop at Trinità dei Monti and other branches followed. His chief activity was the production of beaten silver plate. From 1880, Sotirio, later joined by his sons, Constantine in 1889 and Giorgio in 1890, began to specialise in jewelry, closing the various branches and concentrating solely on the main shop in Via Condotti which was lavishly enlarged in 1934. In addition to the creation of modern jewelry for a very select Italian and international clientèle, the firm keeps a splendid selection of antique silver, jewelry and high quality jade.

Constantine Bulgari has begun an extensive and important study, researching and cataloguing Italian goldsmiths' work, which will be published in a series of volumes of historical

299

Van Cleef and Arpels, brooch in the shape of a bunch of grapes. It is made of gold, silver, brilliants and white and grey pearls. Van Cleef and Arpels collection, Paris.

and critical interest, entitled: *Argentieri, gemmari ed orafi d'Italia*. The first three volumes of this large and important work, the interest of which it is not necessary to stress, are already published. Bulgari's constructive interest, his cultural envolvement with goldware and his enthusiastic work as a collector has put him in the front rank of great jewelers. His grandsons today collaborate in the great firm of their forefathers, with rare dedication and competence.

In addition to those mentioned, other firms of great prestige also maintain a constant high tradition of excellent quality; most worthy of note among them are Asprey of Bond Street, London, founded in 1781; Black, Starr and Frost of Fifth Avenue, New York, founded in 1810 when the city had 175,000 inhabitants; Boucheron of the Place Vendôme, Paris, founded in 1858; Patek Philippe, chiefly watchmakers till 1939, after which they have concentrated increasingly on jewelry; Harry Winston of New York, specialist since 1945 in large stones; and in Italy, Calderoni of Milan, founded in 1840, and Mario Buccellati, founded in 1903.

Jewelry and the Modern Movement in Art

The period of the Art Nouveau style which held sway throughout Europe came to a decisive end with the First World War. The years following it saw the development of new movements and styles in jewelry which were closely related to painting and sculpture, particularly the nonfigurative type. These aesthetic tendencies, based on the theory of 'pure visibility' found satisfactory means of expression in the decorative arts, from the graphic arts to stage design.

Cubism, Futurism, Mondrian's abstracts and and the De Stijl group, the pictures of Klee and above all the work of the Bauhaus school, which attempted to 're-establish the unity and harmony between the diverse branches of the arts', influenced avant-garde jewelry. There was con-

Constantine Bulgari, bracelet of gold and precious stones. The fastening is held by two lions' heads. Gioielleria Bulgari, Rome.

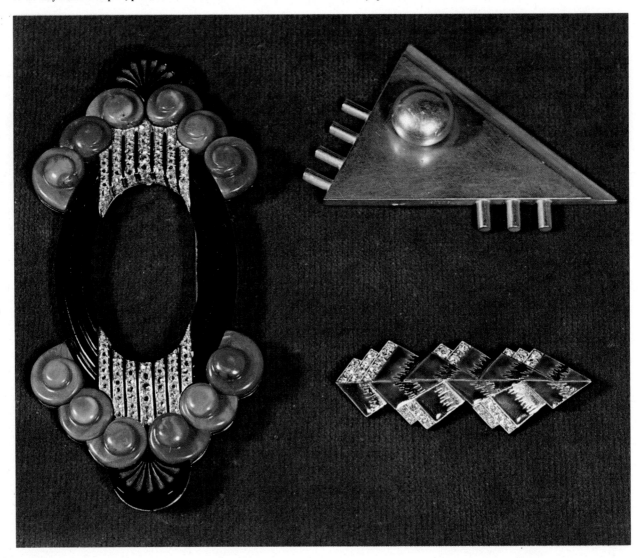

siderable collaboration between artists and craftsmen and by great artistic-industrial firms of the kind mentioned above.

As with Art Nouveau jewelry, in Art Deco works of the 1920s the materials chosen were adapted to express the new stylistic language. The compositions were based chiefly on the play of geometric forms; smooth, polished or satinised surfaces were preferred for precious metals and also steel; diamonds or other precious stones tended to be restricted and used for their colourful effects. For the same reason corals and diamonds, or onyx and emeralds would appear together in one piece of jewelry; difference in the actual value of the different stones did not prevent them being mixed. The sole aim was to create something which

answered the aesthetic requirements of the non-figurative styles in fashion.

Outstanding in this period were various artist-jewelers such as Raymond Templier, Fourquet and René Robert in France, H. G. Murphy in England and Wiwen Nilsson in Sweden. Besides their expressive work, which nearly always bore the signature of its creator or of the jeweler who made it, the market abounded in jewelry made by a large number of anonymous imitators. They, in their effort to copy, enrich and popularise contemporary art forms so as to make them more acceptable to their clients, completely distorted the spirit. By simplification or stylisation, they sought to give an appearance of modernity to traditional compositions. However, despite their technical

perfection, from an artistic point of view these were meaningless. They also applied the same superficial methods of simplification to designs copied from antique jewelry, with disastrous results.

The vogue for pseudo-barbaric jewelry inspired by the work of ancient goldsmiths brought the creation of rustic effects and a look of casual irregularity using gold sheet worked in relief for bracelets, necklaces and brooches. They were composed of designs which were inspired by the appearance of mosaics or of solid gold in its natural state.

In a popular variety of diamond jewelry great technical skill was displayed in the setting of the stones which were linked by very delicate strips of platinum giving the appearance of a cluster of stars or brilliants. In this type of openback setting, made possible by the strength of platinum, the stone is placed in a thin ring of platinum and held in place by claws.

Exceptionally gifted designers such as Schlumberger, Duke Fulco della Verdura, Jean Lucat, Gilbert Albert, in Paris, New York and Geneva collaborated with important firms such as Tiffany and Patek Philippe. In other cases the jewelry bears the signature of the company, Cartier, Van Cleef and Arpels, Boucheron and Winston, not the designer.

Artists Turn to Jewelry Design An important 20th-century development is the interest taken in jewelry by certain internationally famous artists. Braque, Cocteau, Max Ernst, Arp, Man Ray, Dali, Tanguy, Dubuffet, Picasso, Calder, Giacometti, Arnaldo and Gio Pomodoro, Fontana and Afro have all done designs for jewelry.

After the Second World War Calder was one of the first artists to participate in the creation of jewelry, and after him many other painters and sculptors contributed something towards the art of jewelry. Since 1938 he has designed a wide variety of necklaces, brooches and pendants in strips or wire of gold and silver.

Artist-craftsmen of this type have not always aimed for technical accuracy and formality in the lavish jewelry they produced. An exception was the Italian Gio Pomodoro who, while infusing the form and invention of his work with his own personal symbolic vision, took great care over the working of the materials. His sensitively prepared works combined a satisfying completeness with decorative functionalism in the highest sense of the word.

George Braque's jewelry creations, magnificently realised by Heger de Löwenfeld, must be considered an integral part of the artist's vast output. The translation into precious metals of his inspired designs played a part in bringing out the metaphysical and magical aspects of the jewel. Braque's contribution to the art of jewelry, although limited, demonstrates clearly how this branch of the decorative arts can have a validity even in the terms of the figurative arts, as had often happened during the Italian Renaissance period.

The unique pieces designed by Jean Cocteau, 303

Max Ernst, *Small Smiling Chimaera*, made in gold by François Hugo, Paris, 1961. Galerie le Point Cardinal, Paris.

Jean Arp, *Cutout*, made in gold by François Hugo, Paris, 1966-67. Galerie Le Point Cardinal, Paris.

especially brooches, shows his tendency towards Surrealism. Flowers, figures, leafy masks and other zoomorphic and anthropomorphic compositions, created in gold with skilled use of enamels, rubies and diamonds, form the elegant and refined repertoire of the famous writer and painter.

Salvador Dali proclaimed: 'My jewels are a protest against the high cost of jewelry materials. My aim is to show the jeweler's art in its true perspective – where the design and the craftsmanship are of more value than the gems, as in the Renaissance era.' Most of his designs are now in a collection owned by the Owen Cheatham Foundation of New York, and Alemany of New York have the exclusive option to make, in close collaboration with the artist himself, all his designs. His work in this branch of artistic activity is closely related to his pictures. Earrings made in the shape of telephone receivers, brooches made like mouths with ruby lips and pearl teeth, his 'Eye of Time' with a clock's face as the iris, and his snail rings are all part of the ingenious devices of the master of Surrealism.

The famous sculptor Giacometti applied his intellectual artistic skill to jewelry in gilded bronze; Picasso has modelled a number of medallions with bull's heads; and Lucio Fontana produces his large rings with his characteristic style of plain surfaces with occasional slashes or holes.

The increasing output of many countries, including Switzerland, Spain, Germany, the United States, Brazil and Italy, combined with the inspiration of many artists, has very greatly enriched the range of decorative motifs. Some artist-craftsmen have discovered the fascination of the natural crystal structure of uncut stones which the whim of nature endows with an inimitable beauty. Mounted in brooches or pendants, introduced amongst gold branches or set in rings, they often form a most attractive ornament.

Thus the recent tendencies of design in jewelry have been towards the creation of ornaments which distinctly interpret and reflect the artist's creativity and in which the intrinsic value of the materials is of secondary importance to their aesthetic content.

Conclusion A survey of the history of approximately five thousand years of jewelry reveals that from the point of view of the workmanship, ancient jewels do not differ substantially

Lucio Fontana, bracelet with an oval gold plaque. Private collection, Milan.

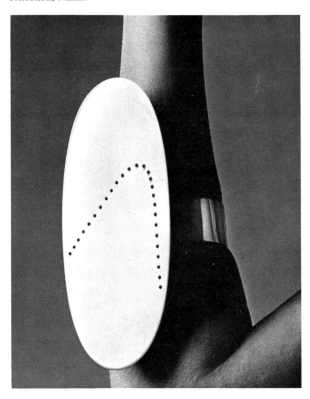

Lucio Fontana, bracelet with an oval gold plaque. Private collection, Milan.

from modern ones. In fact, it can be said that, with the exception of granulation (perfected by the Etruscans), enamelling (which had two great peaks of development, first in the Byzantine era and then in 18th-century France) and the cutting of diamonds and other precious stones, most of the techniques we know today have been in use since the era of the ancient Mesopotamian civilisation. Forms, too, such as necklaces, bracelets, rings and earrings, are very much the same as those used in antiquity.

The main change has been a social one. In the various periods of history until the 18th century, the use of jewelry was limited as much to court circles as it is in tribal societies, which in the less developed regions of the world still today have large ornaments often of considerable artistic interest.

The industrial revolution began the destruction of the old class system of privilege, and, consequently, precious ornaments, among other things, became available to wider sections of the population, losing for ever all their ancient symbolism. There arose the great jewelry and goldsmith companies; famous artists turned their attention to the design and manufacture of art jewelry, at first following the sometimes whimsical stylistic innovations of Art Nouveau and later producing works which were personal expressions of each individual artist.

Mass-produced jewelry became possible with the development of machinery and the widespread manufacture and use of imitation pearls, stones, gems and gaudy alloys and finally the invention of modern materials such as plastic. Jewelry, often not lacking in originality of design, has now become widely available to the poorest for personal adornment. Today, there are even some cases of a return to the ancient custom of painting the body; however it is too early to say whether this, like the extravagant jewelry worn by some young people, is a passing phase or the beginning of a new era of fashion.

Man's desire to embellish himself with precious or apparently precious articles shows no sign of waning, much less of dying; indeed, on the contrary, it would appear that just as it has accompanied man from his earliest being until today, it will continue to be one of his greatest needs.

Giò Pomodoro, bracelet of silver and precious stones, 1956. Private collection, Verona.

305

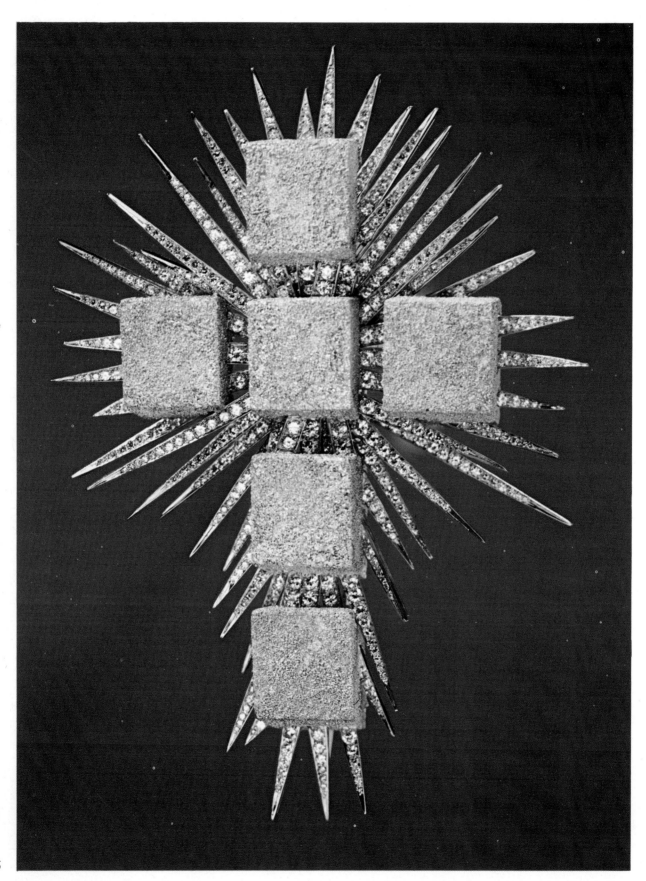

Salvador Dali, *The Gold Cube Cross*. Collection of Sculptured Jewels by Salvador Dali, Owen Cheatham Foundation, New York.

Giorgio de Chirico, *Gli Archeologi*, gold brooch with brilliants and three large pearls, *c.* 1956. Signoria Isabella de Chirico, Rome.

Name	Variety	Hard-ness	Colouring	Deposits	Period of greatest use
Diamond		10	transparent, colourless, blue-white, shades of yellow, green, pink, red, blue, grey, black	India, Brazil, Guiana, north and south-west Africa, Congo, Angola, Tanganyika, Rhodesia, Cameroon, Ghana, Sierra Leone, North America, Australia, Borneo	mentioned by Pliny and Marco Polo; from the 17th century onwards
Corundum	ruby star effect	9	transparent, various shades of red, star effect		mentioned by Pliny, Marco Polo, Albert the Great; rarely used until the 16th century, more frequent from the 17th century
	sapphire, star sapphire	9	blue, pale blue, with star effect	Ceylon, Burma, Siam, Kashmir, Australia, USA (Montana and North Carolina), Madagascar, Urals, Saxony, Bohemia, France	from the 18th century onwards
	aquamarine oriental		pale blue		19th and 20th centuries
	amethyst oriental		various shades of violet, often tending to red		19th and 20th centuries
	topaz oriental		yellow, clear lemon		19th and 20th centuries
Beryl	emerald	7½-8	light green to deep green	Columbia, Upper Egypt, Urals, Siberia, Brazil, Salzburg Alps, North America, Trans-vaal, India, California, Madagascar, Elba	Egyptian, Greek and Roman eras; from the 17th century to 19th century
	morganite		pink, pink lilac		
	aquamarine	7½-7¾	pale blue, transparent	Brazil, Urals, Madagascar, Elba	from the 17th century onwards
Spinel	spinel ruby	8	blood red, transparent to opaque	Burma, Siam, Brazil, Ceylon, Madagascar	Classical era and 19th century
	Balas ruby		red to reddish-violet	Balascia (Afghanistan), India	Classical era, Renais-sance, 18th and 19th centuries
Topaz		8	translucent, yellow-gold, honey-yellow rarely: blue-green, pink, red	in antiquity: Upper Egypt, Saxony today: Brazil, Urals, Siberia, California, Utah, Australia, Mexico, Japan, Madagascar, Ceylon	from the 18th century onwards
Quartz	rock crystal	7	very transparent, colourless	mainly: Alps and other parts of Italy, Tyrol, Silesia, Scotland, Urals, Brazil, Madagascar, Japan	Classical, Byzantine, Barbarian, High Medieval and Renais-sance eras; 17th, 18th, 19th centuries; less popular in modern times

Name	Variety	Hard-ness	Colouring	Deposits	Period of greatest use
	amethyst		transparent; all shades of violet	Brazil, Uruguay, Ceylon, South Africa, Mexico, Madagascar, Russia, Australia, North America, Spain, France, Hungary, Italy	Classical and Renaissance eras, and 19th century
	rose quartz		milky rose-pink; semi-transparent	Brazil, South Africa, Japan, Madagascar, Ceylon, USA, Bohemia, Bavaria, Scotland, Ireland, Italy, Russia	Classical and Renaissance eras, and 19th century
	sunflower quartz		semiopaque, bluish-white, milky, opalescent	Brazil, India, Bohemia, Hungary, Siberia	Classical and Renaissance eras, and 19th century
	falcon's eye		opaque; greyish blue with shimmering streaks of greenish-blue light	South Africa	Classical and Renaissance eras, and 19th century
	aventurine		opaque; red-brown, and green	Russia, India, Tibet, Egypt, Australia, Brazil, Bavaria, Styria, Scotland, Spain, France, Piedmont	19th century
	jasper		white, red, green, blue, yellow, brown, black, opaque, variegated	Saxony, Siberia, Egypt, USA, Brazil, South Africa, Madagascar, Italy (Tuscany)	Egyptian, Classical, High Medieval and Renaissance eras; 19th century
	chalcedony	6½-7	milky, whitish, bluish-grey, greenish, yellowish	Faroe, Iceland, Brazil, Uruguay, Italy	Classical era and 19th century
	blue chalcedony		light blue, blue, opaque	Arizona, Siberia, India, Rumania, Oregon	19th century
	cornelian		blood red, various shades to yellowish-brown	India, Brazil, Arabia, Russia, Siberia, Japan, Germany	Classical era, Renaissance and 19th century
	sard		brown, black-brown, orange-brown, semi-transparent	India, Brazil, Arabia, Russia, Siberia, Japan, Germany	Classical era, Renaissance and 19th century
	chrysoprase		apple-green with white and grey streaks	Silesia, India, Urals, Austria, USA, Canada	Classical era and 19th century
	plasma		dark green, olive, opaque	India, orient, Upper Egypt, Germany	Egyptian and Classical eras
	agate		stratified, green, light blue, white, red, brown, black; semitransparent	Germany, Brazil, India, Asia Minor, China, Madagascar	Classical era, Renaissance and 19th century
	onyx (variety of agate)		striated; white, black or black and red lines or curves		Classical era, Renaissance and 19th century

Name	Variety	Hardness	Colouring	Deposits	Period of greatest use
Andalusite		$7\frac{1}{2}$	whitish, grey, green, olive, red, red-brown, violet; slightly transparent	Andalusia, Austria, Saxony, Brazil, Urals, Ceylon	19th and 20th centuries
Garnet (carbuncle)	hessonite	7	reddish-orange, cinnamon yellow	Ceylon, USA, western Alps, Madagascar, Tyrol, Urals	from the 17th century
	pyrope or Bohemian ruby or Cape ruby	$7\frac{1}{4}$	fiery red	Bohemia, Saxony, Switzerland, South Africa, Ceylon, Scotland, western USA, Brazil	infrequently used in the Middle Ages and Renaissance; much used in 19th century
	almandine or precious garnet	$7\frac{1}{4}$-$7\frac{1}{2}$	violet-red	India, Brazil, Uruguay, South Australia, USA, Madagascar, Greenland, Bohemia, Spain, Austria, Russia, Norway, Switzerland, Hungary, the Alps	mentioned in Pliny; used in the Classical era for engraving; from the 19th century onwards
	demantoid	$6\frac{1}{2}$-$6\frac{3}{4}$	green, yellowish-green	Urals, Val d'Aosta, Val Malenco	19th century
Tourmaline	indicolite	$7\frac{1}{2}$	greenish-blue, light blue	Brazil, South Africa, Urals, Colorado, Massachusetts, California, Kashmir, Madagascar, Bengal	from the 18th century onwards
	rubellite or siberite	$7\frac{1}{4}$-$7\frac{1}{2}$	pink, ruby-red	Russia, USA, Ceylon, Burma, Madagascar, Brazil, China	19th and 20th centuries
	green tourmaline	$7\frac{1}{2}$	shades of green	Brazil, South Africa, Russia, Ceylon, Elba	19th and 20th centuries
	yellow tourmaline	$7\frac{1}{2}$	shades of yellow	Madagascar, Ceylon	19th and 20th centuries
Olivine	olivine or chrysolite or peridot	$6\frac{1}{2}$-7	greenish-gold, olive-green; transparent or translucent	Brazil, Norway, Congo, Australia, Faroe, Egyptian Red Sea coast, Arizona, New Mexico, Ceylon, Burma	Egyptian and Classical eras, Middle Ages, 19th century
Feldspar	orthoclase	6	gold yellow, lemon yellow	Madagascar	20th century
	adularia or moonstone	6	transparent, colourless, green, pearly, milky bluish-white	Ceylon, Brazil, USA, Australia	19th and 20th centuries
	oligoclase or sunstone	6	almost opaque, greyish-white background, flecked with gold particles	Norway, Russia, Siberia, USA	19th century

Name	Variety	Hard-ness	Colouring	Deposits	Period of greatest use
	labradorite	6	opaque, grey background, flecks of all colours	Labrador, Russia, Finland, USA, Sweden, Canada	19th century
Opal	precious opal	$5\frac{1}{2}$-$6\frac{1}{2}$	semitransparent, milky white tending to blue with shimmering rainbow-like colorations. Rarely: yellow, red, green, blue and black	Czechoslovakia, Mexico, Australia, Honduras, Guatemala, USA, Japan	used occasionally in the Roman era; 19th century
	fire opal		transparent to opaque, hyacinth-red, reddish-yellow, orange, wine-red, brownish-yellow. Rarely: iridescent, red or green streaks	Mexico, Faroe, Nevada, Australia	19th century
Chrysoberyl	chrysoberyl	$8\frac{1}{2}$	pale yellow, pale green, from transparent to opaque	Brazil, Ceylon, USA, Madagascar	known in the Classical era; 19th century
	golden chrysoberyl or chrysolite		old gold, yellow-gold tending to greenish	usually Brazil and as above	known in the Classical era; 19th century
	oriental cat's eye		green or yellow mixed, showing streaks of reddish, bluish or violet light	Ceylon, Brazil	known in the Classical era; 19th century
	alexandrite		emerald, dark and olive green	Russia, Ceylon, Tasmania, Rhodesia	19th century
Zircon	precious zircon	$7\frac{1}{2}$	transparent to translucent; shades of green, yellow, grey, violet	widely found: Norway, Sweden, Canada, Madagascar, Ceylon, Siam, Australia	from the 18th century onwards
	jacinth		orange-red, red, dark red, light red, violet-red	as above, Ceylon, Indochina, Siam, South Africa, Brazil	19th and 20th centuries
	starlite		blue, bluish-green, electric-blue	Siam	19th and 20th centuries
	colourless zircon or Matara diamond		transparent, colourless	same as the other varieties, Ceylon (Matara), Siam	19th and 20th centuries
Sodalite	lapis lazuli or lazurite	5-$5\frac{1}{2}$	opaque; sea-blue, dark or light blue, tending to green or violet; specks of gold due to inclusion of pyrites	Afghanistan, Russia, Siberia, Chilean Andes	Mesopotamia, Egypt, Classical era, Renaissance, 17th, 19th and 20th centuries
Turquoise		5-6	opaque; apple-green, green, skyblue, light	Iran, Turkestan, Tibet, Sinai peninsular,	Egypt (from the 3rd millennium BC), Pre-

Name	Variety	Hard-ness	Colouring	Deposits	Period of greatest use
			and dark blue, black, brown or white inclusions	Arabia, USA (New Mexico and California), Australia, South Africa, Silesia, Saxony	Columbian era, Renaissance, 19th and 20th centuries
Jade or Jadeite		6½-7	opaque or transluscent; not uniform; basically white or greyish tending to pink or lilac-blue; specks of emerald green or light green	Burma, Turkestan, China, Tibet, Mexico, Costa Rica, New Zealand, Alaska, Greece, western Alps	Pre-Columbian era, the Far East in prehistoric times; in Europe in the 19th century onwards
Nephrite or Jade		5½-6½	opaque or transluscent; grey-white, grey-green, grass green, yellowish, brown, reddish	Turkestan, China, Russia, Siberia, New Zealand, North Caledonia, Venezuela, Brazil, Peru, Alaska, Switzerland	Pre-Columbian era, the Far East in prehistoric times; in Europe in the 19th century onwards
Malachite		3½-4	composed of copper; transluscent or opaque; emerald or dark green; mottled with dark or light bands	Urals, Rhodesia, Katanga, Chile, USA, Australia, Rumania, France	19th century
Marcasite		6-6½	opaque, gold yellow, metallic	Folkestone (UK), Bohemia, Czechoslovakia, Saxony, France, Mexico, USA	19th and 20th centuries
Amber or Succunite (fossilised resin)		2½-3 (and 1½)	transparent, semi-opaque, transluscent, variegated and mottled; from clearest to darkest yellow, tending to red and brown; also blue, violet and green	Baltic coast, Friesian islands, Rumania (rumenite), Burma (birmite), Galicia, France, Spain, Russia, Canada, San Domingo	from prehistoric to modern times
Jet (black lignite)		3-4	opaque, brown, black	Whitby and Cleveland (Yorks), Spain, France, Saxony, Russia, Colorado	19th century

Bibliography

CELLINI, B.	Due Trattati sull' oreficeria e sulla scultura.	Florence	1568
ROBBIO, G.	Dizionario istorico ragionato delle gemme, delle pietre e di minerali.	Naples	1824
CASTELLANI, A.	Antique Jewellery and its Revival.	London	1862
	Italian jewellery as worn by the peasants of Italy collected by Mr. Castellani.	London	1868
CASTELLANI, A.	Della Oreficeria Italiana.	Rome	1872
TEOFILO	Diversarum Artium Schedula. Edizione critica di A. Ilg, Vol. VII.	Vienna	1874
LUTHMER, F.	Goldschmuck der Renaissance.	Berlin	1881
FONTENAY, E.	Les bijoux anciens et modernes.	Paris	1881
BAPST, G.	Histoire des Joyaux de la Couronne de France.	Paris	1889
PLINY	Naturalis Historia–Edizione critica Teutneriana a cura di L. Jan e B. Mayhoff.	Leipzig	1892-1933
HAVARD, H.	Histoire de l'orfèvrerie française.	Paris	1896
FURTWANGLER, A.	Die antiken Gemmen (3 vols.).	Leipzig, Berlin	1900
RUCKLIN, R.	Das Schmuckbuch.	Leipzig	1901
MENGARELLI, R.	La necropoli barbarica di Castel Trosino in 'Monumenti antichi dei Lincei, XII'.		1902
RADACZEK, K.	Der Ohrschmuck der Greichen und Etrusker	Vienna	1903
CLIFFORD SMITH, H.	The King's Gems and Jewels at Windsor Castle in 'Connoisseur' IV, V.		1902-1903
BARTH, H.	Das Geshmeide–Schmuck–und Edelsteinkunde (2 vols.).	Berlin	1903
FALKE, O. von and FRAUBERGER, H.	Deutsche Schmelzarbeiter des Mittelalters.	Frankfurt am Main	1904
MARSHALL, F. H.	Catalogue of the finger rings, Greek, Etruscan and Roman in the Departments of Antiquities, the British Museum.	London	1907
CLIFFORD SMITH, H.	Jewellery.	London	1908
SCHLOSSER, J. von	Die Kunst und Wunderkammarn der Spätrenaissance.	Leipzig	1908
BELLUCCI, G.	Gli amuleti.	Perugia	1908
BASSERMANN-JORDAN, E.	Der Schmuck.	Leipzig	1909
BAUER, M.	Edelsteinkunde 2nd edition.	Leipzig	1909
BOEHN, M. von and FISCHEL, O.	Menschen und Moden im 17, 18 und 19 Jahrhundert (5 vols.).	Munich	1909
WILLIAMSON, G. C.	Catalogue of the collection of jewels and precious works of art, the property of J. Pierpont Morgan.	London	1910
	Catalogo della Mostra di etnografia italiana in Piazza d' Armi.	Rome	1911
MARSHALL, F. H.	Catalogue of the jewellery in the British Museum.	London	1911
	Peasant Art in Italy in 'The Studio'.	London	1913
PARIBENI, R.	Necropoli barbarica di Nocera Umbra in 'Monumenti antichi dei Lincei'.		1918
JESSEN, P.	Der Ornamentstich.	Berlin	1920
EVANS, J.	English jewellery from the fifth century A.D. to 1800.	London	1921
EVANS, J.	Magical Jewels of the Middle Ages and the Renaissance.	Oxford	1922
EBERSOLT, J.	Les arts somptuaires de Bysance.	Paris	1923
BOEHN, M. von	Menschen und Moden im 16 Jahrhundert.	Munich	1923
DEBO, P.	Alte Ringe.	Pforzheim	1923
FLOERKE, H.	Die Moden der Renaissance.	Munich	1924
DE RIDDER, A.	Catalogue sommaire des bijoux antiques des Musées du Louvre.	Paris	1924
ORSI, P.	Gioielli bizantini della Sioilia in 'Melanges' (Histoire du bas empire) (Schumberger).	Paris	1924
BOEHN, M. von	Menschen und Moden im Mittelalter	Munich	1925
SELIGMANN, T.	L'orfèvrerie carolingienne.	Paris	1927
D'ALLEMAGNE, H. R.	Les Accessoires du Costume et du Mobilier, (3 vols.).	Paris	1928
BOEHN, M. von	Das Beiwerk der Mode.	Munich	1928
BOSSERT, H. TH.	Geschichte des Kunstgewerbes (5 vols.).	Berlin	1928-1932
OSMAN, C. C.	Catalogue of Rings (Victoria and Albert Museum).	London	1930
BURGER, W.	Abendländische Schmelzarbeiten.	Berlin	1930
EVANS, J.	English Posies and Posy Rings.	Oxford	1931
JENNY, W. A. von and VOLBACH, W. F.	Gernischer Schmuck des frühen Mittelalters.	Berlin	1933
EVANS, J.	Wheel-shaped brooches in 'Art Bulletin',	September	1934
CALDERINI, E.	Costume popolare in Italia.	Milan	1934

314

ACCASCINA, M.	*Oreficeria italiana.*	Florence	1934
MORASSI, A.	*Antica oreficeria italiana.*	Milan	1936
BREHIER, L.	*La sculpture et les arts mineurs byzantins.*	Paris	1936
HACKENBROCH, Y.	*Italienisches Email des frühen Mittelalters.*	Basel	1938
SEGALL, B.	*Museo Benaki.*	Athens	1938
BATTKE, H.	*Die Ringsammlung des Berliner Schloss-museums.*	Berlin	1938
BREGLIA, L.	*Le oreficerie del Museo di Taranto.*		1939
COSSAR, M. R.	*L'arte orafa nella Venezia Giulia.*	Trieste	1940
PASZTORY, C. and ALCSUTI	*Les anciens bijoux hongrois.*	Budapest	1941
BREGLIA, L.	*Catalogo delle oreficerie del Museo Nazionale di Napoli*	Rome	1942
SEGALL, B.	*Some sources of early Greek jewellery.*	Boston	1943
GEVAERT, S.	*L'orfèvrerie mosane au Moyen Age.*	Brussels	1943
JACOBSTHAL, P.	*Early Celtic Art.*	Oxford	1944
VOLBACH, F. W.	*Le arti minori in 'Vaticano'.*	Florence	1946
BABELON, J.	*L'orfèvrerie française.*	Paris	1946
CINTAS, P.	*Amulettes puniques.*	Paris	1946
RICKETSON, E. B.	*Barbarian Jewellery of the Merovingian Period.*		1946/47
JANTZEN, H.	*Ottonische Kunst.*	Munich	1947
MACKAY, D.	*The Jewellery of Palmira and its Significance.*	Iraq	1949
JESSUP, R.	*Anglo-Saxon Jewellery.*	London	1950
CLIFFORD SMITH, H.	*Renaissance Jewellery in the Wernher Collection at Luton Hoo* in 'The Connoisseur'.		1950
STOTZ, J.	*Kristalle–Edelsteine–Metalle.*	Heilbronn	1951
FLOWER, M.	*Victorian Jewellery.*	London	1951
EVANS, J.	*A History of Jewellery.*	London	1953
SITWELL, H. D. N.	*The Crown Jewels and Other Regalia in the Tower of London.*	London	1953
BRADFORD, E.	*Four Centuries of European Jewellery.*	London	1953
RIECL, A.	*Industria artistica tardo-romana, trad. di. B. Forlati Tamaro e M. Ronga Leoni.*	Florence	1953
BATTKE, H.	*Geschichte des Ringes.*	Baden-Baden	1953
AMANDRY, P.	*Les bijoux antiques, Collection Hélène Stathatos.*	Strasbourg	1953
AMANDRY, P.	*Les trésors de l'orfèvrerie du Portugal, Catalogue of Exhibition, Musée des Arts Décoratifs.*	Paris	1954
SIVIERO, R.	*Gli ori e le ambre del Museo Nazionale di Napoli.*	Florence	1954
WOOLLEY, L.	*Excavations at Ur.*	London	1954
THOMA, H.	*Kronen und Kleinodien.*	Munich	1955
SCHONDORFF, E.	*Schmuck und Edelsteine.*	Munich	1955
MONACO, G.	*Oreficerie Longobarde a Parma.*	Parma	1955
BECATTI, G.	*Oreficerie antiche dalle minoiche alle barbariche.*	Rome	1955
ROSSI, F.	*Capolavori d'oreficeria italiana.*	Milan	1956
COCHE DE LA FERTE, E.	*Les bijoux antiques.*	Paris	1956
STEINGRABER, E.	*Antique Jewellery.*	London/ New York	1957
DEGANI, M.	*Ori e argenti dell' Emilia antica. (Catalogo della Mostra).*	Bologna	1958
BULGARI, C. C.	*Argentieri, gemmari e orafi d'Italia (2 vols).*	Rome	1958
BARINI, C.	*Ornatus muliebris. I gioielli e le anticho romane.*	Turin	1958
LIVINGSTON, L.	*Dali. A Study of his Art in Jewels. The collection of the Owen Cheatham Foundation.*	Greenwich	1959
CAVENAGO BIGNAMI, S.	*Gemmologia, pietre preziose e perle.*	Milan	1959
DEGANI, M.	*Il tesoro romano-barbarico di Reggio Emilia.*	Florence	1959
BRADFORD, E.	*English Victorian Jewellery.*	London	1959
SHOENFELD, J. F.	*Designing and Making Hand-Wrought Jewellery.*	New York	1960
TWINING, LORD	*A History of the Crown Jewels of Europe.*	London	1960
	Catalogue of the Melvin Cotman Collection of Ancient and Medieval Gold.	Ohio	1961
HIGGINS, R. A.	*Greek and Roman Jewellery.*	London	1961
PACK, G.	*Jewellery and Enameling.*	Princeton	1961
BRUTON, E.	*The True Book about Diamonds.*	London	1961
GOODDEN, R. Y.	*International Exhibition of Modern Jewellery 1890.*	London	1961
CHARENSOL, G.	*Dix siècles de joaillerie française* in 'La revue des modes' no. 11.		1962
CARDUCCI, C.	*Ori e argenti dell'Italia antica.*	Milan	1962
SNOWMAN, A. K.	*The Art of Carl Fabergé.*	London	1962
LIPINSKY, A.	*Gli splendidi gioielli della Corte Normanna in Sicilia* in 'Arte figurativa' no. 10.		1962
GRANDJEAN, S.	*L'orfèvrerie du XIX siècle en Europe.*	Paris	1962
GRANDJEAN, S.	*Ori e argenti dell'Italia antica–Catalogo Mostra al Palazzo Reale.*	Milan	1962
HARRIS, J. S.	*An Introduction to the Study of Personal Ornaments of Precious, Semi-precious and Imitation Stones used Throughout Biblical History.*		1962-63
	Gold and Silverwork, Pre-Romanesque Art and *Folk Art* in 'World Encyclopedia of World Art'.	London New York	1962-68
DEL RENZIO, T.	*Letter from Paris: Modern artists turn to Jewellery* in 'Apollo'.	London	May 1963
GRAHAM, H.	*Modern Jewellery.*	London	1963

MORASSI, A.	*Il tesoro dei Medici.*	Milan	1963
VOLBACH, W. F.	*Monili dell'Asia, dal Caspio all'Himalaya. Catalogo mostra a Palazzo Brancaccio.*	Rome	1963
EYDOUX, H. P.	*Le grandes dames de l'archéologie.*	Paris	1964
KAISSERLIAN, G.	*La gioielleria, l'oreficeria e l'argentaria in Italia.*	Rome	1964
ROSSI, A.	*Oreficeria popolare italiana. Catalogo Mostra al Museo dello Arte e Tradizioni Populari.*	Rome	1964
LIPINSKY, A.	*Oreficeria, argentaria e gioielleria nel tardo Impero e nell'Alto Medioevalo.*	Ravenna	1964
DEMORIANE, H.	*Bijoux étonnants* in 'Connaissance des Arts'.	Paris Feb. 1964	
RHEIMS, M.	*L'objet 1900.*	Paris	1964
LIPINSKY, A.	*Ori, argenti, gioielli del periodo tardo-romano, paleocristiano e paleobizantino in Italia fino al movimento iconoclasta.*		1965
LIPINSKY, A.	*Ori, argenti, gioielli del secolo periodo aureo bizantino in Italia dall' avvento della dinastia macedone alla caduta di Costantinopoli.*		1965
HOFFMANN, H. and DAVIDSON, P.	*Greek Gold Jewellery from the age of Alexander.*	Mainz	1965
RHEIMS, M.	*L'art 1900.*	Paris	1965
STOVER, U.	*Freude am Schmuck.*	Gutersloh	1965
TESCIONE, C.	*Il corallo nella storia e nell'arte.*	Naples	1965
	The art of personal adornment. Catalogue of Exhibition, Museum of Contemporary Crafts.	New York	1965
STEINGRABER, E.	*L'arte del gioiello in Europa dal Medioevo al Liberty.*	Florence	1965
BOOT, G.	*Jugendstil–Kataloge des Hessischen Museums.*		1965
STEINGRABER, E.	*Der Goldschmied.*	Munich	1966
JODIN, A.	*Bijoux et amulettes du Maroc punique* in 'Bulletin d'Archeologie Marocainne' VI.		1966
OLIVER, A. Jr.	*Greek, Roman and Etruscan Jewellery* in 'The Bulletin of the Metropolitan Museum of Art'.	New York	1966
STEINGRABER, E.	*Oreficeria dal Rinascimento al Liberty.*	Milan	1966
COARELLI, F.	*L'oreficeria nell'arta classica.*	Milan	1966
COCTEAU, JEAN	*Catalogue of Exhibition, Museum für Kunst und Gewerbe.*	Hamburg	1966
RANDALL, R. H. Jr.	*Jewellery Through the Ages* in 'Apollo'.	London Dec. 1966	
BELLI BARSALI, I.	*L'oreficeria medievale.*	Milan	1966
BAUER, J. & A.	*A Book of Jewels.*	London	1966
BREGLIA, L.	*Oreficeria.*	Rome	1958-66
RANDALL, R. H.	*A Mannerist Jewel* in 'The Bulletin of the Walters Art Gallery' XX.		1967
GOLDBERG, T., and others	*L'orfèvrerie et la bijouterie russes aux XV-XX siécles.*	Moscow	1967
	Catalogue of the exhibition Europa 1900, Musee des Beaux Arts, Ostend.	Brussels	1967
WILSON, M.	*Gems.*	New York	1967
WILSON, M.	*Catalogue of the exhibition Die Wiener Werkstätte modernes Kunsthandwerk von 1903-1932.*	Vienna	1967
GRAMATOPOL, M. & GRACIUNESCU, V.	*Les bijoux antiques de la collection Marie et Dr. G. Severeanu du Musée d'Histoire de la ville de Bucarest.*		1967
BUTLER, P.	*Jewellery through the Ages* in 'Apollo'.	London April 1968	
FISHER, C.	*Adornments of Antiquity, Etruria, Greece and Rome* in 'Apollo'.	London April 1968	
WILLS, G.	*The Russian State Jewels* in 'Apollo'.	London Oct. 1968	
JAMILA BRIJ BRUSHAN	*Indian jewellery, ornaments and decorative designs.*	Bombay	
RIGHETTI, R.	*Incisori di gemme e cammei in Roma dal Rinascimento all' Ottocanto.*	Rome	
JESSEN, P.	*Meister des Ornamentstichs aus vier Jahrhunderton.*	Berlin	
VEVER, H.	*La bijouterie française au XIX siècle.*	Paris	

Index

The numbers in italic indicate illustrations

Acknowledgements

Photographs not listed below were supplied by the museum. Alinari, Florence 55 bottom, 190 top; AME 18, 22, 26, 41 top, 42, 92, 124, 147 bottom left, 151 top, 152 left, 158 bottom, 165, 229 top, 296 left; Avignone 133; Bacci, Rome 9, 27 bottom right, 29, 30, 31 bottom, 33 top, 36, 54, 55 centre, 56/57, 59, 67, 68, 69 top left, 93, 114, 118 top and bottom, 120 top, 121, 137, 140 right, 142 top right and bottom, 156, 239 bottom, 243 left, 253 top, 255, 256, 258, 301, 307; Bevilacqua, Milan 27 top right, 28 bottom, 31 top, 43 bottom left, 46, 50, 51 bottom, 52 top right, 55 top, 58 top, 61 bottom, 64 bottom, 76, 77, 82 top, 83, 89, 95, 97, 113 bottom, 174 top, 177 left, 179, 180, 181, 182, 185, 193, 194, 205, 222, 226, 259, 279; Blauel, Munich 174 bottom; Brunel, Lugano 132 top right, 178 top, 183 left, 188 top left, 198 centre; Bulloz, Paris 6/7, 107, 108, 109 left, 249; © 1959 Owen Cheatham Foundation, New York 306; Ciol, Casarsa 142 top left, 168 bottom, 169; Cozzi, Milan 273; Dal Gal 305 bottom Dominique Darbois 12, 15 top right; Da Re, Bergamo 195; De Biasi, Milan 90; De Selva, Paris 293 bottom; Electa, Milan 187 top right, bottom left and bottom right, 192 bottom; Wolf-Bender's Erben, Zurich 15 bottom right; John Freeman, London 25 bottom, 94, 122, 154, 155 top left, 163 centre right, 171 bottom, 189, 191 top, 196 right, 201 top, 204 top left and right, 208, 212, 213, 217, 224, 236 top, 237, 241 left, 244 bottom left, 246, 261, 266, 267; Giraudon, Paris 25 top, 72, 74, 79 top right, 105, 109 right, 112 bottom, 163 bottom, 172, 175, 240 left, 242 right, 248, 250, 251, 260, 268; Guido Gregoretti 73 top, 231; Dan Grigorescu 123 top, 140 left, 166 top right, centre and bottom right; Soloman R. Guggenheim Museum 78; André Held, Ecublens 23; Hirmer Verlag, Munich 17, 32, 33 bottom, 35, 39, 45 top right and centre right, 47 top and bottom, 48, 49, 58 bottom left, 65, 66, 104, 106, 108, 130 top left and right, 131, 136 top, 147 bottom right; Jacqueline Hydé, Paris 303, 304; Kodansha, Tokyo 102, 111 bottom, 177 right; C. H. Krüger-Moessner, Munich 63, 112 top, 113 top; Isolde Luckert, Berlin 120 bottom; Mandel 43 top and bottom right, 254; Marzari, Milan 192 top; Mercurio, Milan 186 top right, 188 centre right, 191 bottom; Meyer, Vienna 151 bottom; Ugo Mulas, Milan 305 top; Pagliarani 164 bottom; Perissinotto, Padua 40, 41 bottom; Ritter, Vienna 294 top, 295; Scala, Florence 52 top centre and bottom, 53, 58 bottom right, 64 top, 98, 128, 149 bottom, 153, 160, 178 bottom right, 196 left, 218, 239 top left; Scarnati, Paris 225, 245, 257, 265 top, 282, 285 bottom, 286, 289, 290, 292, 298, 299, 302; Services Photographiques, Versailles 166 bottom left, 197 bottom right; Steinmetz, Munich 80, 85, 138, 170, 239 top centre; Stockmann, Munich 141, 203, 204 bottom, 206, 235, 241 right; Thomas Photo, Oxford 164 top right; University Press, Oxford 132 top left; Van Cleef and Arpels, Paris 300; Harry Winston, New York 281; G. Wipfler, Pforzheim 70 bottom, 71, 118 centre, 214, 285 top, 287, 293 top.